D1605034

Gypsies and the British Imagination

Hubert von Herkomer, "A Gipsy Encampment on Putney Common" (detail).

Gypsies

& the

British

Imagination,

1807–1930

Deborah Epstein Nord

Columbia University Press
New York

Columbia University Press

Publishers Since 1893

New York Chichester, West Sussex

*Columbia University Press wishes to express its appreciation for assistance given
by the University Committee on Research in the Humanities and Social Sciences
at Princeton University toward the cost of publishing this book.*

Library of Congress Cataloging-in-Publication Data

Nord, Deborah Epstein.

Gypsies and the British imagination, 1807–1930 / Deborah Epstein Nord.

p. cm.

Includes bibliographical references and index.

ISBN 0-231-13704-4 (cloth : alk. paper)

ISBN 0-231–51033-0 (electronic)

1. English literature—19th century—History and criticism.

2. English literature—20th century—History and criticism.

3. Outsiders in literature.

4. Romanies in literature.   I. Title.

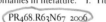
PR468.R63N67 2006

820.9'352991497—dc22   2005034050

Columbia University Press books are printed on permanent
and durable acid-free paper.

Printed in the United States of America

c 10 9 8 7 6 5 4 3 2 1

Designed by Lisa Hamm

This one is for my sons,
Joseph Solomon Nord and David Epstein Nord

Contents

Illustrations

Acknowledgments

ONE OF the pleasures that accompanies the completion of a project like this one is the opportunity to thank those people who have supported, encouraged, and contributed to it over a long period of time. I am grateful, first of all, for the ongoing support of the University Committee on Research in the Humanities and Social Sciences at Princeton University, which funded my research for a number of summers and a trip to England in the spring of 2000. In the final stages of writing, a grant from the American Council of Learned Societies enabled me to take a crucial full year's leave from teaching to complete my book.

At the Gypsy Collections at the University of Liverpool, Katy Hooper and other staff members welcomed me and helped with valuable research advice. I am grateful for permission to use materials, both manuscripts and photographs, in the Gypsy Lore Collections. At Princeton University, two groups of resourceful graduate students in my seminar "Race, Nation, and Englishness," on nineteenth-century literature, inspired my thinking and added fresh insights to my work. I have published very little of what follows in this book, but editors and readers who commented on my article "'Marks of Race': Gypsy Figures and Eccentric Femininity in Nineteenth-Century Women's Writing," *Victorian Studies* 41, no. 2 (1998), gave me confidence to pursue this project at an early stage. I have benefited greatly from being able to present some of this work to receptive and critically astute audiences at the Victorian Studies Conference of Western Canada; the North American Conference on British Studies; the conference "Locating the Victorians" in London; the colloquium "Europe and the Gypsies" at the State University of New York at Stony Brook; a graduate student and faculty group at Hunter College, New York; a nineteenth-century seminar at the University of Chicago; and the Victorian Colloquium at Princeton.

Colleagues, students, and friends have given me intellectual sustenance: they responded to my work, shared their own with me, and sent Gypsy references my way on a continuing basis. I am grateful for the interest and advice of Carol Armstrong, Daniel Blanton, Natalie Davis, Lou Deutsch, Maria DiBattista, Lisa Fluet, Edward Groth, Ian Hancock, Mary Harper, Richard Kaye, Howard Keeley, Uli Knoepflmacher, Beth Machlan, Peter Mandler, Arno Mayer, Gage McWeeny, Jeff Nunokawa, Susan Pennybacker, Ellen Pollak, Jim Richardson, Eve Rosenhaft, Christine Stansell, Susan Stewart, Lisa Tickner, Katie Trumpener, and Judy Walkowitz. Kate Flint has been a devoted and immeasurably helpful reader and interlocutor. I am also extremely grateful to Michael Ragussis, who read the manuscript with care and intelligence. I am indebted to the work of scholars, especially George Behlmer and David Mayall, who wrote about Gypsies in nineteenth-century Britain long before I began this project. This book stands on the shoulders of their scholarship. At Columbia University Press, Jennifer Crewe has been a highly encouraging and astute editor. I am grateful for her interest in this book and her stewardship of its publication. The illustrations for the book were gathered with the invaluable help of Alexandra Neel. Her excellent eye and intrepid approach to digital reproduction of images have enabled me to give this book an otherwise impossible visual richness.

My most personal debts are a good deal harder to define. I hope it is not too self-indulgent to say that sustaining the career of an academic woman of a certain age and life experience requires the understanding and encouragement of other, like-minded women. I am forever thankful for the friendship of Maria DiBattista, Ellen Pollak, and Chris Stansell. They have been an inspiration to me for many years. The Program in the Study of Women and Gender has been my second home at Princeton, and I am delighted to be able to acknowledge Barbara Gershen, its academic manager and presiding muse. My students in the program have been a gifted and spirited bunch. Finally, I am sustained by a family that combines, in equal parts, great warmth, humor, and intelligence. I dedicate this book to my beloved sons, David and Joseph. My husband, Philip Nord, patient, funny, and wise, continues to be my most resourceful—and certainly my most loving—critic.

Gypsies and the British Imagination

Introduction

Children of Hagar

I<small>N</small> 1930, the gypsiologist John Sampson, librarian of the University of Liverpool and leading member of the Gypsy Lore Society, published a volume he had labored over with love for many decades. He called it *The Wind on the Heath: A Gypsy Anthology*. With its frontispiece a beautifully colored painting by Augustus John (figure 1), it contains more than three hundred selections—excerpts from novels and plays, entire poems, journal entries—culled from the works of great writers, mainly, although not exclusively, British. Shakespeare, Milton, Bunyan, Gay, Clare, Fielding, Keats, Wordsworth, Hazlitt, Lamb, Scott, Howitt, Arnold, Browning, George Eliot, Hardy, Meredith, and George Borrow—the nineteenth-century writer most closely associated with recording Gypsy ways—are represented, as are members of the Gypsy Lore Society, founded in 1888 to collect and preserve the cultural artifacts of Gypsy life, and many of their Edwardian progeny. Although Sampson intended the volume to convince readers of the "glamour that enwraps the Gypsy race" and promote the idea of the Gypsy as "touchstone to the personality of man," I begin with it simply as evidence of the ubiquity of the idea of the Gypsy in British literature and culture.[1] Readers alert to the Gypsy presence in British texts might not be surprised by the breadth of Sampson's anthology, and students of Victorian literature certainly would find it confirmation of what they already suspected: that the "gipsy brat" Heathcliff, Matthew Arnold's scholar-gypsy, Edward Rochester's Gypsy masquerade, and Maggie Tulliver's defection to a Gypsy camp on the outskirts of town reflect the persistence of a widespread dependence on the tropes of Gypsy life in British writing and culture. And although Sampson's anthology does not make it explicit, Gypsies were an object of fascination not simply for creators of literature throughout centuries, but for

FIGURE 1 Augustus John, *Spanish Gitana*, ca. 1921 (oil on canvas). (Private collection. © The Fine Art Society, London)

John Sampson used John's painting as the frontispiece for *The Wind on the Heath* (1930), retitling it *Head of a Gitana*.

ethnographers, historians, philologists, social and legal reformers, graphic artists, and journalists.

Sampson's anthology offers a starting place for thinking about the Gypsy as one of the primary "surrogate and . . . underground sel[ves]" of British identity. The phrase is Edward Said's, used to describe the place of the Orient in European imaginations.[2] Said's critical perspective is especially useful in regard to the Gypsies because it renders the complexity and ambivalence of an orientalist mentality, insisting on the importance of imagination, identification, and desire, as well as of relations of power, domination, and repression. The Orient, as place and idea, provided Westerners with careers (the East *is* a career, said Benjamin Disraeli in his novel *Tancred, or the New Crusade* [1847]), scholarly pursuits, opportunities for masquerade and the refashioning of identity, and an escape from the strictures of European bourgeois culture. And in many important respects, fascination with Gypsies in Britain was a form of orientalism.[3] "Gypsies are the Arabs of pastoral England," declared the gypsy lorist Henry Crofton, "the Bedouins of our commons and woodlands."[4] Like the "Oriental" or the colonized, racially marked subject, the Gypsy was associated with a rhetoric of primitive desires, lawlessness, mystery, cunning, sexual excess, godlessness, and savagery—with freedom from the repressions, both constraining and culture building, of Western civilization. Gypsies were the victims of oppression, harassment, and discrimination and of persistent efforts to outlaw and destroy their way of life (figure 2).[5] They operated as a field for the projection of what was both feared and desired in that part of the British cultural self that was denied, reviled, or prohibited. Gypsies functioned in British cultural symbolism as a perennial other, a recurrent and apparently necessary marker of difference that, like the biblical Hagar and Ishmael, represented an alternative and rejected lineage.

Unlike colonial subjects, however, Gypsies were a domestic or an internal other, and their proximity and visibility were crucial features in their deployment as literary or symbolic figures. Their familiarity lent them an exoticism that was, at the same time, indigenous and homely. When the speaker in William Wordsworth's poem "Gypsies" (1807) comes upon an "unbroken knot" of sleeping Gypsies on his rural travels, when Jane Austen's Harriet Smith is accosted by begging Gypsy children on the outskirts of Highbury in *Emma* (1816), or when George Eliot's Maggie Tulliver runs off to join the Gypsies camped in a lane in *The Mill on the Floss* (1860), no one, either characters in these texts or nineteenth-century readers, would register shock at the invasion of English landscapes by a foreign people. Indeed, these Gypsies are British, if not in citizenship, then certainly in permanent domicile and, most likely, country of origin. David Mayall, historian of Gypsies in nineteenth-century Britain, remarks, for example, that the most virulent anti-Gypsy racism on the part of the English most often was reserved for foreign Gypsies—from Greece, Serbia, Hungary, and other lands in eastern and southern Europe—who took refuge in Britain in the late nineteenth and early twentieth centuries.[6] Arthur Morrison's "The Case of the Missing Hand," one of the Martin Hewitt stories, includes a band of Gypsies who turn out to be members of the Lee family, a well-known English clan. The one Gypsy who is "much darker . . . than any other present" is from Romania, and his suspicious behavior, together with his distinctive swarthiness, immediately make him a suspect in the crime that Hewitt is

FIGURE 2 John Garside, "Gypsies and Gentiles." (From John Sampson, *The Wind on the Heath* [London: Chatto and Windus, 1930])

Garside's Gypsy stands in front of a sign that offers a reward of 10 shillings for the rounding up of "Rogues and Vagabonds," a category that included Gypsies.

investigating.[7] Although British Gypsies were considered alien, they were, at the same time, imagined as long-standing features of English rural life and, in some nostalgic views of the English past, signify the very essence of true and ancient Britishness (figure 3).

And yet, as all these literary examples suggest, Gypsies tended to exist not in the midst but on the periphery of British settlement, so they were present but separate, often within view but almost never absorbed, encountered but seldom intimately known. In *Emma*, the geographic point of Harriet's encounter with the Gypsies precisely marks, albeit comically, the cultural borders of provincial community, beyond which a young lady should not roam without protection. Only because the Gypsy band that approaches her is unfamiliar and yet known by rumor and reputation could Harriet be so frightened by what amounts to a

FIGURE 3 John Garside, "Field and Sky." (From John Sampson, *The Wind on the Heath* [London: Chatto and Windus, 1930])

Garside's is a classic image of a secure and inviting Gypsy camp.

group of rowdy children or Emma so eager to make her friend's encounter into an elaborate tale of danger, rescue, and romance. Indeed, the Gypsies' place in Austen's novel exemplifies the mix of foreignness and familiarity, exoticism and homeliness that characterizes their role in British imaginative life.

Jonathan Boyarin has called these alien but domestic groups "the other within." In an essay concerned primarily with European Jews, Boyarin recognizes the Gypsies as a parallel group. Both possess "transnational (or at least non-national) and stubbornly distinct minority identities," and both have histories in pre-Holocaust Europe that tend to be overshadowed and obscured by the events and atrocities of World War II.[8] Like the Jews, with whom they were frequently paired throughout the nineteenth century and beyond, the Gypsies were a people of diaspora, wanderers with no state of their own and thus dispersed to reside among all nations. "They have gone wandering about as pilgrims and strangers," wrote John Hoyland, a Quaker reformer, yet "they remain in all places, as to custom and habits, what their fathers were."⁹ Also like the Jews, they appeared to retain their separateness and their customs.

Walter Scott and George Eliot—both of whom were drawn to stories of dispossession, cultural multiplicity, and national identity—devoted novels and poems to Gypsy and Jewish plots: Scott's *Guy Mannering* (1815) and *Ivanhoe* (1819) and Eliot's *The Spanish Gypsy* (1868) and *Daniel Deronda* (1874–1876). George Borrow's alter ego Lavengro is fascinated by Jews, their language, and their separateness and regards the fragility of their modern survival as analogous to that of the English Gypsies, about whom he writes. The Romany themselves circulated myths of shared Jewish–Gypsy ancestry, primarily in the story of the two "Jew brothers," Schmul and Rom-Schmul, who lived at the time of Christ. While the first brother was reputed to be delighted at the Crucifixion, the second wanted to save Jesus from death if he could. Finding this impossible, Rom-Schmul stole one of the nails destined to pierce Christ's feet. For this reason, one nail had to suffice for both feet, resulting in the overlapping of Christ's legs and the conversion of Rom-Schmul, the original ancestor of all Gypsies, to Christianity.¹⁰ Jews and Gypsies haunted each other throughout the nineteenth century as persecuted and stateless peoples, amounting to each other's "strange, secret sharer[s]," a term that Said borrowed from Joseph Conrad to refer to the paired discourses of orientalism and anti-Semitism.¹¹

Yet the differences—both mythic and real—between the two groups shaped literary representation as well. Jews may have occupied a reviled or, at least, suspect place on the edge of the British world, but they mingled with polite society, if only as business associates, moneylenders, and tradesmen. Gypsies, who were imagined as dwelling at the other end of the economic spectrum from reputedly rapacious and wealthy Jews, maintained a tangential relationship to the economy and a social and geographic distance from British communities. Whether underworld criminal, like Fagin in Charles Dickens's *Oliver Twist* (1837–1839), or prosperous charlatan, like Melmotte in Anthony Trollope's *The Way We Live Now* (1875), the Jew in Victorian fiction is almost always associated with urban—or cosmopolitan—cultures and with greed and overreaching. Seldom, except for Rebecca in Scott's *Ivanhoe* and her fictional descendents, are Jewish characters romanticized or idealized, even in a condescending and distorting way.¹² Gypsy ways of living and subsisting—vagabondage and rural wandering—could, however, play a role in bohemian mythmaking and in dreams of escaping from stifling respectability. Even though London and its environs attracted the bulk of the Gypsy population, at least during the nineteenth century, Gypsies most often were cast in literary texts as pastoral figures, allied with an aesthetic of the picturesque and with protests against modern encroachments on unsettled lands.¹³ A striking exception to this pattern is Dickens's Pancks, the self-declared "gipsy" and "fortune-teller" in *Little Dorrit* (1855–1857). Pancks, in truth a good man who exposes the hypocrisy and sham of his boss, Mr. Casby, and helps uncover the secret of the Dorrit family's fortune, functions as a front man or middleman, collecting rents from the poor inhabitants of Bleeding Heart Yard for Casby, the real gouger and exploiter of the novel. Not only is Pancks an urban Gypsy, but he plays an economic role often associated with Jews.[14]

Some historians and writers, among them Eliot, also emphasized a difference of history between Gypsy and Jew. Many regarded Jews as conscious of their history and aware of their origin, while Gypsies, they argued—with no sacred texts, clearly defined homeland, or written histories—lacked a rich and solid basis for either a national identity or a propitious future. Furthermore, the Jews' elevated, if eclipsed, role in the history of Christianity gave them a cultural status that the Gypsies, presumed by many to be heathens, could not enjoy. Gypsies and Jews also differed in the matter of a putative home. Even before the political project of Zionism, Jews looked toward a specific land, with its attendant history, as their home and conceived of themselves as a people in exile. For Gypsies, no idea of a place of origin or fantasy of return informed their sense of self or yearning for redemption although, as we shall see, Eliot struggled in *The Spanish Gypsy* to endow them with both.[15]

Origins

The most pervasive theme in writing and thinking about Gypsies throughout the nineteenth century, however—and the feature that most clearly distinguished them from Jews and other minority groups—was the mystery of their origin. Since the arrival of Gypsies in England and Scotland in the early sixteenth century, British chroniclers and officials believed them to have come from Egypt, and thus called them Egyptians.[16] As late as 1743, legislation that prohibited fortune-telling referred to its likeliest practitioners by this name, and, even when the epithet fell out of favor, the short version—Gypsies—stuck.[17] By the late eighteenth century, philologists and historians began to identify the Gypsies' place of origin as India, largely because of vocabulary that Romani, their language, shared with Hindustani (and, behind that, Sanskrit).[18] In 1787, the German linguist Heinrich Grellman published a lengthy ethnological study of the Gypsies and ended it with an assertion that, contrary to popular belief, they came from "Hindostan" and were likely identifiable as the lowest caste of Indians: "Parias; or, as they are called [there] Suders."[19] A translation of Grellman's book appeared in England in 1807, and John Hoyland's history of the Gypsies, aimed at their moral and religious rehabilitation, floated Grellman's thesis about their origin a few years later. Hoyland's title, *A Historical Survey of the Customs, Habits, & Present State of the Gypsies: Designed to Develope the Origin of This Singular People, and to Promote the Amelioration of Their Condition*, sounded the keynotes of popular interest in the Gypsies: customs, habits, origin, and the need for conversion. His text also promoted the idea of a scientific search for the truth of their beginnings.

Despite Grellman's and Hoyland's work early in the century, those who wrote about the Gypsies seemed unwilling to relinquish the belief that their origin was ultimately still mysterious. The debate about their genesis (and the reasons for their initial exodus) became a perennial feature of texts that centered on Gypsies. The ostensible ambiguity of their derivation animated the imaginations of various commentators, who, even while acknowledging the power of the Indian hypothesis, would, with great relish, offer alternative speculations of their own. Perhaps the Gypsies were the descendants of Ishmael, the son of Hagar and Abraham, cast out by his father in favor of Isaac to wander the earth.[20] Were they, in fact, Egyptians, who had made their way to Europe while doing penance for withholding hospitality from the Virgin Mary and her son?[21] Or were they actually German Jews who, unfairly blamed for the plague of 1348, had hidden in the forests to escape persecution?[22] Gypsies themselves clung to a number of myths about their origin. In a memoir published in 1970, Silvester Gordon Boswell, an English Gypsy, includes a variation of the Rom-Schmul story to explain Gypsy origins: "That's my belief. That's what I've been taught." His version features no Jews but only a nameless first Gypsy, a metalworker, who was asked to make nails for Christ's Crucifixion. Boswell finds redemptive possibilities in the disappearance of the fourth nail: "[The Gentiles] are realising that the Gypsies done a *good* turn by taking it away instead of adding it to the other three."[23] Although thieves, the original Gypsies might one day be thanked for their efforts to lessen the suffering of Christ.

The reputed mystery of the Gypsies' homeland became, in other words, a necessary and stubbornly preserved staple of thinking about and imagining Gypsies. Their literary representation was intimately connected to an obsession with origins of all kinds—linguistic, personal, and national. A people "without" origins came to stand, paradoxically, for the question of origins itself and to be used as a trope to signify beginnings, primal ancestry, and the ultimate secret of individual identity. Comparative philologists who recognized correspondences between Romani and Indian languages were part of a larger movement in Germany and England that began to consider Sanskrit as "the elder sister of the classical and Romance languages, and . . . the Teutonic as well" (figure 4).[24] This ancient language might yield clues to the histories of different peoples and to the connections between disparate races and their civilizations. Some philologists believed that, as J. W. Burrow puts it, "if all languages could be shown to be related, one could establish the single origin of the human race."[25] The search for linguistic and human origins gave Romani an elevated status among certain early-nineteenth-century philologists and ethnologists, and claims for its

188   HISTORICAL SURVEY

words was sent to James Corder, Broadstreet, Bloomsbury. He obtained from the Gypsies in his neighbourhood, the translation affixed to them.

English.	Gypsey.	English.	Gypsey.
One	Yake	Hot day	Tal-dewes
Two	Duêe	Ear	Kau
Three	Trin	Day	Dewes
Four	Stor	Night	Raut
Five	Pan	White	Parnau
Ten	Dyche	Sheep	Bolko
Head	Charro	Hog	Borlo
Eyes	Yock	Fish	Marcho
Nose	Nack	House	Kare
Bread	Mor	Gold	Sonnekay
Bread & butter	Kil-mor	Silver	Rupe
Beer	Limbar	Dog	Jukou
Hair	Bâlo	Horse	Grarre
Cold day	Shil-dewes		

When it is known that Gypsies are unacquainted with letters, and that James Corder, who took from the mouths of those in the parish called St. Giles, the preceding Gypsey

OF THE GYPSIES.   189

words, did not know of Grellmann's vocabulary, the coincidence appears very remarkable; but it is still more so with the Turkish Gypsey specimen by Jacob Bryant, exhibited also in the 8th Section. Robert Forster of Tottenham, who has been a coadjutor in this work, transmitted the following collection of words obtained from Gypsies in his neighbourhood.

Gypsey.	English.	Gypsey.	English.
Parnee	Water	Shill-deues	Cold day
Jewcal	Dog	Taldu	Hot day
Maurau	Bread	Moila	Ass
Kil-maurau	Bread & butter	Gur	Horse
Livenar	Beer		

In the conversation a clergyman had with the Bosswell gang, as published in the Christian Guardian for 1812 and 1813, they told him *Chum,* was the sun; *Chuu,* the moon; *Kalmàro,* bread and butter; and *Livina,* drink. The first two of those words almost exactly accord with Grellmann's vocabulary, and the latter as nearly with Robert Forster's and James

N 3

FIGURE 4 Romani words and phrases, with their English translations. (From John Hoyland, *A Historical Survey of the Customs, Habits, & Present State of the Gypsies* [York: Darton, Harvey, 1816])

importance found their way into the more fantastical speculations of writers like George Borrow, who ventured that Romani might turn out to be the "mother of all languages in the world" and a "picklock, an open sesame" to the study of language itself.[26]

When John Sampson refers to the Gypsy as "the touchstone to the personality of man" in the preface to *The Wind on the Heath*, he has some of this philological speculation in mind, but he also implies a conviction that the Gypsies played an important role as ur-ancestor to humankind. If Gypsies are represented in literature and other kinds of writing as primitive, it is not only to underscore the ostensibly underevolved nature of their customs and traditions in relation to advanced British culture, but also to suggest that they occupy a primal spot in the history of civilizations and contain in their culture clues to essential humanity that might otherwise be lost. For some writers, this meant that the Gypsy could remind modern men and women of a time before the corruptions of modernity corroded their souls. For others, who regarded the Gypsy as a pastoral figure, Gypsies could conjure an older, preindustrial England, a golden age before enclosure, urban encroachments, the railway, and other defilements of nature. In "The Scholar-Gipsy" (1853), Matthew Arnold famously associates Gypsies with resistance to the "strange disease of modern life." In many of his lyrics, John Clare evokes Gypsies as emblems of both liberty and safety: they seemed to him to live a life free from social constraints and protected from contemporary dangers. Members of the Gypsy Lore Society regarded Gypsies as remnants of a golden age, the human equivalents of village rituals and rural customs long forgotten. In a slightly different register, Walter Scott made Meg Merrilies, the Gypsy sibyl of *Guy Mannering*, at once the embodiment of the "old ways" threatened by new legal and class arrangements and the symbolic maternal presence in the life of his hero, Harry Bertram. In Scott's novel, Gypsies are associated with the complex and partly shrouded origins of both a culture and an individual.

Kidnapped

As in *Guy Mannering*, the mystery of the Gypsies' ancestry makes its way into numerous fictional narratives in the form of stories of vexed personal identities and displaced protagonists. In Scott's novel, Harry Bertram has been separated from his past and has no idea that he is the son and heir of a Scottish laird. In *The Mill on the Floss*, Maggie Tulliver interprets her own physical and temperamental differences from her family—especially, her mother and aunts—as evidence that she actually was born to Gypsies and ended up in the wrong world. Eliot's narrative poem *The Spanish Gypsy* tells the story of a fifteenth-century Spanish princess who discovers that she is, indeed, a Gypsy. The parentage of Heathcliff, the so-called gipsy brat of Emily Brontë's *Wuthering Heights* (1847), remains a permanent mystery: an orphan snatched from the streets of Liverpool by Mr. Earnshaw, he may have come from abroad through the port of the city, be the illegitimate son of the man who brings him home to Wuthering Heights, or have descended from non-English and certainly non-Anglo-Saxon stock. Even Arnold's scholar-gypsy, at once an Oxford student and a Gypsy, develops a muddled and protean identity over time.

These stories of hidden or ambiguous identity, all variations on the changeling plot, were clearly influenced not only by mysteries of Gypsy origin, but also by long-standing myths of Gypsy kidnappings, themselves the products of cultural anxieties about difference. Legends of kidnapping and child swapping had long been associated with Gypsies, and accusations of such crimes haunt them to this day.[27] A combination of proximity and distance fostered English fantasies that Gypsies were close enough to switch one of their children with an English child without detection and yet remote enough to place that child permanently out of the reach of his parents. So, the idea went, a child could grow up in a Gypsy family, lost forever to her own. Probably the most famous story of Gypsy kidnapping—or near-kidnapping—involved Adam Smith, who was said to have been taken as a small boy and returned a few hours later.[28] The thought of losing the great political economist to a Gypsy band seemed so horrifying that the tale became a useful admonition to wayward or recalcitrant children. The father of the painter Augustus John warned his children that if they "walk[ed] abroad on market days . . . they should be kidnaped by the gypsies and spirited away in their caravans, no one knew where."[29] This possibility became a staple of nursery rhymes, the premise for the plots of popular fiction, and even the stuff of lullabies that mixed comfort and threat:

> Hush nae, hush nae, dinna fret ye;
> The black Tinkler winna na get ye.[30]

Parents also apparently teased their naughty children, much as Mrs. Tulliver does in *The Mill on the Floss*, by telling them that they must be the offspring of Gypsies, not born of English parents.

David Mayall has suggested that the habitual association of Gypsies with kidnapping grew out of the need to account for blue-eyed, fair-haired Gypsy children, who simply did not fit the swarthy, raven-haired stereotype.[31] Indeed, many recent accusations of child stealing have arisen merely from sightings of Gypsy adults accompanied by blond children.[32] In the nineteenth century and earlier, when genetics was unknown and paternity could not be proved, suspicions about true parentage were often close to the surface. Tales of kidnapping and child swapping, in other words, reflect the myth of group homogeneity, as well as the belief in absolute distinctions among racial, national, or ethnic types that almost all groups—but especially dominant ones—hold dear. Gypsies should not have fair children, and the Tullivers should not have a dark-skinned child; otherwise, we cannot be sure of exactly who we are and where we belong. The perpetual and imaginatively powerful divide between light and dark affords cultures one convenient way of drawing the line between self and other. (The belief in detectable class differences operates similarly but with another set of identifying characteristics, such as speech or comportment.) The implicit impossibility of making such neat distinctions, however, haunts all societies, eroding their confidence in the purity of any race or discrete group. Kidnapping stories, captivity narratives, and foundling plots express the anxiety created by adhering to an absolute and inherently fallacious separation between peoples and offer reassuring explanations for differences within groups that exist universally.

Kidnapping stories and Gypsy narratives, as well as the larger tradition of foundling or bastard plots, also signal something of the fundamental mystery of individual origins that, even in an age of scientific sophistication, haunts human psyches. Uncertainty about identity and fantasies about parentage form the basis for Freud's theory of the "family romance." According to Freud's schema, the child's feelings of resentment or sexual rivalry lead him (the child is male for Freud) to imagine that he is adopted, in reality the offspring of parents of higher social standing, whose superiority elevates the child's image of himself and simultaneously diminishes the stature of the "adoptive" parents, primarily the father.[33] In eighteenth- and nineteenth-century fiction, the child's fantasy became the novelist's plot: Tom Jones discovers that his mother is not a maid but the sister of his prosperous and kindly surrogate father, Squire Allworthy. Oliver Twist, although born and raised in a workhouse, learns that his father has willed him a fortune and that his mother is of genteel birth. The child-stealing stories associated with Gypsies in folklore and fiction lend themselves to the imagined plot of family romance and the literary plot of the foundling. *Guy Mannering* follows this paradigm: Harry Bertram, like Oliver Twist, turns out to be a well-born heir.

There is another version of the family romance and its literary manifestations, however, that involves the fantasy not of social aggrandizement and aspiration, but of lowly or stigmatized birth. The desire to rival and defeat the parent can also express itself as the wish to escape from the bonds of obedience and confor- mity through the discovery of a secret non-English, non-white (to the extent that Englishness is defined as white) self. Many of the protagonists of Gypsy plots and the writers who gravitated to Gypsies as subjects of art imagined that they had been switched at birth as a way of explaining their inability or unwilling- ness to adhere to parental expectations. They rationalized their personal idio- syncrasies, eccentricities, or feelings of being "out of place" in the world by inventing a Gypsy lineage. Michael Holroyd tells us that Augustus John longed to be "someone other than his father's son" and went from imagining himself a descendant of Owen Glendower, the last Welshman to hold the title Prince of Wales, to posing as a Gypsy.[34] These narratives of alternative birth—whether that of Augustus John, George Eliot, or Maggie Tulliver—suggest that the longing to be something other than English, Welsh, or Scots was, for some, as powerful and certainly as generative as the fear of losing or diluting their class position, nationality, or race. In the Gypsy version of the family romance, psychologi- cal anxiety about and desire for difference are combined with a rebellious zeal against the perceived homogeneity of Anglo-Saxon culture.

Gender Heterodoxy

Writers who used Gypsy plots and figures also often chafed against patterns of gender conformity. They tended to invent Gypsy characters who deviated from conventional forms of masculinity and femininity. When we think of nine- teenth-century French traditions of Gypsy representation, sirens, seductresses, and exotic female beauties come to mind. The best-known of these femmes fatales—Victor Hugo's Esmeralda and Prosper Merimée's, then Georges Bizet's,

Carmen—emerged from fantasies of heterosexual male longing.[35] Early-nine-teenth-century English commentators noted the lasciviousness and abandon of Gypsy women's dancing, and late-nineteenth-century male bohemians, includ-ing some members of the Gypsy Lore Society, conjured Gypsy beauties as objects of desire.[36] But by far the most interesting and memorable literary Gypsies in the nineteenth-century English (or Scottish) tradition are heterodox in their relation-ship not to chastity but to norms of either masculinity or femininity. Scott's Meg Merrilies, immortalized in poetry, drama, and painting, combines elements of feminine and masculine appearance and affect; Arnold's scholar-gypsy, flower-laden and languid, is a vaguely androgynous dropout from university and manly professional pursuits. These figures launched a tradition of literary Gypsies who transcended the divide between male and female and, through their association with racial differences that loosened the bonds of convention, could circumvent rigid standards of gender difference.

In Freud's theory of the family romance, the male child's fantasy of secret, superior birth expresses his desire to (literally) lord it over his father, perhaps in the context of Oedipal competition for his mother. As the scion of an imag-ined noble father, the son achieves mastery over his real one and thereby estab-lishes—at least in the abstract—his adult masculinity. In the alternative family romance, with its fantasy of lowly or exotic birth, the son can be said to overcome his father through rejecting a certain idea of mastery and opting out of conven-tional manly success. The "Romany ryes," or English gentlemen who fostered their own identification with Gypsies, sometimes through language study and sometimes through vagabondage and bohemian habits, rebelled against the strictures of respectability and the demands of bourgeois manhood.[37] Poets like John Clare, Matthew Arnold, and even the ambivalent William Wordsworth used the Gypsy as, among other things, an alter ego free from the shackles of the daily grind and from the modern world of getting, spending, working, and obey-ing the law. The pastoral, indolent, and sometimes passive male Gypsy of their poems offers a contrast—and a comforting one—to conventional and exigent models of nineteenth-century manliness.

Arnold's scholar-gypsy, to return to him once more, provides an antidote to the "sick hurry" and "divided aims" of "modern life," not by undertaking heroic or noble actions but by "leaning backward in a pensive dream, . . . fostering in [his] lap a heap of flowers" and avoiding contact with the contaminants of civili-zation.[38] George Borrow's Lavengro, the prototype, along with Arnold's scholar, of the "Romany rye," gives up on both worldly success and heterosexual union to roam in solitary fashion the forests and dingles of Britain and, ultimately, the world. As we shall see, his relationship to the masculine efficacy of his father, a soldier and boxer, works itself out through his identification with Gypsies and pursuit of an unsettled, peripatetic existence. Even Scott's hero Harry Bertram, who finally does resume his rightful place, rank, and title, wanders for years as a nameless, homeless man whose dispossession and rootlessness mirror those of the Gypsies banished by his father. The Gypsy, imagined as an itinerant outside the economic and social structures of British life, becomes a trope for nonproductive work, refusal of ambition, and the delicacy and softness—the implied effeminacy—of the unsalaried and unharnessed male.

Scott invented Meg Merrilies, the "ancient sibyl" and Gypsy witch of *Guy Mannering*, as a hybrid figure, at once Scottish and "Eastern," male and female. She is six feet tall and of "masculine stature," and her voice hits high notes "too shrill for a man" and low notes "too deep for a woman."[39] The biological mother of twelve children and the surrogate mother of Harry Bertram, she occupies a powerful maternal position and conforms to the image of the mythic female seer. But she is also the leader of her people, the fiercest defender of the rights of her tribe, and the Gypsy who swears to avenge their persecution at the hands of the local laird. She is, then, both masculine and feminine in the roles she plays and in the manner of her dress and speech. This outsize Gypsy leader helped establish the figure of the androgynous—or masculin-ized—female Gypsy in nineteenth-century literature. There are traces of Meg not only in many contemporaneous works of art, but also in the Gypsy "mother" and fortune-teller played by Edward Rochester in Charlotte Brontë's *Jane Eyre* (1847) and in the character of Fedalma, the Spanish princess who discovers that she is the daughter of a Gypsy chieftain, in George Eliot's *The Spanish Gypsy*. Fedalma, who begins as a romantic heroine destined for a great love match, ends as a celibate leader of her people, the inheritor of her father's mantle, for whom both love and feminine attire are prohibited.

A number of the works of Eliot, the nineteenth-century writer most interested in the literary uses of the Gypsy, exemplify what we might call the female version of the family romance. Although Freud had a hard time imagining a girl's fantasy of social aggrandizement in connection with hostile Oedipal feelings (perhaps because the father, not the mother, establishes family rank and social standing), we can easily see a novel like *Jane Eyre* in terms of the model of the family romance.[40] Jane outclasses her reviled Aunt Reed by marrying Edward Rochester (although her desire for independence takes its toll on Rochester's health and property). But in Eliot's variation, especially in *The Spanish Gypsy* and briefly in *The Mill on the Floss*, the fantasy of stigmatized, rather than elevated, birth frees the heroine from the cultural and literary requirements of the marriage plot. The eccentric female, whether heroine or author, imagines herself a Gypsy as a way of escaping from the exigencies of conventional femininity. The Gypsy's habitual swarthiness becomes a marker not simply of foreignness, of non-Englishness, but of heterodox femininity as well. In the girl's family romance, a fantasy of social stigma masks rebellion against or even defeat of the mother. The mother, cus-tomary model and reproducer of exemplary femininity, is replaced by an alien and exotic template that enables the heroine to reinvent womanly identity.

Dissociation

The phenomenon of dissociation refers not, like kidnapping, to a trope but to a mode of representation and its evolving history. Over time, Gypsy identity or, if you will, the quality of "gypsiness" came to be abstracted and separated from Gypsies themselves. It could be argued that there is always an inevitable dissociation between any marginal social group and its representation in literature or in the dominant culture, but, in the case of the Gypsies, the gap between people and image has been especially profound. This is evident on the level of casual language, in which the word "gypsy" can refer to an itinerant dancer or stage performer, a kind of moth, a type of cabdriver, an open-air meal, or an individual—perhaps a scholar—who moves frequently from job to job or place to place.[41] These uses barely call to mind the actual people from which they were derived, nor do they carry the stigma of insult, so neutral do they seem and so wholly separate from any original referent.

A similar dissociation operates between Gypsies and their characterization in literary texts, in which, as Katie Trumpener puts it, "literary traditions [are conflated] with living people."[42] Trumpener argues that this trend deepened over time, reached its ghastly climax during the Holocaust, and extends to the present day, with harsh and even brutal consequences.[43] Although my discussions of nineteenth-century poems, novels, sketches, ethnographies, periodical articles, laws, memoirs, and, to a lesser extent, graphic images support important parts of Trumpener's claim, I offer a few modifications of her argument at the outset. First, although many writers confused symbol with actual people without any irony, some used this conflation self-consciously and pointedly. Both Jane Austen and George Eliot mock their heroines—Emma Woodhouse and Maggie Tulliver, respectively—for failing to distinguish between fiction (or myth) and reality in the matter of Gypsies. In a brief but salient episode in *Emma*, after Harriet Smith returns from her traumatic encounter with the Gypsies on Frank Churchill's steadying arm, the story of her ultimately benign experience with what was, after all, a group of children begins to circulate through Highbury as a drama of terror to be savored and retold. Emma turns the incident into a tale of romance and chivalry, feeling sure that the potential lovers were thrown together by an unprecedented ordeal. Emma's misreading of the event is consistent with her misperceptions of romantic attachments throughout the novel.

In addition, Emma fails to grasp that Frank was fortunately placed to rescue Harriet because he had just come from visiting his secret love, Jane Fairfax. Austen seems to be commenting both on Emma's "imaginist" tendencies (and self-delusions) and on the excessive insularity of Emma's world, in which stories of danger and romance are concocted from the mildest contact with figures whose meanings themselves derive from story and myth.[44] Like Emma's nephews, who spin Harriet's chance meeting with the beggar children into the "story of Harriet and the gypsies," Maggie Tulliver first envisions her escape to the Gypsy camp on Dunlow Common as a fairy tale.[45] "It was just like a story," Maggie thinks, delighting in being addressed as a "pretty lady" and treated, she imagines, like a queen.[46] The narrator's language undercuts Maggie's childish illusions and arrogant assumptions about the Gypsies' enthusiasm at her arrival. Her confidence becomes panic as she realizes that the Gypsies have no interest in her and as her idealization of them turns to unfounded fear. Both Austen and Eliot deploy the "literariness" of Gypsies: they not only make use of a well-established shorthand of evocation (Austen's Gypsies do not even have to appear in the narrative), but also debunk familiar stereotypes as a way of commenting on their heroines' myopia and delusions. The phenomenon of Gypsies' factitiousness in cultural representation becomes part of the fabric of fiction itself.

Second, the separation between Gypsies and their representation began benignly in the mid-nineteenth century and grew out of the sympathetic identification of writers like Arnold, Borrow, and Eliot with the marginality of Gypsies.[47] The space that opened up between image and actual people was created by the "Romany rye" and other fellow travelers whose own eccentricities and dissenting postures toward Victorian society caused them to gravitate toward the Gypsy as representative outsider. In works like Arnold's "The Scholar-Gipsy" and "Thyrsis" (1866), Borrow's *Lavengro* (1851) and *The Romany Rye* (1857), and Eliot's *The Spanish Gypsy*, we see empathy and intense identification at work, but we also see that the alienated writer or artist begins to stand in for and replace the Gypsy in a cultural discourse that threatens to occlude the already partly invisible object of sympathy. By the late nineteenth century, this eclipse became nearly total and, in some cases, took on a more insidious caste. The members of the Gypsy Lore Society, bohemians and scholars who studied Romany language and customs, were in the paradoxical position of bringing Gypsy culture to light and, at the same time, obscuring it through the force of their own projections.

In certain literary works of the turn of the century, the problem created by dissociation between rhetoric and referent is not projection but caricature: a use of the Gypsy as sign or symbol that is completely emptied of reference to reality, history, or experience. In Arthur Conan Doyle's story "The Adventure of the Speckled Band" (1891), a mystery and its solution turn on a Gypsy band (both tribe and headgear) that is never seen. The evocation of the speckled band is sufficient to cast suspicion on an invisible group of people because of the associations—many of them literary—that accrued over time between Gypsies and criminality. Whereas Austen undermines the myth of Gypsy criminality and demystifies the off-stage Gypsy band in *Emma*, Conan Doyle depends on and never dispels the image of marauding Gypsies that he can conjure with little more than a word or two.

In a third modification of Trumpener's theory of the "literariness" of the Gypsy, I suggest that this form of metonymic representation reaches a dead end in D. H. Lawrence's novella *The Virgin and the Gipsy* (1930). In his story of a middle-class young woman's sexual awakening through her encounters with a charismatic male Gypsy traveler, Lawrence makes use of well-established stereotypes of the physically compelling, emotionally primitive Romany, but he also ultimately challenges them by exposing their reliance on ignorance and misperception. Lawrence both exploits and debunks the cultural myths of Gypsies' elemental passions, association with nature, inarticulateness, and perpetual anonymity. At the end of his story, Lawrence gives his Gypsy an identity and a voice, reversing—or at least exposing—the trend toward the invisibility and namelessness of the literary Gypsy.

Finally, I consider the partly written, partly dictated autobiography of Gordon Boswell, a British Gypsy born in 1895, and the brief statement of John Megel, an American Gypsy who was an informal representative to the United States Holocaust Memorial Council. These texts offer an opportunity to speculate on the connections between writing and self-consciousness in the Gypsies' emergence from the realm of the literary into a history composed by themselves. Boswell writes a personal history that directly or indirectly controverts a number of myths about Gypsy life. Megel suggests that the Holocaust enabled—or forced—Gypsies to recognize themselves as historical subjects and to articulate (through testimony and through institutions like the Holocaust Museum) their relationship to the devastating experience of genocide as well as to a largely unwritten collective past. "Through awareness of the Holocaust," Megel writes, "we will become aware of our own history. . . . [W]e can't prepare for the future until we understand our past."[48] The bitter irony of this point of view notwithstanding, Megel proposes that Gypsies begin to wrest the narratives of their own experience from others and effect social and even political change through claiming possession of the record of the past.

In tracing this movement in the representation of the Gypsy from ancestral kin to phantom and then to historical subject, I want to pose some general questions about the benefits, limits, and liabilities of identification. British literature is filled with apparently sympathetic evocations of Gypsy life. Identification is almost always the source of this sympathy, even for someone like John Clare, who had a keen sense of the economic and political realities that Gypsies faced and the harassment to which they were subjected. Is it possible, we might ask, to champion the Gypsies in their oppression without engaging in the potentially distorting process of personal identification? Without the mechanisms, both psychological and fictional, of fantasies or tropes of family romance, kidnapping, and infants switched at birth? When does identification exceed its ethical bounds and become a kind of projection that obscures even the partial reality of the real Gypsy? At what point is the Gypsy obliterated in the writer's own search for expression of self, nostalgia for a golden age, or critique of modernity? I have chosen in this book to focus on the Gypsy as surrogate self to the British writer because the most powerful and influential images of Gypsies in the literature of the nineteenth century convey the general longing to reimagine or expand British identity through a wider vocabulary of images and types. This focus should not, however, obscure the fact that Gypsies, like the children of Hagar—although viewed with fascination and desire, understood as a parallel line of descent or the road not taken—remain an abandoned alternative to and a mere proxy for the British self.

It will be clear that I do not follow a teleological line of argument in relation to the persecution of Gypsies in the twentieth century. That is, I consider nineteenth-century British representations of Gypsies and Gypsy life not as preludes to the exterminatory policies of the Holocaust, but as expressions of a variety of attitudes, some highly discriminatory and racist, others sympathetic and tolerant. In this regard, Jonathan Boyarin's argument about the occlusion of the pre-Holocaust European Jew from history is helpful. The horror of the Holocaust, he writes, eclipses the lives of European Jews before the 1930s and makes it almost impossible not to read backward from events that render all earlier forms of anti-Semitism and distorted characterization insidious and potentially violent.[49] The situation of the Gypsies is not, of course, absolutely equivalent, in that even their fate at the hands of the Nazis has been partly occluded, sometimes by an exclusive emphasis on the suffering of Jews. Neither can the relatively sparse documentation of their lives in the nineteenth century be compared with the extensive record available for many European Jewish communities. For these reasons, it may seem offensive to some to concentrate on what is essentially a history of representation, in a manner largely separate from the events of twentieth-century persecution. My aim, however, is to illuminate the cultural meanings of a pervasive and strikingly resilient tradition of representation in the nineteenth century and the early decades of the twentieth, in a time before and outside of genocide.

A Word About Definitions and Terminology

The word "Gypsy" is used throughout this book, even though it is a misnomer bestowed by non-Gypsies and has come to be understood as a term of opprobrium by many of the people it is used to describe. Because the word is used in most of the texts I am writing about, this simply makes my discussion of those works less confusing. I do at times, however, also employ "Romany," the name that is currently preferred in English-language writing. Some English, Canadian, and American Gypsies have referred to themselves as Romanichals. French Gypsies are manouches and eastern Europeans, Rom or Roma. In German-speaking countries, members of the principal Roma group are Sinti. In order to avoid confusion, I have followed Angus Fraser's lead in using the word "Romani" for the Gypsies' language and "Romany" for the people themselves.[50]

The question of terminology is, to some degree, inseparable from the question of identity. It is not my intention to explore or resolve this issue—rather, my task is to examine myths of identity and conventions of representation—but I wish to acknowledge the controversial and sensitive nature of this matter. Some historians and social anthropologists, especially those with a Marxist bent, have settled on a definition that is based largely on economic categories, occupation, and mode of subsistence. Judith Okely speculates that Gypsies may be a people who "chose to reject wage-labour rather than be proletarianised."[51] She maintains that intermarriage between immigrants and indigenous groups of tinkers, peddlers, pilgrims, and other itinerants occurred so early and so extensively over the centuries that it is difficult to regard Gypsies as a coherent and consistent ethnic or national group. The impulse to see Gypsy customs or even language as having originated in an Indian past, she claims, can indeed be a racist one.[52] David Mayall, who has a similar point of view, emphasizes the idea of the Gypsy as a "racial construct" fostered by gypsiologists determined to find "pure" strains of Gypsies and Romani.[53] Pointing to the documented frequency of intermarriage in the nineteenth century, Mayall wishes to "deconstruct" the image of an authentic Romany culture. Wim Wellems takes the argument that the Gypsy is a social construction even further. He is critical of what he calls the "ethnographic viewpoint," with its "primordial" assumption that Gypsies "constitute a single people with a number of specific characteristics of their own."[54]

Although Okely, Mayall, and Willems rightly direct their critiques at those who both romanticize and revile Gypsies because of a fantastic and insidious belief in racial purity, their efforts at deconstruction are problematic for those who wish to claim a Gypsy identity that has a recognizable linguistic, cultural, and ethnic core. After the Holocaust and certainly since the 1960s, international efforts have been undertaken to claim and document a varied but coherent Gypsy past and, despite the degree of intermingling and national variety, a cohesive and discernible Gypsy identity.[55] The founding of the Gypsy Council in London in 1966 and Ian Hancock's creation of the Romani Archives and Documentation Center there in 1962 (in 1976 the center moved to the University of Texas at Austin) are but two examples of these efforts at political organization and cultural and historical preservation and retrieval.[56] In a recent survey of answers to the question What is a Gypsy? Mayall identified Ian Hancock, Angus Fraser, Thomas Acton, and Donald Kenrick as believers in an "ethnic/racial" or "ethnocentric" classification. He categorizes Judith Okely as a member of the opposing "ethnic/cultural" school, which argues that nomadic ancestry, rather than Indian origin, accounts for the ethnic identity of the Gypsies. Not surprisingly, Mayall maintains that the "key point of contention" between these two groups "remains that of origins."[57] With many others, I believe that Gypsy identity is a matter of both personal self-definition and history. Varieties of experience and culture and the commonness of intermarriage over centuries affect other transnational groups as well but do not nullify the realities of, say, Jewish or Armenian identity and history—or histories. Misplaced and racist beliefs in the homogeneity of minority groups do not invalidate the power or felt reality of minority identity.[58]

Finally, there is the use of the word "race," a highly elastic and elusive concept that is ubiquitous in nineteenth-century references to Gypsies. Any reader of nineteenth-century writing knows that the term is used very loosely, without a precise or consistent definition. When Gypsies or Jews or, for that matter, Italians are referred to as a race in English texts, a number of meanings of the word coalesce: a group descended from common ancestors, a nation or tribe, a group identifiable as decidedly non-English in appearance and habit. When, at the beginning of *Silas Marner* (1861), the narrator speaks of a "disinherited race," he (or she) employs all these connotations to describe an indigenous but alien-seeming class of men—linen weavers who had left the towns to settle in the countryside.[59] A more specifically anthropological definition of race had also been in use since the 1830s and 1840s, when debates about monogenism and polygenism entered ethnographic discourse. Were all human beings, despite differences among civilizations, descended from a single seed, or did each race—by some accounts, five, and by others, three—have its separate point of origin?[60]

Color of skin was considered a determining factor of race, certainly in the division of the three "great races"—Negro, Chinese, and European (or Caucasian)—but also in the habit of designating arguably dark-skinned peoples, like Gypsies, as a race. No matter how vague the meanings of the word, it almost always implied a group with shared characteristics, although such traits could be either biologically or culturally generated.[61] As the anthropologist George W. Stocking, Jr., makes clear, even as late as the mid-nineteenth century, the use of the word "race" did not connote a "rigidly biological determinist approach." "Given the belief that the habitual behavior of human groups in different environments might become part of their hereditary physical makeup," he writes, "cultural phenomena were readily translatable into 'racial' tendencies."[62] When Gypsies were referred to as a race, then, as they invariably were, the epithet implied a number of characteristics—from dark skin, foreign origin, and inherent inferiority to common ancestry, culture, experience, and sensibility. The word "race" could express a desire to designate ostensibly separate and identifiable "non-English" groups, just as it could convey bigotry, revulsion, and certainly disavowal. I have used the term in this book largely without quotation marks, even though its definitions in the nineteenth century clearly differ from those in the twenty-first.

1

A "Mingled Race"

Walter Scott's Gypsies

I N T H E last decades of the eighteenth and early decades of the nineteenth
century, when etymologists, antiquarians, historians, missionaries, and
reformers began to piece together the story of the European Gypsies, they
returned again and again to the question of the origin and extraordinary longevity of these people, with their deep and extensive past in Europe. The narrative
of their ubiquity and ancient presence in the West was almost always accompanied by assertions of their cultural uniformity: their nature was lasting and stable
and everywhere the same. Commentators marveled that Gypsies had been in
Britain from the first decades of the sixteenth century and had arrived in Germany a century before, possibly as early as 1417, and delighted in puzzling over
their precise route of entry.[1] Had they come from Egypt or from India? Were
they descended from the Ishmaelites, "destined by divine proscription ever to
remain a wandering irreclaimable people"?[2] Or were they remnants of the ten
lost tribes of Israel, or part of the "mixed multitude" that had fled Egypt *with* the
Jews?[3] Students of Gypsy history appear to have clung tenaciously to the ambiguity of the Gypsies' lineage, as though the mystery of their origin were crucial to
the role they played in the imaginations of scholars, writers, and readers alike. It
seemed most remarkable that Gypsies had remained fundamentally unchanged
for centuries and spoke a consistent and codified language, not "a fabricated
gibberish," as some had once believed.[4] "They remain ever, and in all places,
what their fathers were—Gipseys," wrote Heinrich Grellman, the first important chronicler of European Gypsies, introducing a theme that often would be
repeated. Life among varied and enlightened civilizations apparently had not
transformed the Gypsies, and their customs and habits were both homogeneous
and consistently anachronistic.[5]

Alongside this narrative of consistency and homogeneity, however, a counter-narrative took form. Although historians and proto-ethnologists did not explicitly challenge the dominant notion that Gypsies had a distinct and lasting character as a people, they, often inadvertently, acknowledged elements of variation, inconsistency, and assimilation. Gypsies certainly had a deep and discrete past in Europe, but they had not remained unchanged, nor were they everywhere, in all ways, the same. Grellman begins *Dissertation on the Gipseys* (1787) by arguing that the Gypsies' "Oriental" attachment to custom and habit of remaining isolated from those among whom they lived accounted for their unvarying nature.[6] But he goes on to undermine both the sense of their consistent identity and the notion of their absolute separateness. Early on, he catalogues the variety of names given to this people throughout Europe: the French call them bohémiens; the Dutch, Heydens; the Moors and Arabs, Charami; the Spaniards, gitanos; the Germans, Italians, and Hungarians, Tzigany; the Transylvanians, Pharaoh nepek; the Clementines in Smyrna, Madjub; the Bucharians, Diajii; the Moldavians, Cyganis; the English, Egyptians.[7] This multiplicity of names, which unsettles Grellman's own assertion that they "remain ever, and in all places, what their fathers were—Gipseys," is related, of course, to the Gypsies' much disputed ancestry (the French call them "bohémiens" believing that they came from eastern Europe, and so on). So in a fundamental way, Grellman implies, Gypsies were different things to different nations, and their essential identity differed widely from theorist to theorist. "Sometimes," he muses, "the Gipseys are Hebrews, then Nubians, Egyptians, Phrygians, Vandals, Sclavonians, or . . . perhaps some other nation."[8]

Grellman maintains that Gypsies did not intermarry with other peoples and so remained unchanged in bodily characteristics over generations. They were readily identifiable as a distinct and uniform race. But he also argues that their swarthy coloring was more the result of "education, and manner of life, than descent" and wonders how non-Gypsies "should . . . be able to distinguish a Gipsey if taken when a child from its sluttish mother, and brought up by some cleanly person."[9] John Hoyland, a Quaker historian of Gypsies in Britain, whose *Historical Survey of the Customs, Habits, & Present State of the Gypsies* owed a great deal to Grellman's work, expresses similarly contradictory views of the Gypsies' integrity as a people. He first claims that Gypsies never married anyone who was not of Gypsy extraction and then remarks that Scottish Gypsies, at least, were "much intermingled with our own national out-laws and vagabonds."[10] Perhaps trying to reconcile his own conflicting assertions, Hoyland insists that when Gypsies *did* marry "strangers," the new members of the clan took on the manners of the Gypsies and their progeny always had "the tawny complexions, and fine black eyes of the Gypsey parent, whether father or mother."[11] The dominant myth of Gypsy identity, then, was that it was constant and consistent, while the strength of empirical observation, a comparative glance at Gypsies throughout the various European countries, and anecdotal evidence about intermarriage suggested a wholly different reality: one of mixture and variation, of an ancient presence that had, over centuries, become an integrated, although not wholly assimilated, part of European culture and had not remained completely insulated or unchanged in the nations of the West.[12]

Europeans favored the notion of Gypsy homogeneity because it reassured them about their own distinctness and national or "racial" integrity. The idea of an intermingled people raised anxieties about the permeability of boundaries between groups and the possibility of mixture on both sides of the presumed Gypsy–European divide. The common myth that Gypsies kidnapped so-called European children and raised them as their own expressed this nervousness about intermingling and accounted for it in a manner that apparently seemed more reassuring than the specter of willed miscegenation. (In the American context, of course, stories of racial blending and unaccountably dark "whites" or light dark-skinned people, focused on Native Americans, with whom Gypsies were often compared, and African Americans.) The accidental or forced mixing of races could explain why Gypsies, who were habitually described as raven-haired, swarthy, even black, sometimes had blue eyes and fair hair. But in England, at least, it might also account for those Anglo-Saxons who were uncharacteristically or inexplicably dark-skinned or dark-haired.[13] Anglo-Saxon homogeneity was also a much-prized myth, and aberrant appearance or even character could be imagined, sometimes whimsically and sometimes earnestly, as the result of misplacing, losing, or mistakenly acquiring a child.

Stories that coupled Gypsies with kidnappings, foundlings, switched babies, and mistaken identities abounded in cultural lore and popular narrative. Gypsies appear to have lived close enough to settled communities to steal English babies and yet distant and peripatetic enough to keep such children hidden. A favorite and oft-repeated kidnapping legend concerned Adam Smith, rumored to have been taken by Gypsies as a boy for just a few hours. "It is curious to think," wrote one particularly alarmist commentator in the mid-nineteenth century,

> what might have been the political state of so many nations, and of Great Britain in particular, . . . if the father of political economy and free-trade . . . had had to pass his life in a Gipsy encampment, and, like a white transferred to an Indian wigwam, under similar circumstances, acquired all their habits, and become more incorrigibly attached to them than the people themselves; tinkering kettles, pots, pans, and old metal, in place of separating the ore of a beautiful science from the debris which had been for generations accumulating around it.[14]

This legend carried particular force as a parental admonition. If the great Smith, a man so important to the building of British civilization, found himself in danger of absorption into an alien tribe, so, too, might any careless child. The threat of kidnapping became a staple of nursery rhymes, lullabies, and teasing to coax children into proper behavior. But the opposite notion, that a Gypsy child could end up in the English world, had great imaginative force as well. Parents might scold a naughty or even an unconventional child by saying that the "tinkers" had stolen their real offspring and left a Gypsy in his or her place.

On the child's side, of course, the fantasy of alternative parentage—what Freud called the family romance—often took the form of imagining more elevated, or nobler, ancestry.[15] This was apparently so with certain Gypsies themselves. According to Walter Simson, a contemporary of Walter Scott and the author of an early series of articles on Gypsies for *Blackwood's*, Gypsies, too, had their own version of family romance: "If . . . you enquire at the Gipsies respecting their descent, the greater part of them will tell you that they are sprung from a bastard son of this or that family of noble rank and influence, of their own surname."[16] But the fantasy of alternative parentage might also express an English child's feeling of anomalousness or oddness—of not being ordinary or fully "English," of not fitting in—and a Gypsy lineage was often invented as the likely or even wished-for explanation of difference. Many of those who wrote about Gypsies throughout the nineteenth century either imagined themselves or were imagined by others to have Gypsy ancestry, and many were drawn to stories of people who had, for one reason or another, fled the English world and been absorbed into that of the Gypsies. Simson recounts the tale of a gentleman of considerable wealth and property who "abandoned his relatives" and married into a Gypsy family, with whom he traveled the countryside. It was said that at times he resided on his own estate, "disguised, of course, among the gang, to the great annoyance of his relatives, who were horrified at the idea of his becoming a Tinkler."[17] Simson himself, when he roamed throughout Scotland in the 1820s, engaged in what he called "Gipsy-hunting," collecting Romany customs and vocabulary, and came to be known by the Gypsies themselves as a "gentleman Gipsy."[18] He was among the first, along with George Borrow, of the "Romany rye," the scholar-gypsies who became aficionados, patrons, and fellow travelers of the Gypsies.[19]

As fascinated as nineteenth-century historians and other commentators were by the separateness and distinctness of Gypsy identity, then, they also were powerfully drawn to the exchanges, crossings over, and porous boundaries between the Gypsy world and their own. Real and imagined meetings with Gypsies, the myth of kidnappings by Gypsies, and the frequent translation of individual experiences into stories with great cultural appeal and currency helped establish Gypsy plots and characters, as well as scenes of encounters

with Gypsies, as common features of nineteenth-century fiction. The Romantic fascination with the foreign and exotic and the hospitable form of the bildungsroman, with its emphasis on riddles of origin and identity, also prepared
the ground for Gypsy subjects. But the single most important literary influence on the nineteenth-century fascination with Gypsies and their role in the
cultural imagination was Scott's novel *Guy Mannering*. The narrative became
a source both for historians, who recycled Scott's account of Scottish Gypsies
as though it were authoritative, and for novelists and poets, who used *Guy
Mannering*'s kidnapping plot and Gypsy heroine as prototypes for their own
inventions. Scott's novel works against the myth of a discrete Gypsy identity—
although it creates a myth of another sort in the figure of Meg Merrilies—and
gives the Scottish Gypsies a local and distinct history that emphasizes their
status as a hybrid and ancestral people.

Prototypes and Ancestors

In his novel *Guy Mannering, or, The Astrologer* (1815), Walter Scott offers his
readers a version of the history of Gypsies that emphasizes their deep and mystical presence in the Scottish past, their intermingling with the Scots themselves,
and their vulnerability to the vagaries of historical, political, and economic
change. His are not Gypsies of a static and constant character, impervious
to alteration and untouched by other people and ways of life, as many commentators in this period imagined them. Scott set his novel in the 1770s and
1780s, reflecting both his personal and familial experience of Gypsy history and
the sense, articulated by his colleague Walter Simson, that the late eighteenth
century had been the Gypsies' heyday, after which their status and viability in
Scotland declined.[20] But Scott's Gypsies also occupy an iconic place in the collective cultural memory of the Scottish people and seem, at times, to stand
in for the prized national past that Scott, as an antiquarian, was committed to
retrieving.[21] Their association with an ancient and dimly remembered history, a
memory of origin, and a complex identity is played out in the novel on the level
of the individual experience of the young hero, Harry Bertram, and his connection to the Gypsy "sibyl," Meg Merrilies, one of Scott's most charismatic and
celebrated characters. The memory of this primal figure links Bertram to his
past, helps him reconstruct his nearly erased identity, and serves as a confirmation of the need to preserve—or, at least, remember—the cultural amalgam of
which the Gypsy is a part.

Meg Merrilies, "harlot, thief, witch, and gypsy," had a life of her own outside Scott's novel throughout most of the nineteenth century and played an
archetypal role in popular culture, the meaning of which is all but lost to us.[22]
She was the subject of the poem "Meg Merrilies" (1818) by John Keats, inspired

another called "The Gipsy's Malison" (1829) by Charles Lamb, became the central character in a successful dramatization of *Guy Mannering* that featured the famed Sarah Egerton as Meg, and was painted in at least seven portraits between 1816 and 1822.[23] This "Meg-mania," as one critic has phrased it, underscores the powerful, imposing, and exotic visual qualities of this figure: her great and mannish height; her wild-haired and red-turbaned head; her garb, which combines "the national dress of the Scottish people with something of an Eastern costume"; and her air of "wild sublimity" (1:36).[24] She is written as a virtual stage character, compared explicitly in the narrative with Sarah Siddons, and always evoked pictorially, as though Scott meant her for the subject of a picturesque tableau (2:284).[25] But Meg Merrilies also captured the imagination of Scott's audience as an emblem of fate and a reader of the future—she is referred to as an "ancient sibyl"—and as an ancestral figure. Neither wholly female nor wholly male, she is a woman of "masculine stature," with a voice whose "high notes were too shrill for a man, the low . . . too deep for a woman" (1:19, 203).[26] Hybrid in a variety of ways—male and female, Scottish and "Eastern"—she transcends distinctions of sex and nation and occupies the position of an ur-parent or original forebear.

Walter Scott himself claimed a wild and mixed ancestry. From his antiquarian research, the respectable lawyer's son drew what John Sutherland calls a "mythic genealogy."[27] It began with a sixteenth-century outlaw border hero and his ferocious daughter-in-law Meg Murray, the "ugliest woman in four counties," whose name must have influenced Scott's choice for his Gypsy witch. Another favorite antecedent was the seventeenth-century "Beardie," a vehement and loyal Jacobite whose portrait hung on the wall of the novelist's study. His attachment to these ancestors and to the stories of their exploits extended to his belief that he resembled them physically, bore no likeness to his own mother and father, and was a "throwback" to earlier generations of the family.[28] The romance of this undoubtedly invented—or at least chosen—lineage is reflected in *Guy Mannering* and conjoined with Scott's memories of the legend of Jean Gordon, a Jacobite Gypsy of the Yetholm clan, and her granddaughter, Madge.[29]

Both Gordons were reputed to have been six feet tall—a trait that Scott gave to Meg Merrilies—and to have made lasting impressions on the people, especially the children, who met them. Jean's legend centered on her fierce and fatal loyalty to the Jacobite cause, a political disposition that Scott could and did romanticize—in his accounts of Jean Gordon and in *Waverley* (1814)—from a distance of some seventy years. For Walter Simson's series of articles for *Blackwood's*, he wrote a description of Jean Gordon's death:

> She chanced to be at Carlisle upon a fair or market day soon after the year 1746, where she gave vent to her political partiality, to the great offence of the rabble of the city. Being zealous in their loyalty when there was no danger, in

proportion to the tameness with which they had surrendered to the Highlanders in 1745, the mob inflicted upon poor Jean Gordon no slighter penalty than
that of ducking her to death in the Eden. It was an operation of some time,
for Jean was a stout woman, and, struggling with her murderers, often got her
head above water, and while she had voice left, continued to exclaim at such
intervals, "Charlie yet! Charlie yet!" [30]

Scott ends his account of the legend of the Gypsy's death by inserting his own
childhood response to the event. "When a child, and among the scenes which
she frequented," he writes, "I have often heard these stories, and cried piteously
for poor Jean Gordon." The tale of sacrifice and stubborn allegiance moved the
child and, ultimately, made its way into the Gypsy character and novel of 1815.
Almost eighty years later, Andrew Lang, Scottish man of letters and folklorist,
wrote an introduction to an edition of *Guy Mannering* that includes this excerpt
from the *Blackwood's* article and then moves on to talk of Jean Gordon's granddaughter, Madge. Lang claims that his own "memory is haunted by a solemn
remembrance of a woman of more than female height, dressed in a long red
cloak, . . . whom I looked on with . . . awe."[31] He quotes yet another witness,
who recalled this "remarkable personage, of a very commanding presence and
high stature," from his own childhood: "I remember her well; every week she
paid my father a visit for her *awmous* [alms], when I was a little boy, and I
looked upon Madge with no common degree of awe and terror." The complex
association between these outsize female figures and deeply etched memories
from childhood form a basis for the affective and psychological drama of Harry
Bertram's story in *Guy Mannering*.

One final aspect of Scott's personal experience proved crucial to the particular history of the Scottish Gypsies that he wrote into *Guy Mannering*. In the
year preceding the publication of the novel, he had taken a tour of northern
Scotland and seen the effects of the "Clearances," landowners' efforts to evict
old tenants from their property in order to make better economic use of their
farmlands.[32] Although a landlord himself and so identified with landlords' interests, he lamented the evidence he saw of these changes in social relations and
landscape during his trip to the Orkney Islands. "How is the necessary restric-
tion to take place, without the greatest immediate distress and hardship to these
poor creatures?" he wondered of three hundred displaced tenants who had been
living on Lord Armadale's estate. "If I were an Orcadian lord," he continued in
his diary of the journey, "I feel I should shuffle on with the useless old creatures,
in contradiction to my better judgement."[33] Scott's ambivalence about the social
and moral consequences of the "Clearances" informed the plot of *Guy Mannering*, in which it became a question about the Scottish Gypsies' place both in
society and in history, as well as a way of dramatizing the individual and communal dangers of banishing the past.

Dispossession

Intertwined with the history of Meg Merrilies and her Gypsy tribe in *Guy Mannering* is the story of a lost heir, Harry Bertram, and his Oedipus-like saga of wandering, exile, and recovery of identity. Bertram, the prospective laird of Ellangowan, and the Gypsies who have lived on his family's lands for genera-tions share the fate of dispossession; indeed, it is the "clearance" of the Gypsies from their home at Ellangowan that appears to lead to the forced separation of young Harry from his patrimony. The plot turns on the drama of kidnapping, playing pointedly on the common association of Gypsies with that crime, and the novel casts India—symbol of the British Empire—as the offstage scene of exile and ill-fated adventure. Scott employs the Gypsies—and Meg Merrilies as their representative—to endorse a particular relationship with the past, a notion of polyglot culture (Sutherland calls the novel a "maelstrom of lan-guages, jargons, idiolects, and dialects"), and a wariness of new social and eco-nomic arrangements.[34] The mechanism for realizing this vision in the novel is memory, particularly the semiconscious, almost hallucinatory memory of earliest, infantile attachment to a place and, more important, to an archetypal, surrogate mother.

The novel begins, like the story of Oedipus, with a prediction about the ulti-mate fate of a child. An Oxford-educated astrologer, the Guy Mannering of the title, has wandered northward to Kippletringan, in Scotland, and finds himself at Ellangowan House just as its owner's son and heir is being born. Manner-ing casts the baby's horoscope, his celestial calculations revealing that the child Harry will meet with captivity or sudden death and will be especially vulnerable at three crucial points in his life. Mannering is intrigued by the Gypsy Meg Merrilies's spinning, a competing means of divining the boy's future (figure 5). He encounters her as he wanders through the ruins of the original Ellangowan Castle, the ancient seat of the family, where she sits in an apartment, weaving together multicolored threads and intoning a "charm"—"Twist ye, twine ye!" (1:37). The spinning and chanting culminate in Meg's measuring the length of the thread she has produced to determine the boy's future. She reckons for the child not a "haill" but a long life, a span of seventy years marked by three traumas or breaks and subsequent recoveries. Unlike Mannering, Meg sees in Harry Bertram's fate the possibility of triumph: "he'll be a lucky lad an he win through wi't" (1:37).

This appearance of Meg in the novel is notable for a number of reasons. First, her prophecy is placed in opposition to Mannering's. Will the Gypsy's or the astrologer's prediction prove correct? Aside from setting in motion the mystery of the plot, this question pits the erudition of the English scholar against the wild ways of the Scottish Gypsy. Earlier, the laird has hinted at this competition when Meg offers to tell the child's fortune as soon as it is

FIGURE 5 R. S. Lauder, "Meg Merrilies Spinning the Charm of the Heir of Ellangowan."
(From Walter Scott, *Guy Mannering* [London: Clay, n.d.])

born and the laird rejects her offer, assuring her that "a student from Oxford
that kens much better" how to make such predictions will do so by the stars
instead (1:22). Second, the scene locates Meg within the decaying walls of the
laird's ancient castle, not by her cauldron in a forest or Gypsy encampment,
and so identifies her with the "auld wa's [old ways]," as she will later refer to the
traditions of patronage and privilege associated with the landowning class. As
we shall see, the haunting and sublime site of these ruins plays an important
role in the hero's eventual recovery of memory and self. Finally, Mannering
glimpses the Gypsy through "an aperture." Spied on as she performs her secret
rituals — "he could observe her without being visible himself" — she assumes an
elevated and powerful place, conveying to Mannering the "exact impression of
an ancient sibyl" rather than the air of a deranged Gorgon, which she conveyed
earlier (1:22). A figure likely drawn from fairy tale as well as myth, Meg is associated with fate and the hidden rites of femaleness — not to say, female sexuality.[35]

Critics have noticed the frequency with which characters in the novel perceive events dimly, through apertures or small openings.[36] It is Meg who is most often spied in this way, and her power as a figure in the novel (and, possibly, beyond it) derives from her association with what Freud calls "primal phantasies" — that is, the memory or fantasy of something secret, sexual, and hidden that is only partly seen and understood.[37]

As Harry grows up, Meg's "ancient attachment" to the Bertram family is transferred to the child. When he is ill, she lies all night outside his window and chants rhymes to speed his recovery. When he wanders from home to "clamber about the ruins of the old castle," she follows and retrieves him. When he ventures forth to places unknown, she "contrive[s] to waylay him . . . , sing him a gypsy song, . . . and thrust into his pocket a piece of gingerbread" (1:66). So constantly does she attend to him and watch over him that Harry's mother, who is sickly, indifferent, and pregnant with a second child, becomes suspicious of the woman who has, in effect, taken her place. Harry's rambling ways and Meg's presence cause general concern, and his tutor, the sentimental Dominie Sampson, fears that "this early prodigy of erudition [will] be carried off by the gypsies, like a second Adam Smith" (1:67). Both Harry's mother and Dominie misread Meg's role: she protects rather than threatens the child, and her loyalty to the Bertrams, rather like Jean Gordon's loyalty to the Stuarts, is indestructible. But the fate of Adam Smith is not to be avoided, and at five, the first of the child's vulnerable ages according to the astrologer's predictions, Harry is kidnapped.

With Harry's kidnapping, Scott sets up the expectation that the Gypsies have committed a crime "consistent with their habits," but he also gives the reader reason to believe that the crime is an act of at least understandable, if not forgivable, vengeance. Scott inserts the Ellangowan Gypsies into a history that combines a particular interpretation of their presence in Scotland with the recent events, not directly involving Gypsies, of the "Clearances." In chapter 7 of the novel, he evokes a Gypsy history that begins with segregation and outlawry; moves deliberately to integration, domestication, and salutary coexistence; and ends with banishment. A century earlier, the narrator records, Gypsies were little more than "banditti" who roamed about the countryside, stealing, begging, drinking, and fighting. In time, however, they lost the "national character of Egyptians" through intermarriage with Highlanders and thus became a *"mingled race,"* both their numbers and the "dreadful evil" they produced decreasing (1:57 [emphasis added]). They learned trades — primarily tinkering and earthenware-making — and practiced the arts of music, fortune-telling, and legerdemain. Scott's Gypsies not only are a mixed and substantially tamed group, but also maintain a symbiotic relationship with Scottish landowners or "settlers." Meg's tribe, for example, has dwelled on the estate of Ellangowan for generations, enjoying the lairds' protection and paying in return with services

FIGURE 6 Clark Stanton, "The Departure of the Gypsies." (From Walter Scott, *Guy Mannering* [Boston: Estes and Lauriat, 1892])

and combat in times of war. Scott also identifies the Gypsies ethnologically: they are "Pariahs," like "wild Indians among European settlers," and, although attached to a settled group, are judged according to their own "customs, habits, and opinions" (1:60).[38] Separated by class and culture rather than by nationality from the landowning Scots, they live by different practices and mores but enjoy a "mutual intercourse of good offices" (1:61). Scott takes pains to establish an identity for the Gypsies that is subject to historical change and that exists and evolves in a process of exchange with other groups. They are not a timeless, insular, or undiluted people, as many observers and historians of the Gypsies had maintained. By the start of the narrative, then, Scott's Gypsies are part of the fabric of disparate groups that make up the Scottish nation. The laird of Ellangowan interrupts this history of amelioration and integration when he banishes the Gypsies from his land and sends them into exile.

Although the laird has ignored trespassing laws, he now feels compelled to enforce them because he has been made a "conservator of the peace." He issues an order to remove the Ellangowan Gypsies, sets a deadline, and then resorts to "violent measures of ejection" (1:68). Like the lords of Orkney, whose enactment of the "Clearances" Scott had noted with great ambivalence, the laird of Ellangowan separates this tribe from its "ancient place of refuge" (1:70). He observes the exodus of the Gypsies from his lands with a "natural yearning of heart" toward those he has known for so long (figure 6) and is confronted suddenly with the figure of Meg Merrilies, dressed in red turban and looking like a

FIGURE 7   "The Curse of Meg Merrilies." (From Walter Scott, *Guy Mannering* [London: Ward, 1878])

"sibyl in frenzy" (figure 7). In a set piece that was later sketched, painted, acted on the stage, and described in verse, Meg curses Bertram for this rude displacement of her people:

> There's thirty hearts . . . yonder, from the auld wife of an hundred to the babe that was born last week, that ye have turned out o' their bits o' bields, to sleep with the tod and the blackcock in the muirs! Ride your ways, Ellangowan. Our bairns are hinging at our weary backs; look that your braw cradle at hame be the fairer spread up,—not that I am wishing ill to little Harry, or to the babe that's yet to be born,—God forbid,—and make them kind to the poor, and better folk than their father! (1:72)[39]

Although, if Meg is to be taken at her word, the laird's children have nothing to fear from her, and although there are smugglers close at hand who might easily engage in the crime of kidnapping, Harry's subsequent disappearance is blamed on the Gypsies and understood as a direct result of this curse. The novel offers the reader the example of Adam Smith, the lore of Gypsy kidnappings, and the specter of a fierce and wrathful Meg Merrilies, but it does so in tandem with a crime committed *by* the laird *against* the Gypsies, and, in the end, it controverts most of the evidence that associates the Gypsies with this misdeed. Meg is nonetheless banished from the country as a "vagrant, common thief, and disorderly person," a charge commonly used to rid locales of Gypsies throughout Britain and Scotland (1:97).[40] The irony is obvious: Meg is banished as a vagrant because she has been ordered off the land that was her home. The act that exiles her also makes her an outlaw. By the middle of the novel, both Harry Bertram and the Gypsies have become dispossessed and homeless wanderers.

Empire and Its Discontents

Myths and narratives of Gypsy kidnappings, like that of Adam Smith, would dictate that Harry Bertram—if, indeed, taken by Meg or her people—be raised as a Gypsy in an unseen but nearby enclave. Such is not the fate of Harry, who was taken to Holland by smugglers immediately after his kidnapping and forcibly apprenticed to a commercial house, before being posted by the firm to India. In the unnarrated seventeen years between Harry's kidnapping and his return to Scotland, Guy Mannering also ended up in India, where he has had a successful military career but a chaotic and miserable personal life. In retrospect, the narrative informs the reader of certain salient events that occurred abroad, most important a falling out between Mannering and Harry—now called "Brown" and unknown to Mannering as Harry Bertram—who, detesting the life of a counting-house clerk, became a soldier in Mannering's regiment. The older man suspected Brown of being his wife's lover, and the two fought a duel in which Mannering was supposed to have killed Brown. Mannering's wife died in a state of grief and alienation, leaving a daughter, Julia, possessed of "piercing dark eyes, and jet-black hair of great length, . . . vivacity and intelligence, . . . shrewdness . . . [and] humorous sarcasm" (1:177). Neither dead nor living the life of a Gypsy, Brown/Bertram, prompted by inchoate desires, returns to Kippletringan. In the intervening years, his mother has died in childbirth, and his father has perished a broken, presumably heirless man, his estate sold to an arriviste named Glossin. Brown's identity is a mystery to all, including himself. Mannering, longing to redeem his life and that of his daughter, also returns to Scotland and the vicinity of Ellangowan House, hoping to purchase the estate and there "nurse the melancholy that was to accompany him to his grave" (1:122).

Some of the most interesting recent analyses of *Guy Mannering* have focused on its imperial themes and motifs, what Katie Trumpener calls the novel's inauguration, along with Jane Austen's *Mansfield Park* (1814), of "a new analytic model for describing the workings of the imperialist unconscious."[41] Peter Garside points to the text's frequent yoking of Gypsies and Indians and concludes that Scott knew current theories identifying India rather than Egypt as the Gypsies' land of origin. He also argues that the eviction of the Gypsies from Ellangowan reflects not only the domestic "Clearances" that Scott observed, but the expulsion of villagers in Bengal by landowners attempting to enlarge their estates.[42] Trumpener's ambitious reading of *Guy Mannering* emphasizes the way it continually folds the domestic into the imperial and the imperial into the domestic, draws parallels between misdeeds abroad and those at home, and generally advances an "interpenetration" of these two spheres in narrative, ideological, and psychological terms.[43]

These readings seem compelling, particularly as correctives to the long-standing critical silence about what Edward Said calls the "structure of attitude and reference" created by imperialism in Western culture and, especially, British fiction.[44] *Guy Mannering* may be among the first English or Scottish novels to contain an offstage colonial interlude in which disinherited sons and penniless scholars go abroad to make fortunes, have adventures, or at least make lives for themselves. This narrative pattern was to be repeated again and again in nineteenth-century fiction. But, having observed this, I want to identify with a bit more precision what this interlude signifies in Scott's novel. If, by the end, the "wide world and its problems disappear," as Trumpener writes, if there is finally a suppression of political and moral complexities associated with empire, there is also in the novel a decidedly skeptical view of imperial adventure.[45] For all that empire proves an arena for personal advancement, it also threatens a potentially dangerous rupture with a vital domestic past.

In *Guy Mannering*, India is a site of anarchic passions, near-fatal Oedipal dramas, and, most important for Scott, suspect means of achieving wealth and position and thereby overturning traditional hierarchies of privilege and responsibility. It is a place of exile that enriches some, like Mannering, whose life it also destroys, and thwarts others, like Harry, whose very degradation enables him ultimately to reclaim the privilege that is rightfully his. The machinery that threatens Harry's inheritance and the renewal of the House of Ellangowan combines and links the efforts of the villainous smuggler Hatteraick, who engineers the boy's kidnapping; the grasping and corrupt magistrate Glossin, who colludes in the kidnapping so he can seize Ellangowan; and the Dutch commercial house Vanbeest and Vanbruggen, where Harry is placed by the "brutal tyrants of his infancy" (the smuggler and an accomplice) and which sends him to India (2:291). Glossin, who seeks to dismantle the old ways through an illegitimate use of power, is the novel's central villain: through him, colonial commerce is associated—perhaps even equated—with the common crimes of smuggling and kidnapping. Colonial wealth and power, like Glossin's new money, also threaten the old ways, in economic and class terms. Scott indicates his wariness of—not to say, disdain for—the kind of status that is to be gained through both colonial commerce and the rise of a ruthless arriviste like Glossin by a small detail: the usurper of the Bertram property has commissioned an "escutcheon for the new Laird of Ellangowan" and must wait his turn until fake coats of arms are produced for two Jamaican traders (2:147).[46] All these pretenders are alike, and all are suspect. Glossin's pursuit of wealth robs Harry of his birthright and, like colonial commerce, promises a kind of geographic dislocation that disrupts connections with the past and the places that enshrine it. As Ian Duncan puts it, "Glossin establishes a false order, based on ambition, avarice and fraudulent legality, the evil psychic energies of historical change."[47] The bogus nobility of Glossin and the Jamaican traders unites them in the process of regrettable change and, by implication, the perpetration of dislocations of new wealth and colonialism.

For Harry Bertram, rootedness in place and past constitute the very identity that he has lost. His return from India and exile will restore this identity, and it is Meg Merrilies, the figure most deeply associated with his beginnings, who will act as the prime agent of that restoration. The tragic Oedipal story of Harry's presumed affair with Mannering's wife and nearly fatal duel with his father-surrogate, Mannering, is to be replaced by a triumphant Oedipal story of Harry's filial redemption, reunion with the originary mother Meg, and union with Julia Mannering, whose dark beauty and forceful character suggest a tamed—and thus acceptable—version of the Gypsy.[48] The treachery of Mannering's misplaced jealousy, likened by him to the rage of Othello, is traded for the heroism of another racially marked, although indigenous, other, the Scottish Gypsy Meg Merrilies (1:117).

Primal Memories

Like an amnesiac, Brown/Bertram must relearn his identity, and it is, first of all, his encounters with Meg, still on the scene, that produce this gradual recognition and retrieval of the past. The sight of Meg triggers memories of certain primal experiences that, at the outset, he cannot quite place or distinguish from dreams: "He was surprised to find that he could not look upon this singular figure without some emotion. 'Have I dreamed of such a figure,' he said to himself, 'or does this wild and strange-looking woman recall to my recollection some of the strange figures I have seen in Indian pagodas?'" (1:204). The answer to both speculations is, of course, no, and, although the question implicitly links Gypsy and Indian, it also distinguishes them from each other.[49]

Meg's foreignness is only apparent or, perhaps, only partial, for she connects Harry to an authentic and specifically local past. Memory is not simply personal, not simply the agent of a retrieved identity, but also historical, geographical, and essential to the restoration of a particular social order. And it is Meg, the Gypsy, who is at the center of memory for Harry. She is also the one who has worked surreptitiously, even in his absence, to keep his inheritance within his reach. Meg "occupies the site of origins," observes Ian Duncan, "[and] tirelessly guides, instructs, saves and provides until the homecoming and recognition are fulfilled."[50]

Because Glossin, the new owner of Ellangowan and engineer of Harry's removal as a child, wants to obliterate the past, memory is his enemy. In a highly dramatic, gothic scene of recognition, the returned Harry approaches Ellangowan Castle, in whose ruins Guy Mannering first saw and heard Meg spinning the child's fortune. Harry, still struggling to make sense of the hazy memories evoked by seeing Meg and Ellangowan and now described as "the harassed wanderer" (having become a species of vagrant or Gypsy himself), muses on the eerie sensation of déjà vu:

> "Why is it," he thought . . . , "why is it that some scenes awaken thoughts which belong, as it were, to dreams of early and shadowy recollections such as my old Brahmin Moonshie would have ascribed to a state of previous existence? Is it the visions of our sleep that float confusedly in our memory, and are recalled by the appearance of such real objects as in any respect correspond to the phantoms they presented to our imagination? How often do we find ourselves in society which we have never before met, and yet feel impressed with a mysterious and ill-defined consciousness that neither the scene, the speakers, nor the subject are entirely new . . . ? It is even so with me while I gaze upon that ruin. . . . Can it be that [it has] been familiar to me in infancy?" (2:135)

The ruins, like Meg herself, spark in Harry a primal memory, indistinguishable from dream or from the psychological trick of déjà vu. Both connect him to his childhood, when he clambered on the ruins and Meg followed him, as well as to his family's ancient history. This history—personal, familial, and in some sense national—is what exile in India and the usurper Glossin threaten to interrupt, to sever. As Harry contemplates the ruined castle, Glossin approaches and, for the first time since Harry's return, recognizes him. Instinctively, Glossin knows that he must be cautious "lest he should awaken or assist, by some name, phrase, or anecdote, the *slumbering train of association*" (2:137 [emphasis added]). It turns out to be a phrase—the Bertram motto—that awakens certain associations in Harry, prompting him to remember a rhyme and then a ballad from his childhood.[51] When Glossin proceeds to curse ballads and balladeers, Scott, for whom both ballads and Gypsy lore were products of antiquarian researches into

Scotland's precious past, marks him indelibly as a man who imperils memory, culture, history, and the future.

Brought by memory and association back to the truth of his identity, Harry is embraced by the friends of his youth as an *enfant trouvé*. Hazy memories of the kidnapping seep into his consciousness, and he recalls, above all, falling into the arms of a tall woman "who started from the bushes and protected me for a time" (2:249). Gathered with the retainers of the old laird, Harry sees Meg appear again before him, "as if emerging out of the earth" (2:276). In a scene that rivals in its almost operatic theatricality that of Meg's cursing of Harry's father, the Gypsy is evoked as a towering, "gigantic" shape that belongs as much to ancient, elemental forms of nature as to humankind. She rises from the ground, like a tree or a rock, and, in her "wild sublimity," she is a figure of prophecy, primeval origin, and justice. Just as she protected the rambling and then the abducted child, she has looked after his interests in his absence, knowing—because of her own predictions—that he would live a long life. The miniature exiles and returns of his earliest childhood adventures are replayed in the exile abroad and return to Scotland of his adulthood. "I shall be the instrument," Meg tells Harry, "to set you in your father's seat again" (1:258). She exposes the smuggler Hatteraick, who spirited Harry off to Holland, and, even more important, the role of Glossin, who supported the kidnapping because it worked to his advantage. For this, she is shot and killed by Hatteraick in the last pages of the novel.

But Harry, a fortunate Oedipus, who has happily survived the efforts of those who tried to destroy him as a child, will be reunited with his lands and his inheritance. Meg Merrilies dies a martyr to the restoration of the Ellangowan lineage and to the resumption of the "auld wa's." Harry gazes on the "wild chieftainess" as she lies dead before him and cries over the corpse of "one who might be said to have died a victim to her fidelity to his person and family" (2:305). Meg Merrilies mimics the heroic Jean Gordon, who died a similarly stubborn victim to fidelity and who, like Scott's Gypsy, remained loyal to a group of people whose interests were not obviously her own. Scott's hero reproduces the novelist's own boyhood sorrow as he "cried piteously" for the poor woman who had drowned rather than betray the Jacobite cause. But if Meg Merrilies helps restore Harry's title and family inheritance, she also links him, through her very being and maternal relationship to him, to a more ancient and fundamental lineage, one that has deep roots in the Scottish past. And although the novel must culminate in the confirmation of Harry's legitimacy, it also flirts with and produces a kind of shadow illegitimacy for him. Glossin tries to claim that Harry is a bastard, his father's "natural son," and thus not the legitimate heir to the Ellangowan property (2:313). To prove him wrong, Harry's supporters introduce the laird's actual illegitimate son, a seafaring man from Antigua (no less), thereby establishing a double for Harry Bertram whose own vexed origins help maintain the sense of Harry's complicated and symbolically "mingled" lineage.

The Middle Way

What, then, does *Guy Mannering*, a story of kidnapping and restored inheritance, suggest about the discursive role of the Gypsy? And what was the novel's legacy in the nineteenth century, as it influenced literary representations of Gypsies, launched the enduring and generative figure of Meg Merrilies, and helped determine the "truth" of Gypsy character in the general culture? To begin with, the novel responds to and deploys the myth of Gypsy kidnappings in order to expose it as just that—a myth—and makes the representative Gypsy figure protective of rather than a threat to both the life and the rights of the disinherited laird. It does so by pointing a finger at the avaricious upstart Glossin, the real criminal, and by suggesting that the new ways of gaining status and wealth are far more insidious than the old ways of vagabondage and patronage, which the Gypsies and the lairds embody. But the effect of this exoneration, as it were, of the suspected kidnappers is a complicated business. The trope of Gypsy kidnapping is still at the center of the plot; Harry Bertram does, after all, fulfill the legend of Adam Smith; and the Gypsies are given a powerful and important motive for a deed that they nonetheless did not commit.[52] It is possible that Scott's nineteenth-century readers were better placed to understand his glorification of Meg than we are, in large part because of the particular contours of Scott's conservative impulses. His vindication of the Gypsies is part of a more complex conservatism than some have allowed, as is his wariness of imperial adventure and gain. Georg Lukács defines Scott's conservatism and "honest Tory[ism]" as an attempt to chart for himself a "middle way" between the "ardent enthusiasts" of the Industrial Revolution and capitalist growth, on the one hand, and their "pathetic, passionate indicters," on the other.[53] Scott is able to sympathize with those who are displaced by new economic and social arrangements, just as he is able to celebrate the greatness of the clans and their "primitive order," but he is unable to repudiate fully the new developments responsible for this displacement.[54] The "middle way" of *Guy Mannering* includes both justification and historicization of the Gypsies' role in Scottish culture, as well as the recognition that modern "clearances" must necessarily disperse them and remake Ellangowan as an estate free from their ancient presence.

Meg's role in Harry's preservation not only vindicates the Gypsies' honesty, but also upholds privilege and indigenous tradition, which ought to include making room for the now dispersed Gypsies on the land of Ellangowan. With Meg's death, however, and the scattering of her people—all twelve of her children are, like the twelve tribes of Israel, dispersed into an unnamed diaspora—this seems a hollow proposition, and the novel's conclusion suggests that only in death will Meg truly be believed: "When I was in life, I was the mad, randy gypsy that had been scourged and banished and branded . . . what would hae minded *her* tale? But now I am a dying woman, and my words will not fall to the ground" (2:300). Scott's vision is, nonetheless, ultimately an inclusive and reformist one. Even as the elder Bertram banishes the Gypsies from his land, he feels remorse at the thought that, although they were indeed idle and vicious, no one had "endeavoured to render them otherwise. . . . Some form of reformation ought at least to have been tried" (1:70–71). Scott's Gypsies, already a "mixed," hybrid people, are part of an imagined multicultural nation, their potential return to Ellangowan a conservative but utopian symbol of cultural retrieval. Indeed, Scott uses a Gypsy as the mouthpiece for tradition and places her squarely in the center of the drama of both personal and cultural memory. You suppress these people at your peril, his story implies; yet the novel ends with their presence fully erased.

Is *Guy Mannering*, then, a story of extinction, a vision of the Gypsies' salutary disappearance from the Scottish scene?[55] Yes, in the sense that the Ellangowan Gypsies cease to be a visible presence by the close of the novel. But they are dispersed—not extinct—and already intermingled with other Scottish groups. Their local legacy, in the form of the new laird, suggests that their ways and influence survive. Gypsy identity has been transferred, albeit temporarily and obliquely, to the new laird. Harry has wandered the world dispossessed, homeless, nameless—Gypsy-like—and, as a consequence, has returned a laird unlike any his father might have imagined. When Meg curses Harry's father, she also issues a kind of blessing in wishing that his children might be kinder to the poor and "better folk than their father" (1:72). On Harry's return as an adult, she predicts that he will be "the best laird . . . that Ellangowan has seen for three hundred years" (2:200). It is his exile and experience of suffering, which he shares with the Gypsies, that will enable him to be a superior laird. So, too, has his filial tie to Meg Merrilies, the symbolic begetter of a reinvigorated Scottish line, connected him spiritually and viscerally to ancient modes of being and ruling. And his marriage to Julia Mannering, she of the long, jet-black hair and shrewd nature, joins him to a woman who bears at least a fleeting resemblance to the Gypsy Meg.[56] As Michael Ragussis has observed in his discussion of *Ivanhoe*, Scott envisions history as "a lengthy process of racial mixture, . . . a record of difference." Just as *Ivanhoe* debunks the fantasy of English purity by "delineating the mixed Saxon and Norman genealogy of the modern Englishman," so does *Guy Mannering* suggest that Gypsies, Highlanders, lairds, and vagrants are part of a mongrel Scottish inheritance.[57]

Meg's Progeny

The legacy of Scott's novel to nineteenth-century ways of imagining Gypsies begins with Meg Merrilies. She lived beyond the novel — in popular culture, on stage, and in verse — but her longevity as a character certainly cannot be ascribed solely to her Gypsy identity. To the degree that she established an archetypal form of Gypsyhood, however, her ancestral role, physical size and shape, and association with childhood memory are crucial. She is the agent and subject of distant, hazy, and early recollections, associated by the hero with maternal solicitude and infantile sensations. Identified, too, with a state of mind that mixes memory and dream—something glimpsed but perhaps really only imagined—she seems to exist in the realm of "primal phantasy," the term that Freud used to describe just such ambiguous recollections. It is possible that Scott was also engaged in imagining or inventing what Freud would later call the "phylogenetic endowment" of such fantasy-memories and Jung would describe as the "primordial image . . . dormant in the collective unconscious." For Freud, this "phylogenetic endowment" allows individuals to reach back in memory beyond their own experiences and personal recollections into "primaeval" events. For Jung, the persistence into the present of images from myths and early religions suggested that "archetypes" exist in the "mental history of mankind."[58] The power of these theories as credible accounts of the individual psyche is not the issue: rather, I want to suggest that Scott's novel seems to claim for Meg, and for the Gypsies whom she represents, just this primeval, archetypal realm that Freud and Jung were to elaborate.[59] Meg is part of the unconscious memory of not only Harry Bertram but the Scottish nation: an ancestral figure, an originary figure, who nonetheless is not of the legitimate ancestral line.

Meg occupies a place in Harry's memory that, in a far more domesticated form, Peggotty occupies in David Copperfield's. The two women, alternative mothers, large in form and alien in social class and custom, fill a "vacancy in [the] heart" of the boy and represent a kind of maternal physicality that does not partake of middle-class femininity.[60] Both are associated with states of half-sleep—David remembers Peggotty seeming to "swell and grow immensely large" as he falls asleep as a child—and with recollections of boyhood trauma from which these women had protected them.[61] Both traumas involve separation: attempts to wrench the boys from their homes—kidnapping in one case and assault by a stepfather in the other—and the deaths of their mothers in childbirth. But Peggotty is, of course, the gentled, Victorian version of Meg. She is neither wild nor mysterious, not the outraged representative of a shunned people, and, although large and shapeless, not manlike in stature.

Indeed, Meg's combination of feminine and masculine characteristics—"androgynous" seems too tame a word for her—reflects the anomalous sexuality with which Gypsies would continue to be associated in the first half of the nineteenth century. Observers often commented on the sensuality and "lasciviousness" of Gypsy women. Heinrich Grellman described the seductive dancing of female Gypsies, and John Hoyland regretted the "indecent gestures" of young girls who rambled and danced with their musician fathers for a few pennies.[62] While these writers decried the louche performances of these women, later authors deployed the Gypsy seductress as a stock figure, the welcome object of male desire. But early in the century, literary texts often used Gypsies to represent ambiguous, masculinized, and sometimes celibate femininity, on the one hand, and effeminate or passive masculinity, on the other.[63] The Gypsy in Charlotte Brontë's *Jane Eyre* is a man—Edward Rochester, of course—masquerading as a woman. With a face "all brown and black" and "elf-locks" bristling from beneath a bonnet, the disguised Rochester quizzes a skeptical Jane and perplexes her with an appearance alien but familiar, female but male.[64] In this guise, Rochester resembles the outsize Bertha, another demonic woman with masculine proportions and strength. Like the dazed Harry Bertram recovering the memory of his identity, Jane responds to the hybrid fortune-teller in a state of disorientation: "Where was I? Did I wake or sleep? Had I been dreaming? Did I dream still?"[65] Calling the Gypsy fortune-teller "mother" and unable to distinguish between dream and reality, Jane replays, if only briefly, aspects of Bertram's relationship to Meg Merrilies. The heroine of George Eliot's *The Spanish Gypsy* appears at the conclusion of the dramatic poem in men's clothing: turbaned, like Meg, and dressed in the manner of her chieftain father, whose mantle as leader of her people she has inherited. And Wordsworth, in his poem "Beggars," evokes the great stature of his Gypsy beggar woman with the opening line: "She had a tall man's height or more."[66] All these characters are in the tradition of the large Gypsy woman, much like Jean Gordon, the prototype for Meg Merrilies, and all combine qualities of mother and leader. They seem to displace and then absorb the fatherly role and join male and female properties in the figure of a genderless primal ancestor.

In the next few decades of the nineteenth century, ancestral associations came to dominate literary and cultural representations of Gypsies, as a result not only of Walter Scott's influence, but also of a general cultural preoccupation with the origin of the Gypsies themselves, with broader questions of vexed individual and collective identities, and with the need to imagine alternative lineages. The anxiety that was both expressed and allayed in stories of Gypsy kidnappings was transmuted into the very material of bildung in *Guy Mannering* and into a parable about remembering and embracing ancient ways. Scott responded to the fascination with the long and widespread presence of the Gypsies in Europe by making them into an emblem of a necessary, deep, and fundamental past. But Scott's Gypsies do not simply represent a static and mystical moment in a distant time. They are subject to history, and they change in an ongoing process of intercourse with those whose lands and imaginations they inhabit. He gives them a political identity by inserting them into a historical situation—the "Clearances"—that did not necessarily involve them and figures them as the objects of legal harassment and persecution.[67] Finally, by representing them as a "mingled race," Scott raises at least the possibility that the hybrid pedigree of the Gypsies is mirrored among the settled and dominant peoples of the nation. Harry Bertram himself incorporates symbolic and affective elements of a Gypsy lineage, and the lairdship he cultivates will scatter but nonetheless preserve the memory of the Gypsies of Ellangowan. In Scott's vision, the old ways will ultimately be transcended but not erased, and the Gypsies, far from being wholly separate, a nation distinct from Britain or Scotland, will be understood to have mingled with dominant cultures and even, perhaps, to have been their progenitor.

2

Vagrant and Poet

The Gypsy and the "Strange Disease of Modern Life"

I N CHAPTER 11 of George Eliot's *The Mill on the Floss*, an aggrieved
Maggie Tulliver runs away from home to join the Gypsies on Dunlow
Common. Feeling like an outcast in her own family and told repeatedly that her dark skin and thick, unruly hair make her look like a mulatto
or a Gypsy, she goes in search of her true kin. Maggie harbors a number of
fantastic preconceptions about the Gypsies. She believes that they are sure to
embrace her as one of their own and even, perhaps, make her their queen and
firmly expects that they live on a common: a "mysterious illimitable common
where there were sand-pits to hide in, and one was out of everybody's reach."[1]
After searching in vast green fields and finding neither Dunlow Common nor
any Gypsies, she discovers them in a lane behind a gate. Eliot uses Maggie's
naïve disappointment to suggest the gap that commonly exists between the
folkloric images and the actual circumstances of Gypsy life. Eliot also alludes
to certain historical developments of the 1820s and 1830s (the period during
which the novel is set) to help direct her readers' attention toward the sometimes harsh realities of Gypsy experience: the enclosure movement, which
prohibited the public use of open spaces, like commons, and vagrancy laws,
which allowed for the harassment and uprooting of Gypsies if they camped on
commons or highways.

After the late eighteenth century and, in particular, after passage of the
Vagrancy Act of 1824, Gypsies were prosecuted not as they had been, as
a nation or "race," but as nomads, "vagrants, rogues, and vagabonds."[2] The
overtly racist content of anti-Gypsy legislation had disappeared in 1783, when
the laws that mandated the imprisonment, deportation, or even execution of
individuals simply because they were Gypsies were repealed. These statutes,

passed in the Elizabethan period, were replaced, however, with legislation that targeted Gypsies through the ostensible crime of vagrancy. Beginning in 1783 and culminating in 1824, Gypsies could be rounded up simply by virtue of their nomadic existence. For the offenses of hawking, peddling, begging, camping on the side of a turnpike, telling fortunes, "wandering abroad and lodging under any tent or cart," or vagrancy (however defined), Gypsies could be prosecuted, fined, locked up, or persistently harassed.[3] They often tried to set up camp in cramped, isolated places—like lanes, as in *The Mill on the Floss*—or to elude arrest and imprisonment by continually moving on. But simply sleeping outside or having no apparent and regular employment could serve as the basis for legal action and, certainly, for persecution of moderate but persistent intensity.

Walter Scott took up the theme of the displacement and homelessness of Gypsies, their status as wanderers and pariahs, and tied it to specific economic and legal developments that he had observed in the Orkney Islands. In a similar but more impassioned manner, the poet John Clare yoked the Gypsies' endangered way of life to the pattern of enclosures that he witnessed and lamented.[4] "There is not so many of them as there used to be," he wrote in an autobiographical fragment on Gypsies, "the inclosure has left nothing but narrow lanes w[h]ere they are ill provided with a lodging."[5] For Clare, as for William Wordsworth slightly before him and Matthew Arnold after him, Gypsies played a role in a changing landscape, but they were also figures in a pastoral tradition. Their literary representation was bound up with particular poetic conventions, with ways of understanding and imagining the landscape, and with the transformations they registered in the countryside around them. In nineteenth-century pastoral, Gypsies were marked both as casualties of rural transformation and as itinerant and vagabond doubles of the poet. For Wordsworth, whose identification with Gypsy wanderers and "travellers" was ambivalent at best, the Gypsy was a primitive, an unevolved fellow resident of the Cumberland hills, whose vagrancy was itself a defining characteristic. Clare, whose father was an agricultural laborer, wished fervently to be of the Gypsies, and the Cambridge-educated Wordsworth to be spared their fate, but both regarded them, as did Scott, as an aboriginal people with their own customs and habits who lived on the always visible periphery of settled society.[6] For Arnold, however, the Gypsy became a focus for modern nostalgia, a preindustrial figure untainted by the "strange disease of modern life." What was primitive but contemporary for Wordsworth and Clare was idealized, allied with the past, and all but invisible for Arnold. Clare's pastoral was inseparable from the economic and political vicissitudes of the people who inhabited the land, whereas Arnold's pastoral expressed an inchoate and abstract sense of loss.

Arnold's Gypsy poems—"Resignation," "Thyrsis," and, especially, "The Scholar-Gipsy"—played a major role in the mid-nineteenth-century creation of the Gypsy figure as a remnant of prelapserian England, a marker of the transition from rural to industrial society that was imagined, in the words of Raymond Williams, as a "kind of fall, the true cause and origin of our social suffering and disorder."[7] As the Gypsies took on this association with a world that no longer existed, they were figured more and more frequently as mythic beings, as phantom visitors from another world, "seen by rare glimpses," like Arnold's scholar-gypsy. A few decades earlier, in Wordsworth's and Clare's day, the palpable loss of common lands and open fields, of settled rural communities and traditions, had been registered with pain and dismay. Williams estimates that between 1775 and 1825, about one-quarter of all cultivated acreage was appropriated by large and usually politically powerful landowners, and he relates these enclosures to the intense feeling for "unaltered nature [and] wild land" in the poetry of the period, as well as to the new emphasis in a poet like Wordsworth on "the dispossessed, the lonely wanderer, the vagrant."[8] In the first quarter of the nineteenth century, as Elizabeth Helsinger has written about a slightly different but related subject, "nostalgia is a luxury the embattled rural scene does not often afford."[9] Toward the end of the century, however, nostalgia had replaced the sense of immediate loss and struggle characteristic of earlier decades, and Arnold, as observer of a world in transition and anatomist of "modern life," began to create the contours and images of longing for a premodern world. As an aspect of this imagery, the Gypsy became, in Arnold's hands, both a more transcendent and a less actual, less corporeal, figure. Indeed, his scholar-gypsy is not a Gypsy at all, but a one-time Oxford student who has abandoned "English" society and who, in a way that has had a lasting effect on the way the poem has been read, *stands in for* the Gypsies.

Wordsworth and Arnold saw themselves and their poetic projects in relation to the patterns of existence that Gypsies, among other vagrants and vagabonds, seemed to embody: wandering, unproductive repetition, cyclical movement, detachment, and marginality. The interesting and, to some, frustrating aspects of this identification in Wordsworth is that he denies Gypsies the same sympathy and charitable interest that he accords almost all other rural vagrants and wanderers about whom he wrote. Arnold, though, who distanced himself from what David G. Riede calls the "passionate, committed, deep empathy of Romanticism," accepted Gypsy existence with apparent equanimity.[10] He imbued the Gypsies' distance from the contentious and distracting hub of society with the serenity of detachment to which he himself aspired. In the process, he removed Gypsies from the context of certain political and historical realities and transformed them into creatures of myth. The paradoxes of Wordsworth's apparent disdain and Arnold's adulation can be understood in the context of certain aspects of the poet's and the Gypsy's relationships to time and space: to repetitive movement, stasis, and intense watchfulness.

"A quiet, pilfering, unprotected race"

In order to understand the complexity of William Wordsworth's and John Clare's variations on the idea of the Gypsy as stock pastoral figure, we begin with the conventional example of Mary Russell Mitford's *Our Village: Sketches of Rural Character and Scenery* (1832). The two sketches that feature Gypsies in this collection offer a crude but representative version of the Gypsy's role in the tradition of late-eighteenth- and early-nineteenth-century picturesque.[11] The homey, occasionally giddy narrator of "The Old Gipsy" and its sequel, "The Young Gipsy," begins by lamenting the paucity of Gypsies in her neighborhood. The reason for this regrettable state is that the town is too well penned, watched, and guarded—too successfully insulated from theft, that is—to be easy prey to "that ambulatory race."[12] "In short," she declares, "we are too little primitive" (436). This "gipsyless" condition is most unfortunate for the landscape painter or lover, she complains. Gypsies—"that picturesque people"—harmonize with nature and complement the rustic scene (436). In an analogy that she will extend later in the sketch, the narrator elaborates on the potentially picturesque qualities of this group by comparing them to wild but unthreatening and aesthetically pleasing animals. Gypsies are the "wild genus," she writes, "the pheasants and roebucks of the human race" (436).

The sketch proceeds to focus on a family of Gypsies the narrator once discovered at a nearby encampment, a group "innocent" in its appearance and happily absent of the "tall, dark, lean Spanish looking men" she would be loathe to encounter alone on an empty path (437). Devoid of threatening masculine sexuality—no thieving or pillaging from this lot—"our village's" Gypsies are headed by a female fortune-teller and answer the demands of the landscape painter: "a pretty picture . . . the group . . . so harmless, poor outcasts! and so happy—a beautiful picture!" (438) (figure 8). This "modern Cassandra," whom the narrator predictably compares with Walter Scott's Meg Merrilies, tailors her fortunes to suit each client and emerges as a colorful and benign, if implicitly dishonest, figure. But her talents are also equated with those of an animal, the narrator's dog May, an "oracle" consulted by the entire village about matters of character and commerce.[13] This prophetic greyhound, her mistress records, "probably regarded the gipsy as a sort of rival, an interloper on her oracular domain" (442). The gently humorous and superficially appreciative tone of the sketch—the old Gypsy is ultimately shrewd in her predictions and the Gypsies are a welcome and picturesque presence—barely masks the narrator's belief in the Gypsies' semihuman status. Like the picturesque pheasants and domesticated dogs of the landscape, but unlike the sexually predatory "Spanish looking men" who might roam elsewhere, these Gypsies are harmless primitives. They possess cunning instincts but exhibit no refined talents or cultivated behavior.

FIGURE 8 "The Old Gipsy." (From Mary Russell Mitford, *Our Village* [London: Bell, 1876])

In Mitford's second Gypsy sketch, "The Young Gipsy," the old Cassandra, "dark as an Egyptian," proves an embarrassment to her granddaughter, a young beauty whose rosy, bright-skinned looks make her worthy of a portrait by Sir Joshua Reynolds. The girl, Fanny, has the chance to marry a non-Gypsy game-keeper and assimilate into English village life, where the "sin of her gipsyism [might be] forgotten" (458). Fanny is "clever and docile, and comports herself just as if she had lived in a house all her days" (458). But her grandmother, the old Cassandra, must decamp, leave town, and disappear so the girl can "pass" as English and suffer no stigma as the granddaughter of a Gypsy fortune-teller. A classic story of upward mobility through the denial of an ethnic past, "The Young Gipsy" belies the benign, if condescending, regard of "The Old Gipsy." Mitford may wax enthusiastic about the picturesque presence of the Gypsies of "our village," but ultimately she imagines a community purged of its dark trick-sters and bolstered by their passable kin. Foreignness and difference are blunted as the light-skinned Gypsy beauty blends into a homogeneous Englishness.

Mitford's contemporary John Clare also made use of the familiar association between Gypsies and the aesthetic of the picturesque, casting them as primitives with distinct, although not alien, moral and social codes. Beyond that, however, his disposition toward Gypsies in his poems and private writings is radically dif-ferent from the genteel condescension of *Our Village*. First, Clare saw Gypsies, as I have indicated, in the political and economic context of enclosure and of deeply unsettling rural change and so regarded them as emblematic of both persecution and liberty. Second, Clare regarded Gypsies as pastoral figures. For him, they not only represented an insulated and authentic state of being to be cherished and celebrated, but appeared as objects of empathy and identification, seemed to offer possibilities for escape and refuge, and were imbued with qualities that the poet aspired to possess (if only partially and temporarily).[14] The Gypsy carried both a political and a psychological charge for Clare, and one was inseparable from the other.

Clare, like Scott, was a collector of ballads and folk traditions and gathered the cultural artifacts of Gypsy life as part of a general retrieval and conservation of local history and custom.[15] Clare was particularly interested in Gypsies for their music and, at first, associated mainly with the Boswells, a nearby "tribe . . . famous for fidd[l]ers and fortunetellers" for the purpose of instrumental instruction: "I usd to spend my sundays and summer evenings among them learning to play the fiddle in their manner by the ear and joining in their pastimes of jumping dancing and other amusements."[16] Not only did he learn to play Gypsy songs, but he wrote down their musical notation in a series of notebooks and, as his biographer Jonathan Bate puts it, saw himself in the "self-appointed role [of] mediator between oral and written cultures."[17] He also picked up their slang and "black arts"—really just the ability to trade on local gossip—and observed their habits, which he catalogued in his fragments of autobiographical writing. Like an ethnologist—and like Henry Mayhew, an urban explorer himself influenced by ethnology—Clare recorded the Gypsies' relationship to religion (ignorance), morality (loose), learning (none), murder (also none), honesty (tenuous), food (badgers and hedgehogs), and tea (great fondness).[18] He believed that what the ignorant wider world interpreted as criminality and viciousness were really cultural differences, and he often preferred the straightforward, unembellished tricksterism of the Gypsies to the hypocrisy of their "calumniators."[19]

In some of Clare's most moving Gypsy poems, he transforms these objects of intense fascination into objects of longing. A sonnet that he began at the age of fourteen or fifteen, "The Gipsies Evening Blaze" (1807–1810), pictures a group of Gypsies at dusk, sitting around a "quivering" fire in a "warm nook," protected from fierce winds by sheep-nibbled, "shrubby" bushes. The warmth and light of the scene attract and invite the speaker of the poem from out of the bleakness of the evening, and it is *his* intensity of feeling and what we might call pastoral longing that begin and end the sonnet. "To me how wildly pleasing is that scene," he begins, before shifting from himself as subject to the Gypsies and their camp and then circling back. "Grant me this life," he pleads in the final line, "thou spirit of the shades!"[20] In the "October" section of *The Shepherd's Calendar* (1827), the narrator catalogues all the "pleasing objects" that might make the poet pause and turn to gaze while proceeding on his "solitary way." Among them are

> . . . gipseys camps in some snug sheltered nook
> where old lane hedges like the pasture brook

Run crooking as they will by wood and dell
In such lone spots these wild wood roamers dwell
On commons where no farmers claims appear
Nor tyrant justice rides to interfere
And but discovered by its curling smoak
Puffing and peeping up as wills the breeze
Between the branches of the colord trees[21]

This Gypsy camp is at once an image of protection and comfort, a secret and hidden nook of cozy pleasure—like the scene in "The Gipsies Evening Blaze"—and a locus of liberty, free from the restrictions of law and the tyranny of those who enforce it.[22] Banished from commons by enclosure, these Gypsies have nonetheless found a rare safe and open spot where they can settle, like the unfettered hedges and brook, "as they will." The poet, who is stopped in his tracks by this picture "that October yields," covets both the freedom and the womb-like security of the Gypsies' pastoral refuge, their "snug shelterd nook."

The canny and enviable ability of Clare's Gypsies to create oases of comfort and warmth in inhospitable surroundings reappears in a late poem, "The Gipsy Camp" (1841), a sonnet that describes a scene much like that in "The Gipsies Evening Blaze":

Beneath the oak which breaks away the wind,
And bushes close in snow like hovel warm.[23]

But in this poem, the camp is "squalid," the mutton to be eaten is "tainted," and the dog that waits for scraps is "half-wasted." These notes of realism prepare us for the ironic and paradoxical final lines:

Tis thus they live—a picture to the place,
A quiet, pilfering, unprotected race.

The Gypsies' "picturesqueness" has been much mitigated by the blunt description of the impoverished camp, so the word "picture" in the penultimate line cannot be read without irony. The double-edged "picture" modulates into the sober and wistful conclusion, a line that maintains in perfect tension the contradictory aspects of the Gypsies' state. They are quiet, but they steal; they steal, but they are unprotected—*by law* as well as by adequate shelter. They are both enemies and victims of the law; their circumstances are picturesque but seedy and foul; they keep to themselves but are parasitic. As Anne Williams has remarked of this line, it is free from "any sentimentality or romantic cliché," an instance of Gypsy representation notable for its understatement and complexity.[24]

Clare demonstrated the same equanimity with regard to the Gypsies, their glories, and their foibles during his period of incarceration for insanity in Matthew Allen's asylum in Epping. In 1841, he planned an escape and chronicled his attempt in his journal.[25] He recorded that, wandering in the forest near the asylum, he fell in with Gypsies who offered to help him run away by hiding him in their camp. Here was the Gypsy life as pure pastoral: escape and haven from the constraints of an oppressive world. But the poet could not afford to pay them for their trouble; the Gypsies wavered in their promise; and, when he went to meet them on the day he planned his journey, they had disappeared. Abandoned by his prospective rescuers, he nonetheless resolved to follow the route they had showed him: "Reconnitered the rout the Gipsey pointed out and found it a legible one to make a movement and having only honest courage and myself in my army I led the way and my troops soon followed."[26] With no expressed disappointment or anger, no admonishment of the peripatetic band, Clare sought to emulate their movements and follow them to freedom. He accepted their nomadic existence and necessary unreliability even as he longed for their liberty and for the comfort and warmth of their makeshift hearth. Clare's imaginative and psychic identification with Gypsies in all phases of his life contrasts markedly with the caricature of Mitford's sketches. Although both treat Gypsies as pastoral and picturesque figures, Clare replaces Mitford's condescension and dehumanizing regard with social critique and poignant longing.

"I was a Traveller then upon the moor"

The conclusion of Wordsworth's "Gypsies" (1807), a poem contemporaneous with "The Gipsies Evening Blaze," expresses a sentiment antithetical to Clare's supplication in the final lines of his poem. In place of "Grant me this life, thou spirit of the shades!" we have "[O]h better wrong and strife / Better vain deeds or evil than such life!" in response to the sight of a group of inert Gypsies on the moors. With considerable passion, both poets call for the intervention of the fates, the first wishing to achieve a destiny like that of the Gypsies, and the second hoping to ward it off.[27] Whereas the sight of a Gypsy encampment inspires longing and desire in one, it triggers a phobic reaction in the other. While Clare laments the "tyrant" laws that harass Gypsies and force them to abandon their temporary homes, Wordsworth seems to endorse the sentiments and reproduce the emphases of these laws. Both of them, Wordsworth no less than Clare, however, see their own lives in relation to those of the Gypsies, and it is the former's complicated and highly vexed identification with the motionless, "unbroken knot / Of human Beings" that I address here. But before discussing what David Simpson calls "one of Wordsworth's prickliest poems," I consider a pair of Gypsy poems that Wordsworth wrote in a very different key: the slightly earlier "Beggars" (1802) and its companion, "Sequel to 'Beggars' Composed Many Years After" (1817).[28] Although these poems do not focus exclusively on the poet's disapproval of what he regards as the doubtful moral status of Gypsies, they do suggest his inability to settle on a consistent response of either sympathy or antipathy.

Wordsworth based "Beggars," an eight-stanza poem about a haughty "Amazonian" or "Egyptian brown" beggar woman, on an incident that his sister Dorothy had experienced while alone and recorded in her journal in June 1800.[29] In Dorothy's account, a woman "tall beyond the measure of tall women," with skin that was dark brown but had "plainly once been fair," came begging at her door.[30] The woman claimed to have come from Scotland and explained that her family could not keep a house, and "so they travelled." Later that day, Dorothy encountered the woman's husband, a tinker, and then her two boys, who were begging as well as chasing a butterfly. They told her that their mother was dead; she answered that she had met their mother that morning (she noticed their strong resemblance to her) and then sent them away with nothing—a clear indication of her disapproval. Later still, she saw the boys with their mother and so was confirmed in her belief that the boys had lied about being orphans.

In "Beggars," Wordsworth keeps the outlines of the story and makes the double act of begging the central drama of his lyric, but effects a few small but telling changes. First, he makes overt the woman's Gypsy identity. In Dorothy's account, there are markers of Gypsy ways—tinkering and traveling—but the woman's dark skin seems to be a product of time and the elements rather than inheritance. Wordsworth, although he never calls her a Gypsy outright, introduces the adjective "Egyptian" to describe the color of the woman's skin. He also masculinizes her by announcing her stature in the first line as "a *tall man's* height or more."[31] An ancestor of both Scott's Meg Merrilies and Keats's "Old Meg," this beggar woman is commanding, almost marshal in her bearing, and it is her unusual appearance that moves the poet to give her alms

> . . . for the creature
> Was beautiful to see—a weed of glorious feature." (ll. 17–18)

But Wordsworth evinces far greater interest in the boys than in their mother. The beggar children are at the moral heart of the poem, and they become the subject of its companion piece, "Sequel to 'Beggars' Composed Many Years After," in which their mother is never mentioned. The boys appear in the original poem as pastoral putti "wreathed" with flowers and laurels, chasing a crimson butterfly, reveling in their utter freedom, and "so blithe of heart" that, had they wings, "they might flit / Precursors to Aurora's car" (ll. 31–34). For the moment cleansed of their "racial" or criminal associations, they ultimately revert to type by begging. The poet quickly tells them that he has given money to their mother—he recognizes in their features "Unquestionable lines of that wild Suppliant's face"—and they answer that she is dead:

> "She has been dead, Sir, many a day."—
> "Hush, boys! you're telling me a lie;
> It was your Mother, as I say!"
> And, in the twinkling of an eye,
> "Come! come!" cried one, and without more ado,
> Off to some other play the joyous Vagrants flew! (ll. 43–48)

And so ends the poem.

Wordsworth leaves out the final confirmation of the boys' relationship to the beggar woman that concludes Dorothy's story, thereby allowing for the possibility of their honesty or, at least, of some misunderstanding between them and the poet—the kind of speaking at cross-purposes found in "Now We Are Seven" (1798), in which death means different things to the child and her interlocutor. The "lie" with which he charges the boys has, in any case, a benign inflection in the poem, and his admonishing "Hush" betrays no anger but only a gentle, avuncular scold. They flit away insouciantly, exhibiting no consciousness of guilt, and their animal spirits outweigh their unreliability in the poet's parting image of them. Only the naming of the boys as "Vagrants" and the jarring yoking of that word with "joyous" in the final line betray uneasiness, a dissonance of tone. The harder note of realism or even of disavowal in the noun, an uncomfortable echo of the category under which Gypsies could be prosecuted, sits awkwardly with the breezy, untroubled adjective that precedes it. Unlike Clare's "pilfering, unprotected race," which balances knowingly the complex and apparently contradictory elements of the Gypsies' state, Wordsworth's "joyous Vagrants" conveys discord, unintended irony, perhaps callousness.[32]

The cast of amorality that Wordsworth lends the Gypsy boys in "Beggars" becomes an aura of innocence in the retrospective "Sequel." The poet now wonders what has become of the "wanton Boys" he imagined and wrote about fifteen years earlier. No longer identified as Gypsies, vagrants, or the children of a beggar woman, they have been transformed into emblems of purity and gladness, "lambs" who "Walk through the fire with unsinged hair," and are forever associated with a time of innocence in the poet's own life. The "Egyptian brown" of the mother's face has been replaced by the whiteness of clouds, the clarity of a brook, the immaculateness of lambs. "They met me in a genial hour," he writes,

> A time to overrule the power
> Of discontent.[33]

Although the poem begins and ends with a question about the whereabouts and well-being of the boys, its central subject is the poet's own departed innocence and wistful reminiscence. Separated from their origins, in the sense of both their parentage and the moral context in which Dorothy and William had initially placed them, the Gypsy boys mutate into abstractions through which the poet can evoke something of himself. He can, in other words, identify with the state of innocence the boys are made to represent, and the tinge of disapprobation in "Beggars" vanishes completely in "Sequel." Together, the two poems suggest something of the ambivalent and vexed sympathy that Wordsworth felt for this subject and prepare us for the strident but unconvincing denial of affiliation with the Gypsies' state of being in his poem of 1807.

"Gypsies"—which earned the opprobrium of William Hazlitt and Samuel Taylor Coleridge, among others, for its moralizing tone—takes as its subject the contrast between stasis, exemplified by the band of inert Gypsies the poet meditates on, and change, enacted in nature, especially in the rising and setting of the sun and the waxing and waning of the moon. Having himself walked to and from a particular destination—we know from his notes that it was Derby—and seeing the Gypsy families camped in the same pose and place on both legs of his journey, the poet begins with a question, "Yet are they here?" and ends with the declaration that even "vain deeds or evil" would be better than this lethargy and paralysis.[34] After twelve hours, he has covered a good deal of ground, the sun has set, the waning moon has risen, the "silent Heavens" have been busy, the stars have accomplished their "tasks," but the "unbroken knot / Of human Beings" has remained precisely as he left them.[35] The poem turns on the speaker's relationship, as a kind of third term, to the unchanging, unproductive Gypsies, on one side, and to busy nature, on the other. His own status in this regard is ambiguous: Who does he more resemble? Can he, as walker and poet, claim a kinship to nature in its cyclic, ever-changing, and awe-inspiring movements? Or is he uncomfortably like the Gypsies, indolent, static, and ineffectual?[36]

The language of the poem, and especially of three lines near the middle, betrays the poet's anxiety about his similarity to the Gypsies and his worthiness as a protégé of nature:

> —Twelve hours, twelve bounteous hours, are gone while I
> Have been a Traveller under open sky,
>   Much witnessing of change and chear,
>   Yet as I left I find them here. (ll. 9–12)

Most striking in its inadvertently ironic reference to the poet and the Gypsies alike is, of course, the word "Traveller," used often by Wordsworth to describe himself as wanderer on the hills and moors and commonly by others to refer to Gypsies. Indeed, Coleridge takes Wordsworth to task for ignoring the fact that "the poor tawny wanderers might probably have been tramping for weeks together through road and lane, over moor and mountain, and consequently must have been right glad to rest themselves . . . for one whole day."[37] Gypsies were represented alternatively as settled (or stagnant), as in Clare's various scenes of Gypsy encampments, or as itinerant (or vagrant), as in Wordsworth's "Beggars." In this poem, Wordsworth chooses the former without, apparently, acknowledging or making use of the possibility of the latter, so when the speaker of "Gypsies" refers to himself as a "Traveller," he seems to separate himself from rather than ally himself with the Gypsies. But traveling combines movement and inertia, purpose and purposelessness in a way that draws poet and Gypsy together, and the word "Traveller" carries too strong an association with Gypsy life to preclude such an alliance, particularly in conjunction with other aspects of these lines.

The speaker has subsisted "under open sky" for the past twelve hours, as have the Gypsies. There is, as well, the question of what he has accomplished in these "bounteous" hours, in this generous and expansive period of time: he has walked, of course, but has returned to the same spot, and he has *witnessed change* and cheer. The poet himself has not undergone change, as have the heavens, but has merely observed it, just as he now observes the "Spectacle" of the Gypsy encampment. If his moral indictment of the Gypsies rests on their changelessness, the poet cannot claim himself exempt from the same charge. As a mere witness to change, he also invites accusations of passivity, sloth, and marginality. The motion of walking to and fro, of going out but coming back by covering the same ground, suggests repetition without purpose, traveling without advancing. In his screed against the poem, Hazlitt mocks Wordsworth as a "patron of the philosophy of indolence" who nonetheless attacks a band of Gypsies for doing nothing. "What had he himself been doing in these four and twenty hours," Hazlitt asks, ". . . admiring a flower, or writing a sonnet?"[38] The distracting syntax of this section's final line — "Yet as I left I find them here" — further complicates the overt disavowal of any correspondence between poet and Gypsies. The two "I"s and "them" bump up against the verbs "left" and "find" in a contracted space, forcing the reader to sort out carefully the nature of the relationship between subject and object, both syntactically and existentially. If the second "I" is taken, fleetingly (and ungrammatically), as the object of "left," the line can be understood as the poet's disappointment at discovering *himself* just as he had been twelve hours earlier. In addition, the first word of the line echoes that of the first line of the poem — "Yet are they here?" — linking the speaker ("I") to stasis and to others who, like him, are still here "in this self-same spot."

As Simpson has argued, the poet's reaction to the Gypsies in this troubling poem is inseparable from his sense of the "ambiguous position of the poet, neither a laborer nor an idler."[39] As poet, he is witness and wanderer, and his nervousness about this aspect of his vocation is registered as a strident and exaggerated protest:

> . . . oh better wrong and strife
> Better vain deeds or evil than such life!" (ll. 21–22)

In "Resolution and Independence," written a few years earlier and published in 1807, the poet explicitly links wandering and a kind of guilty aimlessness with anxiety about his poetic career. He pictures himself as a "Traveller . . . upon the moor," a joyous and carefree reveler in nature's exquisite bounty who plummets from an emotional height of gladness to sudden and deep dejection:

> Far from the world I walk, and from all care;
> But there may come another day to me —
> Solitude, pain of heart, distress, and poverty.[40]

He berates himself for being indolent, for living always in "pleasant thought," for expecting others to work for him—"Build for him, sow for him"—and he thinks explicitly of other poets whose lives have ended in misery. It is precisely his distance from the work-a-day world and from the industry in which others engage that worries him, just as it does in a more covert manner in "Gypsies." As so often happens in such moments in Wordsworth's poetry, a figure—here, a leech gatherer—appears suddenly both to admonish him and to allay his fears. The leech gatherer, too, is an itinerant:

> . . . gathering leeches, far and wide,
> He travelled . . .

And, like the speaker of "Gypsies" and the camp dwellers he observes, he lives in open air:

> From pond to pond he roamed, from moor to moor;
> Housing, with God's help, by choice or chance." (ll. 103–4)

The leech gatherer's ability to comfort, rather than to unnerve or even anger, the poet derives from his fortitude and, perhaps even more important, from his industry. This traveler, unlike the Gypsies as Wordsworth has imagined them, can appear to be without purpose and yet, in fact, be diligent. Invisible work, like gathering leeches and writing poetry, might be work nonetheless, and if one marginal form of labor can be sustained, then so, perhaps, can the other. Wordsworth must suppress the Gypsies' work, make them sedentary rather than itinerant, portray their inactivity as repellent rather than inviting, and classify them as an undesirable type of vagrant—sleeping out of doors, exhibiting no means of subsistence, and, perhaps, breaking the law.[41] He cannot openly claim the Gypsies as his counterparts because, as a collectivity ("Men, women, children"), they carry the taint of "race," immorality, and primitivism. The mother and sons of "Beggars," although dishonest, can be somewhat redeemed because they are beautiful and take pleasure in nature, because they are represented as individuals, separate from their "tribe." Both the leech gatherer and the Gypsies mirror the poet's apparent idleness, but, for reasons that are both psychically and culturally determined, the former can more easily be imagined to reflect an image that gratifies the ego and soothes the cares of the poet.

"I wander'd till I died"

In a startling moment in Isobel Armstrong's chapter on Matthew Arnold in her monumental work on Victorian poetry, she writes of "an uncanny meeting point" between Arnold, the "liberal in crisis," and John Clare, the "peasant poet" who is in many ways Arnold's antithesis. "Both write of dislocation and isolation," she observes, "both are fascinated by Gipsies, traditional outsiders of the culture, both negotiate a bewildering number of poetic voices and traditions, Keats, Wordsworth, song, ballad and political lyric—and both are acutely sensitive to spatial boundary and limit."[42] This unlikely pairing of poets is explained, too, by their attraction to the pastoral mode and their sorrow over "estrangement from . . . earlier environment[s]."[43] Armstrong's acknowledgment of Clare's and Arnold's fascination with Gypsies is crucial, for it serves as a focal point for much else that they share. The Gypsy as a distinctly pastoral figure is linked to the loss and alienation that each registers in his poetry and is deeply connected to a sense of cherished place and the unforgiving character of time and change. The palpable losses of land and space that Clare laments had, by Arnold's time, become more abstract, less tied to the legal and practical realities of enclosure, but Arnold notes these brutal changes as well. "They must live still," he writes of the beleaguered and uncomplaining Gypsies in "Resignation (To Fausta)" (1849),

> . . . and yet, God knows,
> Crowded and keen the country grows;
> It seems as if, in their decay,
> The law grew stronger every day.[44]

These lines lack the anger and edge of Clare's "tyrant justice" in the "October" section of *The Shepherd's Calendar*, but they offer the same association between the laws that dictate oppressive change and the Gypsies' struggle to survive. For both, the Gypsy becomes emblematic of a bitter and always losing battle against what Arnold calls, also in "Resignation," "time's busy touch." What in Clare's poetry appears as the transformation of the land and accompanying shifts in social and economic life, becomes in Arnold "modern life" itself, a more sweeping and more cataclysmic mutation of the spirit, as well as of the world.

If Arnold echoes generally the sentiments of Clare's interest in Gypsies, he quite specifically rewrites and revises Wordsworth's central Gypsy poem. "Resignation" contains an explicit challenge to the older poet's mode of representation in "Gypsies" and an implicit critique of his apparent disdain for the Gypsies' way of life. Others have noted the resemblance of "Resignation" to another Wordsworth poem, "Tintern Abbey" (1798): each is dedicated and addressed to the respective poet's sister (Arnold's subtitle refers to his sister Jane) and commemorates a revisiting, a return to a memorable landscape. David G. Riede sees Arnold's poem as a general rejection of the Wordsworthian view, of both the role of the poet and his deep and passionate engagement with nature.[45] But to the extent that "Gypsies" is, as I have suggested, also a poem about the poetic vocation and the return to a particular scene, it, too, serves as a model after which and against which Arnold fashions "Resignation." He does so by transplanting the scene of the Gypsy encampment from Wordsworth's poem to his own and by radically changing its meaning for the speaker's meditation on the nature of change, repetition, and resignation.

In "Resignation," Arnold uses the occasion of a walk in the Lake District with his sister, first taken ten years before and repeated in the present, to contemplate the painfulness of time's passage and the human habit of circling back to former places and states of being. He begins by ventriloquizing those whose energies are focused fiercely on the realization of a goal, those who quest, battle, or journey as pilgrims: *"To die be given us or attain!"* they would proclaim. For these questing spirits, the act of repeating, of returning — or turning back — is untenable:

> . . . to stand again
> Where they stood once, to them were pain;
> Pain to thread back and to renew
> Past straits, and currents long steered through. (ll. 18–21)

"Thread[ing] back" is precisely what he and his sister have been doing, traveling again "this self-same road" and wondering whether they have changed little or are, rather, only "ghosts" of the "boisterous company" they once were. We glean from her brother's words that the unheard sister expresses some discontent, some regret about this return journey, and so he enumerates a variety of responses to the experience and frustration of repetition for her to consider. After the impatient ones, those who must attain or die, he mentions the "milder natures," those who are resigned, serene, freer because less passionate. Those who have achieved equanimity and calm acceptance in the face of inexorable change and the tyranny of time might be models for him and his sister, for whom this revisiting brings wistfulness and feelings of loss.

The speaker-brother then offers "Fausta" two examples of these "milder natures," a group of Gypsies they have passed on their walk and the generic "poet," who combines intensity—"a quicker pulse"—with detachment:

> Before him he sees life unroll,
> A placid and continuous whole—
> That general life, which does not cease,
> Whose secret is not joy, but peace. (ll. 189–92)

Although it is, arguably, the poet's "sad lucidity of soul" as a model for sister and brother that is of greatest interest in "Resignation," it is not at all clear that the Gypsies' perseverance and stoic acceptance of the passage of time are not equally, if differently, exemplary. In stanza 5, Arnold makes explicit his indebtedness to Wordsworth's "Gypsies" and, like his predecessor, raises the possibility of the Gypsies' resemblance to the traveler who narrates the poem. Only in Arnold's poem, the correspondence is fully acknowledged and the Gypsies are capable of providing moral instruction. Like the poet and his sister and like the traveler of Wordsworth's poem, the Gypsies have "roamed to and fro." Indeed, for this "migratory race," the pattern of returning to a "former scene" and finding remnants—"fragments"—of previous sojourns is a way of life, not simply an occasional experience.

Arnold seems to be answering and correcting Wordsworth, reminding him that it is the practice of Gypsies to be peripatetic, habitually to-ing and fro-ing *like him*, rather than, as the older poet would have it, sedentary and inert. Alluding again to "Gypsies," the poet of "Resignation" remarks on the "dark knots" that the Gypsies form in their huddle around the fire. Arnold's knot, however, consists exclusively of children, while Wordsworth's "unbroken knot" includes "[m]en, women, children" in a promiscuous and indiscriminate jumble of generations and sexes.[46] With apparent deliberateness, Arnold makes innocent the "knot / Of human Beings" that his predecessor obviously viewed with suspicion and distaste. With the image of the children by the fire, he also imbues the scene of the Gypsy camp with a powerful sense of return, of transitory homecoming. This encampment, unlike Wordsworth's, which suggests stagnation, or Clare's, which beckons the poet as a redoubt against the elements, combines the weariness of the Gypsies' travels and their fleeting pleasure in returning to a scene they once knew.

If Wordsworth insists on taking at face value the "Spectacle" of dormant Gypsies, Arnold counters him with the admonition that these habitual travelers, their outward appearance notwithstanding, are not impervious to the wearing vicissitudes of life. They, too, could measure themselves against the past and so feel unease and regret. As he instructs his sister,

> Signs are not wanting, which might raise
> The ghost in them of former days. (ll. 122–23)

By reiterating the word "ghost," which in the previous stanza refers to themselves—brother and sister—Arnold underscores their own resemblance to the Gypsies. Time is the Gypsies' enemy as well. Their joints grow stiff and the winds cold; laws become oppressive and open land scarce. But this "migratory race" will not stop to complain or compare "times past with times that are," but will persevere—"rub through" is the colloquial phrase that Arnold uses—in their customary way.[47] The "resignation" of the Gypsies is very like that of the "poet," although what may be stoicism and stolidity in the former is more considered, more self-conscious and intellectualized, in the latter. The poet's greatest strength is his ability to observe, his watchfulness and disinterestedness. In stanza 6, which evokes the poet's powers of resignation, the language of seeing and watching dominates. The poet "scans," "admire[s]," "looks down," "surveys," "gazes," "leans upon a gate and sees," and "sees" again and again. He can know through detached observation and discernment what others apprehend through experience. Just by witnessing love, the poem suggests, he knows its nature.

Does the poem suggest an identity between poet and Gypsy, both resigned, although differently? "Fausta" is apparently skeptical. To her, both poet and Gypsy seem poor models for mere mortals, but the first appears superior to the common mass of humankind and the second decidedly inferior. We know that the silent sister thinks this because her brother, "scan[ning]" (like a poet) her thoughts, has articulated them for her. Indeed, he continues to read her mind for twelve lines, dilating particularly on "Fausta's" views of the poet as a creature who avoids human experience and never, as a result, sees deeply within it. Does he share her assessments of poet and Gypsy? Does he agree that the Gypsies *"feel not, though they move and see?"* (l. 205). We know that he dissents from her characterization of the poet, for he devotes the rest of the poem to its refutation. But only by extension and by returning to what he has said about the Gypsies' vulnerability and refusal to indulge their feelings can we conclude that he disagrees with her description of the travelers. After speaking in "Fausta's" voice, he never again directly mentions the Gypsies.

Like Wordsworth, who can imagine the leech gatherer in "Resolution and Independence" but not the Gypsy as a model for human endurance, Arnold cannot sustain the implicit yoking of poet and Gypsy in "Resignation." Nor can he overtly urge his sister to emulate the "migratory race" as well as the man of "mighty heart." Put simply, the poet's vocation is noble and his vision complex, while the Gypsy, although resigned, never transcends the realm of the mundane. Nonetheless, Arnold allies the poet and the Gypsy—in part by alluding to Wordsworth's "Gypsies"—as creatures on the periphery of human community and as observers of change who "rub through." His revision of Wordsworth's poem expressly moves the Gypsies from the position of the observed—the "Spectacle"—to the place of the traveler and observer, the wanderer who, like the poet, compulsively returns to where he began.

If Arnold rewrites Wordsworth's "Gypsies" in "Resignation," he rewrites his own Gypsy poem four years later in "The Scholar-Gipsy" (1853). In place of an address to his sister, set in a naturalistic and familiar Lake District scene, Arnold offers a pastoral lyric complete with an opening call to a shepherd and a coda that removes the poem from the Cumner Hills near Oxford to an ancient beach in the Aegean. The poetic realism of "Resignation," which casts the Gypsies as objects of oppressive modern laws, is relinquished in favor of the stylized conventions of the pastoral form; accordingly, the buffeted, weary, stiff, and wind-chilled Gypsy has become an immortal, blithe-spirited apparition of a man. In a striking turnabout, the Gypsy, formerly deployed to evoke human vulnerability and care, is made indestructible and immune to change. In this poem, the figures of Gypsy and poet—or qualities associated with each in the earlier poem—are merged. The scholar-gypsy combines the social marginality and nomadic habits of the Gypsies of "Resignation" with the exquisite watchfulness and ocular disposition of the generic poet of that poem. Whereas the brother-speaker of "Resignation" cannot sustain his praise of the Gypsies' exemplary stoicism, the author of "The Scholar-Gipsy" has no difficulty in representing his Gypsy figure as an explicit ideal. For not only are poet and Gypsy merged, so are insider and outsider, self and other, university student and rustic. The Gypsy has been anglicized.[48] Through this conflation of scholar-poet and Gypsy, Arnold creates not only a highly sympathetic and idealized Gypsy figure, but an emblem of preindustrial nostalgia that would have an effect on Gypsy symbolism and iconography throughout the rest of the nineteenth century. By means of the artifice of pastoral convention and the separation of the Gypsy from history, Arnold imagines the scholar-gypsy as the ultimate exile—excluded from privilege and established community but free from the corroding diseases of modern life (figure 9).

Embedded in the conventional pastoral frame of the poem, between the poet's invocation of the shepherd and his departure by means of the classical world, lies a real and very familiar place: the hills outside Oxford, which the legendary scholar-gypsy was said to have inhabited and where the young Matthew Arnold roamed as a student. For Arnold, it was a place of nostalgic longing and of memories that he feared would themselves disappear. He wrote to his brother Tom that this poem, "The Scholar-Gipsy," was "meant to fix the remembrance of those delightful wanderings of ours in the Cumner hills before they were

FIGURE 9 John Garside, "Scholar Gypsies." (From John Sampson, *The Wind on the Heath* [London: Chatto and Windus, 1930])

quite effaced" and to commemorate "the freest and most delightful part, perhaps, of my life, when with you and [Arthur Hugh] Clough and [Theodore]
Walrond I shook off all the bonds and formalities of the place, and enjoyed
the spring of life and that unforgotten Oxfordshire and Berkshire country."[49]
Although the best remembered parts of the poem—its complaint against the
"sick fatigue," "languid doubt," and aimless striving of modern life—are heavy
with adult weariness and cynicism, other moments, especially those surrounding the description of the scholar-gypsy himself, are infused with sensual pleasure and youthful indulgence. Arnold's shaking off the strictures of university
life and escaping into the delights of spring and countryside are given form
in the poem as the penniless scholar-gypsy's abandonment of the student's life
and its oppressive exclusivity (he "tired of knocking at preferment's door") and
his complete absorption into the "wild brotherhood" of Gypsies. The scholar-
gypsy's narrative revises the traditional Gypsy kidnapping plot to make wholly
voluntary the young man's exile from the world into which he was born. He

becomes a Gypsy and never looks back, and those he has left behind encounter him only rarely. He has dropped out, gone through the looking glass. The fantasy of secret origins has become a fantasy of escape, and the anxiety about the true nature of identity has evolved into an alternative identity freely chosen and embraced.

Although the gulf between the poet and the scholar-gypsy remains wide—the poet ends by repeatedly urging the scholar to stay away from him—they cannot remain wholly separate throughout the poem. Arnold's younger self, the self he sloughed off, is fused with the scholar. As Dwight Culler has phrased it, "Seeing the Scholar-Gipsy and being the Scholar-Gipsy are a process imperfectly distinguished. One sees him by being him and in no other way."[50] The poet's search for the scholar-gypsy begins in reverie, in response to his reading of "Glanvil's book," *The Vanity of Dogmatizing* (1661), which tells the story of an Oxford lad who left the university to seek his livelihood and ended in the company of "Vagabond Gypsies" to "follow their trade."[51] There is a clear logic to Arnold's use of Joseph Glanvill as a source for his poem, for in his book the story of retreat from the mainstream is connected to a particular institution and place: the university that nurtured Arnold and yet exemplified a privileged life of traditional learning and its wilder environs, where he sought release from "the bonds and formalities of the place." But the choice of Glanvill as a source for Arnold's representation of Gypsies is striking for another reason. It goes against the grain of nineteenth-century representation by associating Gypsies with both breadwinning and learning, rather than thieving and ignorance. Glanvill's scholar joins the Gypsies at the outset to make a living and is ushered into the secrets of their "Mystery" only after earning their trust. The scholar explains to old friends who encounter him years after his disappearance that the Gypsies are not "Impostours," as was widely believed, but have "a traditional kind of learning . . . and could do wonders by the power of Imagination."[52] Neither mere parlor tricks nor fakery, their mental powers enable them to guide—and not simply read—the thoughts of others through a kind of telepathy. It is the mind of the Gypsies that interests Glanvill and not their purported criminality, vagrancy, or chicanery. Arnold takes from Glanvill this focus on the Gypsies' "lore" and "arts," seeing them as the possessors of occult knowledge and imaginative powers. Their talents, then, lie not so far from the poet's.

The "I" of "The Scholar-Gipsy" reads his Glanvill looking down on the spires of Oxford, lays the book beside him, and contemplates the "lost Scholar" who frequented that landscape two centuries before. In stanza 7, the poet suddenly shifts the locus of this legend from seventeenth- to nineteenth-century Oxford by indicating that he has seen the scholar-gypsy: "And I myself seem half to know thy looks."[53] With this sentence, the scholar-gypsy becomes either immortal or ghostly and the poet brings himself into some form of communion with the subject of the poem. Unhinged from time, the scholar-gypsy becomes a phantom

for all times and yet maintains the integrity and purity that had resulted from
his initial flight. The poet, half-knowing that he has seen the scholar, tries to
conjure him again. He watches for him in this way:

> Or in my boat I lie
> Moor'd to the cool bank in the summer-heats,
>   'Mid wide grass meadows which the sunshine fills
>   And watch the warm, green-muffled Cumner hills,
>   And wonder if thou haunt'st their shy retreats. (ll. 66–70)

The poet's posture—lying back, in passive enjoyment of nature's scene, and
watching—is transferred in the next stanza to the scholar-gypsy himself. The
poet seems to believe that mimicking the habits and recumbent position of the
scholar will either make him appear or induce a dream of the scholar in his
mind (he appears to have fallen asleep because, after "seeing" the scholar, he
shakes himself awake). Or perhaps this impersonation will simply enable him to
become the scholar-gypsy, to see him by being him, as Culler proposes.

   For the next six stanzas, he evokes the phantom wanderer across the seasons
as an onlooker, a pastoral, even pagan figure whose eyes are his most animated
and powerful organ. Like the poet, the scholar-gypsy floats on the Thames in
his punt, "leaning backward in a pensive dream," with his "eyes resting on the
moonlit stream" (ll. 77, 80). Associated with water, flowers, and fecundity—"fostering in thy lap a heap of flowers"—the scholar is a feminized and happily
indolent figure (a flower child, if you will), framed by a luscious and fertile
scene.[54] In this continuing description of him, two things are emphasized: the
scholar's watching and "eying," on the one hand, and the impossibility of fix-
ing him with one's own eyes, on the other. He is forever vanishing, visible one
moment but gone the next, so those who believe they have glimpsed him from
afar can never be sure that he is really there.

   The scholar-gypsy's ocular disposition, his rambling, and his apparent purposelessness place him in the tradition of poet vagrants and Gypsy wanderers
I have been discussing: Wordsworth's "Traveller . . . witnessing . . . change
and chear"; Arnold's generic poet of "Resignation," who eschews experience
and "sees life unroll" before him; the "I" of "The Scholar-Gipsy," whose "eye
travels down to Oxford's towers" and who lies waiting for the scholar in his teth-
ered boat. From "Resignation," Arnold repeats an image suggestive of the poet's
customary place as an observer on the periphery. "He leans upon a gate and
sees / The pastures and the quiet trees" (ll. 172–73) in the earlier poem becomes
"Thou hast been seen . . . hanging on a gate / To watch the threshers in the
mossy barns" (ll. 103–4). Not only marginal—resting at the gate—and peripatetic, these intent watchers of nature and humankind also seem lacking in efficacy and agency. Neither conforms to conventional manly activity or worldly

engagement. What *are* their "tasks"? we might ask, as Wordsworth asks of the "human knot" of sleeping Gypsies. Distributing stores of "white anemony, / Dark bluebells . . . / And purple orchises," the "spare" figure with "dark vague eyes, and soft abstracted air" seems to have, at best, a decorative and lyrical mission (ll. 87–88, 99). The scholar's feminine associations—with flowers and vegetal lushness—combine with his passivity and apparent lack of purpose to make him a dubious model of nineteenth-century masculinity. Wordsworth reviles the Gypsies of his poem of 1807 at least in part because of his discomfort with their insufficient manhood. The male Gypsy figures conjured by Clare, Wordsworth, and Arnold share a heterodox gender identity with Scott's Meg Merrilies: as she is a masculinized Gypsy woman, they are feminized Gypsy men.

The surprise, then, is that the scholar-gypsy's mission as a creature of the imagination is to aid those overwhelmed by purpose and striving. It is precisely his unconventional relationship to the demands of Victorian manliness that make him a needed antidote to the oppressiveness of contemporary life. Modern man, distracted by too many aims and worn out by unceasing change, needs to conjure the scholar-gypsy as an immortal, unchanging, and hopeful presence:

> Who fluctuate idly without term or scope,
>   Of whom each strives, nor knows for what he strives,
>   And each half lives a hundred different lives;
> Who wait like thee, but not, like thee, in hope. (ll. 167–70)

Arnold represents the contemporary world as a place devoid of concentration and productive constancy. Far better, he suggests, to drop out of sight—to be a "truant boy"—and follow the Gypsy's lore than to live a harried, divided, and empty life. Far better to embrace the "Mystery" than to believe in half-creeds and lukewarm faiths. Not only is a truant and adopted Gypsy to be a lodestar, a source of hope, but the "wisest" of the time seem able only to spew misery and dejection and then to offer numbing and useless comfort. The official poets or sages, whether Tennyson, Carlyle, or someone else, can no longer offer true solace or provide a model of "resignation." Only those who hang on the gate— be they Gypsies, dreamers, or exiles—can proffer transcendence. They do so because they are disengaged from worldly concerns and partisan disputes. As unwitting practitioners of disinterestedness, they possess the quality that Arnold required of the true critic.

In the last five stanzas of the poem is a final paradox, and, in the context of representations of the Gypsy in the nineteenth century, it comes as a striking reversal. In numerous other texts, the Gypsy is depicted as a contaminant, a figure who, although living on the margins of settled society, threatens it with certain contagion. "Despite their self-containment," writes Katie Trumpener, summing up this phenomenon of the imagined Gypsy, the Gypsies' wildness is highly contagious, as their arrival in a new place initiates and figures a crisis for Enlightenment definitions of civilization and nationalist definitions of culture. Here, in the Gypsy camp, is a culture without "culture," transmission without "tradition"—self-knowledge and collective amnesia side by side. Anchored themselves in an eternal present, a self-continuity that transcends context and time, they seem able to remove and replace the memory of others at will. Those who join them—whether as stolen children, "scholar-gipsies," or willing or resistant fellow travellers—seem not only to forget who they are but to lose all sense of time.[55]

Arnold's scholar-gypsy conforms, to a large degree, to the pattern that Trumpener describes. His susceptibility to change ceases when he joins the Gypsies, perhaps even to the extent of defying death. We can imagine that he loses all sense of time, that he has forgotten who he is. But Arnold does not worry about contagion from contact with the scholar; indeed, he regards it as a boon. Rather, he worries about contagion that travels in the opposite direction, about the scholar-gypsy's vulnerability to "infection" from "us." To that end, he implores the scholar to flee "our" presence, and he does so no fewer than four times in the final stanzas of the poem:

> Fly hence, our contact fear! (l. 206)
>
> Wave us away, and keep thy solitude! (l. 210)
>
> But fly our paths, our feverish contact fly! (l. 221)
>
> Then fly our greetings, fly our speech and smiles! (l. 231)

The settled community, or Enlightenment civilization, is quite clearly the contaminant, the diseased and feverish body that will infect innocence through contact. And, consistent with the emphasis in the poem on the scholar-gypsy's mind and imagination, the poet also makes clear that the "strong infection" from which we suffer is of the mind: "our mental strife." At all costs, the scholar-gypsy must avoid us. If not, he risks breaking the spell, inviting distress, courting mortality.

The coda of the poem, which begins just after the poet has implored the scholar-gypsy to flee for the final time, underscores the power and peculiarity of this reversal. The lone "Tyrian trader" sailing the waters of the Aegean is the scholar-gypsy's analogue, and the intruding Greeks, their boats laden with fresh and plentiful cargo, correspond to the society that Arnold has described as suffering "this strange disease of modern life." The trader flees the scene "indignantly," heading for the Atlantic through the Mediterranean and ending at the Iberian Peninsula. There he finds "the dark Iberians," counterparts of the Oxfordshire Gypsies, and settles, at least for the moment, among them. If this reading of the coda is correct, Arnold seems to be suggesting that his beloved Greeks, models of a rich and highly developed culture, are also to be understood as a flawed ideal.

The strivings and accomplishments of modern England or ancient Greece carry with them certain liabilities that, if left unchecked, threaten to infect the pure of spirit. Retreat from "civilization" may be preferable, even if it means disappearing among peoples presumed to be benighted, whether Gypsies or Iberians. The poem suggests, of course, that such peoples are not ignorant or primitive but possess a kind of knowledge and mental strength of their own. Indeed, they have regenerative powers that must be protected from contact with populations that rule and dominate, from ways of thinking and even forms of learning that corrupt and sicken the mind.[56]

Arnold returned to the scene of the Cumner Hills and the subject of the scholar-gypsy in the pastoral elegy he wrote in 1866 to mark the death, five years earlier, of Arthur Hugh Clough. Clough, a fellow poet and one of the university friends with whom he had roamed the countryside surrounding Oxford, appears as "Thyrsis," a poet-shepherd whose quest for the scholar-gypsy Arnold, or his poetic persona, had shared. More conventional than "The Scholar-Gipsy," the elegy makes overt what its predecessor only implies: that the identities of the scholar-gypsy and the poet are, if not interchangeable, then conjoined. "Thyrsis" begins with the poet's recognition of change—"How changed is here each spot man makes or fills!"[57]—and his resolve to find again those things that marked the glory of his youthful rambles: Thyrsis, the scholar-gypsy, and the elm tree whose existence attested to the scholar's immortality. With Thyrsis gone, first self-exiled from this spot and now dead, the poet seeks confirmation that the scholar, at least, lives on. He finds it when he discovers the elm:

> Despair I will not, while I yet descry
> 'Neath the mild canopy of English air
> That lonely tree against the western sky.
> Still, still these slopes, 'tis clear,
> Our Gipsy-Scholar haunts, outliving thee! (ll. 193–97)

What comforts him, however, is not precisely the persistence of the scholar-gypsy in the face of the loss of Thyrsis, but the promise of his own survival:

> Fields where soft sheep from cages pull the hay,
> Woods with anemonies in flower till May,
> Know him a *wanderer still; then why not me?*
>
> A fugitive and gracious light he seeks,
> Shy to illumine; and I seek it too. (ll. 198–202 [emphasis added])

The poet seeks reassurance that the quest itself and the wandering—whether they signify aspiration, poetry, or remaining on the margins—can be sustained and are worth sustaining. The scholar-gypsy's tree offers proof that he still haunts the scenes of the poet's youth; the memory of Thyrsis confirms *him* as a like-minded spirit:

> Thou too, O Thyrsis, on like quest was bound;
> Thou wanderedst with me for a little hour! (ll. 211–12)

And now the poet needs to hear—or to reproduce—the voice of his dead friend comforting him and bidding him to *"Roam on!"*: *"Why faintest thou?"* he hears Thyrsis inquire, *"I wander'd till I died"* (l. 237). Finally, Thyrsis points to the elm tree that crowns the hill and marks it as a sign that "our Scholar" wanders yet.

The elusive scholar-gypsy, the lamented Thyrsis, and the poet himself are of a piece in this elegy. Poet figures, exiles, faithful to their separate and collective missions, they persist in the face of the change that Arnold registers at the very beginning of "Thyrsis" and that serves as a fundamental theme of "The Scholar-Gipsy." Whereas in the earlier poem the line between scholar and poet is clearly demarcated and, for the most part, maintained, in the later one, the two poet friends replicate every aspect of the scholar that is heralded in the poem, except his immortality. Although the poet of "The Scholar-Gipsy" mimics the scholar's recumbent posture on the Thames and eagerly seeks him out, he makes a passionate plea for separateness, for the scholar's need to maintain his distance. In "Thyrsis," the scholar himself is invisible, but the tree that stands in for him establishes the likeness between the phantom "Gipsy-Scholar" and the youthful friends. They all are, or have been, wanderers. The tension that characterizes the relationship between Gypsy and poet in Wordsworth's "Gypsies," in Arnold's "Resignation," and even in "The Scholar-Gipsy" vanishes in "Thyrsis." In this elegy, the scholar-gypsy seems hardly to be a Gypsy at all, making possible the complete fusion of poet, wanderer, phantom, and exile.

Denied access to land that was never legally their own, as a result of the enclosure movement of the late eighteenth and early nineteenth centuries, Gypsies became a symbol for dispossession and homelessness and for ultimate impermanence. They were figures in a changing landscape and emblems of rural transformation and, as a consequence, easily absorbed into pastoral imagery as citizens of a green and better world. For some, like John Clare, vagrancy carried with it possibilities for liberation. He was attracted to the Gypsies' apparent resistance to law and identified with their victimhood. Wordsworth, on the contrary, could not completely separate vagrancy from depravity or excessive inertia, from the lawlessness that the word had come to signify in relation to Gypsy life. To the extent that he nursed anxieties about his own ambiguous relationship to indolence or unproductive labor, he reviled the Gypsies rather than claiming them as kindred travelers. Insistent on their inactive, nearly motionless state in "Gypsies," he could imagine only himself as the detached witness of change and walker "to and fro," failing to see that vagrancy could involve peripatetic and perhaps contemplative, not just sedentary, phases of life.

Despite the difference in their responses to the Gypsies, though, both Clare and Wordsworth focus on stasis in their poetic evocations of Gypsy groups. For Wordsworth, stasis appears repellent and threatening; for Clare, it signals rest, shelter, and home. Both poets also understand Gypsies in the context of particular social and economic patterns: Clare sees them as casualties of enclosure; Wordsworth, as unproductive, taskless, without industry. For them, as for Mary Russell Mitford, the Gypsies were primitives, the bearers of a distinct culture and mode of life that survived in tandem with their own. They were a race apart—less than fully human for Mitford, slothful and uncivilized for Wordsworth, canny and resourceful for Clare.

With Matthew Arnold, the Gypsy's vagrancy and static pose are replaced by circulation, movement, and, finally, wandering. The Gypsies of "Resignation" travel back and forth, returning repeatedly to places they have occupied before, weary, like Wordsworth's Gypsies, but not indolent. They are subject to change, to age and infirmity, to the legal and geographic restrictions that Clare lamented. But in "The Scholar-Gipsy," the Gypsy himself becomes elusive. The hybrid figure of the scholar-gypsy occupies a middle ground between the settled English world and the "wild brotherhood": his new form of identity anglicizes the Gypsy and uncouples the qualities of gypsyhood and the "race" itself. The "wild brotherhood" of the Gypsies remains all but invisible in the poem, their "smoked tents" pitched on the outskirts of Bagley Wood and glimpsed only from a great distance (ll. 111–13), and the scholar figures as their surrogate. But the scholar himself is a ghostly presence, a phantom whose very existence may itself be the poet's projection.

Gypsy identity, then, is greatly attenuated in Arnold's poem, and the poet's desire for the scholar-gypsy's equanimity and grace overshadows the story and the being of the scholar. It is the poet's sympathy with exile and wandering, in both "The Scholar-Gipsy" and "Thyrsis," that defines the contours of Gypsy identity. In this way, the scholar-gypsy serves, as we shall see, as a prototype for the bohemian Gypsy lorist of the late nineteenth century—the Englishman who leaves "society" and voluntarily adopts the social posture of the outcast and nomad. He does not fear for the safety of settled civilizations, as, by implication, Wordsworth appears to in "Gypsies," but frets that Gypsy life and lore will disappear and be forgotten. Intent on preserving and maintaining the imagined

purity of Gypsy culture, the scholar and lorist insist on the contaminating powers of English life, of modern life. No longer the primitive tribe coexisting with
its host culture, Gypsies occupy a frozen, lost, prelapserian, imagined world.
In Wordsworth's pastoral, it is nature that embodies the principle of beneficent
and healthful change and the Gypsies who signify a disconcerting and dangerous stagnation. In Arnold's pastoral, change is associated with human society,
and its powers are insidious and corroding. For him, then, the timeless Gypsies,
immortal and unreal, offer redemption and solace. They do so, however, at the
cost of their identity as both victims of law and agents of history.

3

In the Beginning Was the Word

George Borrow's Romany Picaresque

A LONG WITH Matthew Arnold, George Borrow invented the persona of the mid-nineteenth-century "Romany rye": the gentleman or scholar-gypsy who devoted himself to the preservation of Gypsy lore and abandoned — even for a brief time — settled English life for a nomadic sojourn among the peripatetic Gypsies, a kind of Romany fellow traveler. While clearly a fictional character in Arnold's "The Scholar-Gipsy," a projection of the poet's desire for an aloof, disinterested relationship to modern life, Borrow's rye is part fiction and part self-invention. In two volumes of uncertain genre, *Lavengro* (1851) and *The Romany Rye* (1857), Borrow tells the tale of a man who finds his identity as a wanderer and discovers in the English Gypsies he encounters along the way a template for both vagabondage and authenticity of being.

If Arnold imagines the Gypsy as an antidote to the diseases of modernity, to mindless striving and morbidity, Borrow understands the Gypsy as the antithesis of "gentility," a term he uses to evoke the modern threat of cultural homogeneity.[1] In mid-nineteenth-century England, Borrow believed, the distinctiveness and specificity of Gypsy culture, like that of Jews and Quakers, confronted the danger of assimilation. The continued health of true English eccentricity, with which Borrow has long been associated, depended on the preservation of cultural mixture and distinctness.[2] Like Arnold, he conjures Gypsy life as an escape from conventional masculinity, from the exigencies of manly vocation and worldly success. Like the feminized scholar-gypsy, laden with flowers and lying languidly in his boat, Borrow's rye evades the narrative of masculine efficacy. In Borrow, the flight from normative manliness expresses itself not only in his attraction to Gypsy life but in the very form of his literary works. He produced a kind of picaresque fiction that invites readers to expect both autobiography and bildungsroman, but delivers neither. The unclassifiable form of his writing reflects both his subject—a group of people with marginal status—and his own ambivalent relationship to ambition, accomplishment, and the hallmarks of worldly success. Borrow's rye, who goes by the name of Lavengro, meaning "word master" in Romani, differs from Arnold's scholar-gypsy in forming his deepest attachment to British Gypsies by way of their language. The Romany evoke for him the world of philological exploration and the fantasy of an originary tongue. Borrow's Gypsies stand, above all, for linguistic cosmopolitanism and a dream of ultimate origins—that is, both the multiplicity and the unity of human experience. The "treasure" the Gypsies possess, writes Ian Duncan, is "encrypted in their language" and fulfills "the philologist's true goal, the aura of an ontological lost home."[3]

Borrow's work, largely forgotten today, enjoyed a revival at the turn of the twentieth century, when he was recast as a figure dear to cultural conservatives nostalgic for a prelapserian and preindustrial England. In this version of Borrow's pastoral narratives, the Gypsy plays the role of quaint and benign primitive, a symbol of changelessness akin to the immortal scholar-gypsy of Arnold. Ideological complexity and, often, ambiguity hover over the tradition of pastoral, as over the literary representation of Gypsies. As suggested in the discussions of John Clare and Arnold, the question of whether the Gypsy is regarded as subject to history and change is often deeply connected to the social and political sympathies of the writer and to his ability to see the Gypsy as an actual, not simply a literary, being. Borrow's quixotic ideological stance has been hard to pin down. He has been understood as both conservative and radical, and his reputation over time has varied accordingly. His obsession with language and his attachment to both cultural specificity and cultural variety, I would argue, are the best clues to his place in the history of Gypsy representation.

Borrow's Incarnations

George Borrow, a marginal man of letters who was nonetheless well known in his own time, made his living as a translator, a literary hack, and the author of a series of books that tend to straddle the forms of travelogue and memoir. Borrow based his early, best-selling works on his travels in Europe and elsewhere as an employee of the British and Foreign Bible Society, a Protestant organization committed to distributing Bibles to benighted peoples across the globe.[4] The work of translating and selling Bibles made use of Borrow's linguistic skills and militant anti-Catholicism, a passion that fueled his dislike of both the Oxford Movement and, more idiosyncratically, the gothic fiction of Walter Scott (RR 351–52). The object of this anti-Catholic wrath in *Lavengro* and *The Romany Rye* is a recurring character, to whom I will return, called the "man in black," an itinerant priest who seems to wander the English countryside in search of converts at the behest of the pope.

It was on his travels for the Bible Society that Borrow encountered Gypsies in many lands, discovering in their customs, language, and manner of subsistence a reflection of the British Gypsy ways he knew from his boyhood rambles in the Norwich countryside. In a reversal—or perhaps parody—of the European traveler's dependence on a Western lingua franca like English or French, Borrow's knowledge of Romani, however rudimentary, functioned as a passport to other cultures and formed the basis of his internationalist credo. In a letter to the Bible Society, written in Moscow in 1835, Borrow describes a characteristic visit to Gypsies near Marina Rotche:

> [They] swarmed out from their tents . . . and surrounded me. . . . I addressed them in a loud voice in the dialect of the English Gypsies. . . . A scream of wonder instantly arose, and welcomes and greetings were poured forth in torrents of musical Romany, amongst which, however, the most pronounced cry was: *ah kak mi toute karmune*—"Oh, how we love you," for at first they supposed me to be one of their brothers, who, they said, were wandering about in Turkey, China, and other parts. . . . Their countenances exactly resembled those of their race in England and Spain, brown, and for the most part beautiful, their eyes fiery and wildly intelligent, their hair coal-black and coarse.[5]

This experience of recognition and of Borrow's—or, later, Lavengro's—discovery of "brothers" in unlikely places recurs throughout his works. Gypsies constitute an anchor for his identity and a unifying motif for his encounters with the disparate peoples of the world.

The Bible in Spain was Borrow's most popular and best-received book during his lifetime, *Lavengro* and *The Romany Rye* achieving the status of respected literary works only after his death in 1881.[6] Borrow's biographer Michael Collie believes that the missionary aura of *The Bible in Spain* added to its appeal to the English public in the mid-nineteenth century and that the qualities that accounted for its fame—ostentatious but essentially fraudulent autobiographical details—explain the only moderate success of the later two works.[7] I would speculate that *Lavengro* and *The Romany Rye*, published in the 1850s, frustrated the public's expectation that they were reading an autobiography—whether fictional or not—that promised a teleological frame and a terminus in marriage and vocation. Set on English soil and not offered as a justifiably picaresque travelogue, these two works begin not with embarkation on a journey but with birth, genealogy, and the conundrums of physical and psychic inheritance. Unlike the various narratives of David Copperfield and Jane Eyre, Arthur Pendennis and Maggie Tulliver, Teufelsdröckh and John Stuart Mill, the story of Lavengro ends almost in medias res or, more precisely, as we shall see, in another embarkation.

The popularity of these two mock memoirs after Borrow's death and the revival of his work at the turn of the century tell us a good deal about the trajectory of British attitudes toward and representation of Gypsies in the nineteenth and early twentieth centuries. Renewed interest in Borrow and his writings followed the publication of a two-volume biography by William Ireland Knapp in 1899 and the contemporaneous appearance of cheap editions of his works. (Between 1893 and 1914, for example, sixteen editions of *Lavengro* were published.)[8] Late-nineteenth-century pastoralism and nostalgia for preindustrial England, about which Jan Marsh and others have suggestively written, assigned a particular place to the British Gypsy.[9] The Gypsy Lore Society was itself part of this movement to preserve and revive rural folkways, music, dance, and similar antiquated cultural practices, but others also made the connection between Gypsies and an older, unspoiled England. The composer Ralph Vaughan Williams, who took an interest in English folk music and older musical idioms, planned—but never wrote—an opera based on *Lavengro*.[10] Cecil Sharp, principal of the Hampstead Conservatoire of Music, collected old folksongs from Gypsy women, and Edward Thomas, another early-twentieth-century ruralist and poet, studied George Borrow and wrote Gypsy poems.[11] Borrow emerged as a prototype of the Romany rye and as a kind of putative godfather to those who wished to celebrate the preindustrial past. John Sampson, a leading member of the Gypsy Lore Society and librarian at the University of Liverpool, acknowledged Borrow's centrality to the British literary tradition of Gypsy representation by naming his anthology of Gypsy references *The Wind on the Heath*, a phrase taken from *Lavengro*: "There's night and day, brother, both sweet things; sun, moon, and stars, brother, all sweet things; there's likewise the wind on the heath."[12]

In essays written in the 1880s and 1890s, collected forty years later for an edition of selections from the works of Borrow, Leslie Stephen and George Saintsbury expound on the meaning of Borrow for the late Victorian reader.[13] Saintsbury remarks on Borrow's apparent lack of interest in current events, literary contemporaries, and the dramatic political changes through which he lived. "Who, as he reads [*Lavengro*]," Saintsbury asks, "ever thinks of what was actually going on in the very positive and prosaic England of 1824–5?"[14] This absence of topicality or even contemporary detail enables the reader of the 1880s and 1890s to escape the material realities of his own time, as well as previous eras, and to revel in unreality. Stephen delights in the "half-visionary fragment of fairyland" that Lavengro occupies: "It will never be again discovered by any flesh-and-blood traveller; but, in my imaginary travels, I like to rusticate there for a time, and to feel as if the gipsy was the true possessor of the secret life, and we who travel by rail and read newspapers and consider ourselves to be sensible men of business, were but vexatious intruders upon this sweet dream."[15] In an indulgent tone, Stephen insists that Borrow was a "staunch conservative, full of good old-fashioned prejudices," a bohemian but not in revolt against the established order.[16] A "genuine tramp," a benign dreamer in touch with a land now obliterated by modern inventions like the railroad, Borrow appears to comfort the late-nineteenth-century man of letters.

The Borrow of the fin de siècle and the early decades of the twentieth century, then, is both culturally conservative and bohemian, and, for some, the latter role took on a racier and potentially more subversive quality than Stephen allows. Augustine Birrell—essayist, passionate Borrow admirer, and sometime literary man—devoted an essay to Borrow in his collection *Res Judicatae*, in which he tries to define the "born Borrovian" by evoking Borrow as a kind of outlaw: "down tumbles the standard of Respectability . . . ; up flutters the lawless pennon of the Romany Chal [man]."[17] Daydreaming under the flag of lawlessness, this species of Borrow reader escapes not just modernity but propriety and social convention. Some of the male Gypsy lorists, whose penchant for heterosexual libertinism constituted an important part of their enthusiasm for Gypsy caravanning and rambling, saw in Borrow a kindred sexual spirit. Even Theodore Watts-Dunton, whose sexuality was more complicated and ambivalent than that of his fellow lorist Augustus John, regarded Borrow as an avatar of romantic love and, in homage to the spirit of Romany female beauty, featured two stunning Gypsy women in his novel *Aylwin* (1898) and narrative poem *The Coming of Love* (1898). In his introduction to an edition of Borrow's *Wild Wales: The People, Language and Scenery* (1862), Watts-Dunton characterizes this late work as lacking in glamour. He attributes the straight-laced mood of the tour of Wales and its narrative to the inhibiting presence of Borrow's wife and step-daughter. Because of this constraint, Watts-Dunton concludes, Borrow found it impossible "to indulge in his bohemian proclivities and equally impossible to give his readers any of those romantic coincidences . . . which illuminate his other works."[18] This image of Borrow as sexual bohemian is as much an invention of turn-of-the-century Borrovians as is the notion of Borrow as nostalgia-bound conservative.

Thwarted Bildung

George Borrow's *Lavengro* and *The Romany Rye* provide grist for the nostalgic ruralist's mill. The bulk of Lavengro's story, written in the first person, occupies the 1820s and evokes an England free from reform politics, industrial cities, and even railroads, save as a fantasy of the future. Jasper Petulengro, the Gypsy who becomes Lavengro's "brother," tells of hearing two engineers describing a "wonderful invention" that would necessitate destroying all the old roads and digging up the grain fields in order to put down "iron roads, on which people would go thundering along in vehicles pushed forward by fire and smoke" (*RR*

38). How, Jasper wonders, could the Gypsies pitch their tents on iron roads, protect their families from danger, find places for their cattle to graze? Numerous allusions to boxing and references to stagecoaches and inns of "times gone by" remind us that we are in the world of Pierce Egan and Thomas De Quincey and, perhaps, the earliest Dickens. Ian Duncan has observed that even Borrow's London resembles "the rogues' town of Nash or Defoe [more] than the imperial metropolis of Dickens and Mayhew."[19] That this should be the case, given that the works are set in the 1820s rather than the 1840s or 1850s, does not seem to prevent Borrow's readers from detecting in them an aura of nostalgia or even anachronism. And it is as much the literary form as the temporal setting of these works that establishes their affinity with a premodern era, with the late eighteenth rather than the mid-nineteenth century.

In a statement about his creation Lavengro, Borrow touches on the resolutely picaresque and anti-bildung nature of his narrative:

> [H]e does not become a Captain in the Life Guards . . . nor does he get into Parliament, nor does the last volume conclude in the most satisfactory manner, by his marrying a dowager countess, as that wise man Addison did, or by his settling down as a great country gentleman, perfectly happy and contented, like the very moral Roderick Random, or the equally estimable Peregrine Pickle; he is hack author, gypsy, tinker, and postillion. . . . [H]is tale is not finished. . . . [I]t is probable that he will retain something of his gypsyism. (RR 318)

The fictional and real figures whom Borrow cites convey his kinship with eighteenth-century models, but even these forerunners' narratives, however episodic and rambling they might be, culminate in the resolution of ambition or love. Lavengro, however, retains his "gypsyism," a way of indicating that his haphazard occupation, unfulfilled—even inchoate—romantic yearnings, and unsettled habits will shape the form as well as the substance of his life. "Gypsyism" comes to signify not just the open-endedness of the hero's life but the rambling quality and inconclusive form of the written narrative, so the genre of the work mirrors its peripatetic subject.

Peter Brooks has suggested that the hero's ambition in nineteenth-century texts is a latter-day version of the *picaro*'s scheming merely to stay alive in earlier fiction: "It may be a defining characteristic of the modern novel (as of bourgeois society) that it takes aspiration, getting ahead, seriously, rather than simply as the object of satire . . . , and thus it makes ambition the vehicle and emblem of Eros, that which totalizes the world as possession and progress."[20] The depth and power of this modern myth was so great for nineteenth-century audiences, he goes on, that ambition constituted the very "readability" of a text, the structure by which its meaning might be created or perceived. As Brooks's discussion implies, this myth of ambition—of "possession and progress"—was inextricably

bound up with notions about the achievement of manhood.[21] Lavengro's relationship to the plot of masculine ambition, although familiar to the Victorian
reader, ultimately eludes clarity or resolution.[22] Borrow draws on elements of
family romance, pastoral, and bildung, but he ultimately denies his narrative
and his readers the "readability" associated with the plot of ambition.

In *Lavengro*, the standard Gypsy-foundling story is, not unexpectedly, fused
with the plot of manhood and masculine identification, reinforcing the centrality of the Oedipal struggle to the narrative of family romance. In this book, however, as in some narratives involving heterodox femininity, the child imagines
not a real parent more powerful and prestigious than his own but a true origin
that is socially abased and marginal. Borrow creates a world in which the relations between parents and children generally are tenuous and the knowledge
that each generation possesses of the other is murky and incomplete. "You are
my son," Lavengro's father tells him after hearing that the boy has been devoting
himself to the study of strange languages rather than the law, "but I know little
of your real history" (*L* 175). Later, during Lavengro's unsuccessful sojourn in
London, he befriends a woman who sells apples on London Bridge and tells
her that he cannot be sure that she is not his mother: "How should I make it
out? [he asks] who can speak from his own knowledge to the circumstances of
his birth?" (*L* 257). His particular sense of estrangement within his own family
is inseparable from his sense of physical difference, from both his father and his
older brother. His brother's relation to him is "as light is opposed to darkness":
his brother is the "gay and rapid river," and he is the "dark and silent lake"; his
brother's temperament is "happy, brilliant, cheerful," and his is "sad and melancholy" (*L* 5). The brother is not only light and beautiful but unmistakably
English: "rosy, angelic face, blue eyes, and light chestnut hair . . . one of those
occasionally seen in England, and in England alone" (*L* 5).

Their father, a soldier and one-time boxer, articulates the difference between
his sons in terms that impugn both Lavengro's "racial" identity and his masculinity. Arguing with his wife, who slightly favors Lavengro, about which son
would be the Jacob and which the Esau, he declares: "my first-born . . . is
my joy and pride—the very image of myself in my youthful days, long before
I fought Big Ben [a well-known boxer of the day]. . . . As for the other . . .
Why, he has neither my hair nor my eyes; and then his countenance! why 'tis
absolutely swarthy, God forgive me! I had almost said like that of a gypsy" (*L*
87). The father's near assertion of Lavengro's resemblance to a Gypsy reinforces
the narrator's own expression of affinity with the Romany, but puts it in the context of an Oedipal drama. Family mythology about the boxing match between
the father and Big Ben becomes a leitmotif of manly ritual in the narrative, as
Lavengro must box with the Gypsy Jasper Petulengro before Jasper, defeating
him, offers Lavengro his sister-in-law as a mate and as Jasper himself goes on to
fight "in the ring" in London. But the father's pugilistic past is also inflected by

a drama of color. The last thing the father tells Lavengro before he dies, at the very end of volume 1, concerns Big Ben: "his skin when he flung off his clothes . . . his skin, I say, was brown and dusky as a toad" (L 178). Lavengro's swarthiness aligns him not only with the alien Gypsies but with his father's enemy. His dubious manly prowess—it is his brother who resembles the youthful, vigorous father—prompts him both to test himself through physical struggle and to seek out the company of Gypsies, whose unconventional masculinity will better match his own.

An incident narrated by Lavengro in the first pages of the text introduces the idea of his apparent foreignness, linked both to racial difference and to linguistic precociousness. One day when he was a small boy, a "travelling Jew" appeared at the door of the farmhouse where Lavengro's family dwelt. Reminiscent of other uncanny strangers (the Malaysian, for example, who suddenly lands on the "opium-eater's" doorstep in the Lake District in De Quincey's *Confessions of an English Opium Eater* [1822]), this old man comes and goes like an apparition and carries prophetic powers. Introducing Lavengro to the old peddler, a maid refers to the boy as slow of speech and somewhat weak in the head. The old Jew observes the child sitting on the floor and drawing "strange lines in the dust" and declares him sweet, Jewish-looking—having "all the look of one of our people's children"—and preternaturally clever. He further judges Lavengro to be "a prophet's child," already able to write and engaged in tracing "holy letters" on the dusty ground (L 7–8). The old man was the only adult, Lavengro tells us, who ever formed a good opinion of him when a child. The incident of the Jewish peddler first marks Lavengro as a being whose identity cannot be explained by his obvious parentage. The old man functions as a precursor to the Gypsies, who will claim Lavengro as one of their own and will do so through the medium of an alien language. The scene mystifies knowledge of such languages, as though to suggest that it is innate and grounded in some deep racial inheritance, and it associates Lavengro with the written rather than the spoken word. The family romance of this narrative, like that of other Gypsy stories, establishes the hero as a wanderer, misfit, and potential pariah—a child whose strangeness must be explained through race.

As in a typical bildungsroman, then, the narrative launches Lavengro in search of identity and origin. What is the nature of his true lineage, in a symbolic if not a biological sense? Where does he belong and with which family? What will he become and where will he find his fortune and his mate? The early death of his brother intensifies his sense of inadequacy—"He was taken, and I was left"—and, conjoined with an Oedipal struggle displaced from father onto brother, sends Lavengro in search of a brother rather than a parent (L 73). This he finds in the shape of Jasper Petulengro, whose Romany family he encounters first on his boyhood rambles. Mrs. Petulengro's skin, he remarks, is "dark and swarthy, like that of a toad"—like his, that is, and Big Ben's (L 29).

FIGURE 10 E. J. Sullivan, "Jasper Petulengro." (From George Borrow, *Lavengro* [London: Macmillan, 1896])

The Petulengro parents, impressed with Lavengro's snake-charming talents and ability to read to them from his favorite book, *Robinson Crusoe*, command their own son and this boy "to be two brothers" (*L* 34). Although Jasper appears only sporadically in the early chapters of the narrative, his fraternal presence is a steady anchor for Lavengro's identity—a replacement for the dead brother and an outward affirmation of his kinship with the Romany (figure 10).

The question of Lavengro's education and vocation, like that of identity, winds through the first two books of the three-book *Lavengro*. Will he become a soldier, like his father; a lawyer, like the man to whom he is apprenticed; a translator of texts from the languages he studies almost compulsively? As each possibility emerges, it is either immediately scrapped or undermined, most often because the straightjacket of professionalism never suits the self-described wanderer: "from my infancy," he writes of himself, recalling the roving child Harry Bertram in *Guy Mannering*, "I was accustomed to travelling and wandering" (*L* 9). Lavengro the narrator has difficulty keeping his early efforts at professional education in focus, as though they were eclipsed in his memory by the aliens and vagabonds who became his sometime companions. "I would fain describe him," Lavengro says of William Taylor, the gentleman lawyer who attempted to prepare him for the law, "but figures with which he has nought to do press forward and keep him from my mind's eye; there they pass, Spaniard and Moor, Gypsy, Turk, and livid Jew" (*L* 115). His ready acquisition of languages—Arabic, Danish, Hebrew, Irish, and, of course, Romani—convinces him that he might make his fortune in London as a translator, and so, after his father dies, he leaves Norwich for the metropolis. A young man's typical journey to London ensues, and its standard features are present: riding for a hundred miles on the top of a coach, finding "dank and filthy" lodgings in a narrow street, encountering the waifs and strays of the urban scene, hawking his literary creations without success. The city swallows him for a time, offering him adequate but demeaning employment and sending him repeatedly to London Bridge in search of relief for his suicidal despair, and then it spits him out. Now an apparent failure, he will not retrace his journey back home but will wander on foot into the countryside, "leaving my subsequent movements to be determined by Providence" (*L* 312). Leaving the anti-Eden of London, he appears to reverse the direction of Adam and Eve's ejection from Paradise. From this moment in the text, Lavengro's trajectory circumvents any bid for fortune or fame and evades the ambitious plot of bildung. He has not yet, however, reached the complete "freedom from desire" that Duncan identifies as the ultimate requirement for the hero's overall liberty in Borrow's work.[23]

Thwarted Pastoral

In *Lavengro* and *The Romany Rye*, romantic desire finds its place, not unexpectedly, in a pastoral setting.[24] On the tramp after leaving London, Lavengro encounters Jasper Petulengro once again and decides to follow his advice to settle in Mumper's Dingle and work at the blacksmith's trade—that is, take up the life of a Gypsy (figure 11). The dingle, or wooded valley, becomes Lavengro's womb-like home:

> It was a deep hollow in the midst of a wide field, the shelving sides were overgrown with trees and bushes, a belt of sallows [shrubby willow trees] surrounded it on the top, a steep winding path led down into the depths . . . ; at the bottom was an open space, and there I pitched my tent, and there I contrived to put up my forge. "I will ply here the trade of *kaulomescro* [blacksmith]," said I. (*L* 444)

Delighting in the odor of hissing horse hooves and singing a Gypsy song, Lavengro becomes a pastoral man. Protected from the world, housed by nature, and

FIGURE 11 E. J. Sullivan, "I was lying on my back at the bottom of the dingle." (From George Borrow, *Lavengro* [London: Macmillan, 1896])

engaged in a trade that he deems "poetical," he finds balm for his city-worn spirit. He needs only an Eve to complement his Edenic life. Isopel Berners, the mate he finds, matches his idiosyncratic and solitary being (figure 12). Alone and peripatetic, having "travelled the country melancholy," she was born and raised in a workhouse, is immensely tall and strong for a woman (Lavengro compares her to Brunhilde, the serpent-killing Valkyrie), and knows some Romani from her life on the rural roads. Lavengro invites her to live with him and vows to teach her Armenian, a deeply romantic gesture to Lavengro, the word master, but of doubtful significance to Isopel (*RR* 39). They take up residence in Mumper's Dingle and live, like any number of biblical forefathers and -mothers, as "the first occupiers of the ground" (*RR* 28). Not only first man and woman, Adam and Eve, they also play the roles of Abraham and Sarah, first patriarch and matriarch, especially when Lavengro coaxes the reluctant Belle to emerge from her tent and greet their visitors: "We . . . should consider ourselves in the light of hosts," he urges, mimicking Abraham, "and do our best to practice the duties of hospitality" (*RR* 28).[25]

FIGURE 12 E. J. Sullivan, "Belle." (From George Borrow, *Lavengro* [London: Macmillan, 1896])

The unintended consequence of Abraham and Sarah's hospitality in Genesis, of course, is the announcement of future progeny and the begetting of a new race. Lavengro wishes for the same outcome and proposes to Belle that they leave this temporary paradise and emigrate to America, a truer Eden, where they can "settle down in some forest" and have children (*RR* 95). This dream of procreation notwithstanding, Lavengro will never father a new people in a new world. Frustrated by his peculiar and ambiguous manner of courtship and convinced, as others, of his madness, Belle Berners leaves him: "Isopel had deserted me, and was gone to America by herself, where, perhaps, she would marry some other person, and would bear him a progeny, who would do for him what in my dreams I had hoped my progeny would do for me" (*RR* 105). The pastoral dream, as well as the dream of heterosexual love, eludes him. So, too, will the redemption of his own vexed origin through reproduction. What progeny might "do for" him is give him a place in the world and a lineage of his own: not the family into which he was so confusingly born and not the Gypsies, with whom he feels a not fully authentic kinship. Belle, herself a woman with Romany affinities—she is a rootless outcast and vagabond—is distinctly not a Gypsy, and Lavengro rejects the idea of a union with Jasper's sister-in-law Ursula. Living and working in Mumper's Dingle convince Lavengro that he cannot sustain his Romany masquerade: "It was much more agreeable," he concedes, "to play the gypsy or the tinker than to become either in reality" (*RR* 83). Belle had represented his chance to discover a third way of being, to be an outsider who discovers his own promised land.

Readers of Borrow often have claimed that the consummation that eludes Lavengro in reproducing and emigrating also escapes him in sexual matters. Puzzled over as celibate, asexual, even autistic, he appears to many to be chaste throughout his narrative.[26] The editor and poet W. E. Henley, one of Borrow's greatest late-nineteenth-century fans, identifies Lavengro's story as "entirely unsexual"—"the book does not exist in which the relations between boy and girl are more miserably misrepresented than in *Lavengro* and *The Romany Rye*"—and classifies him with other nonsexual, if chivalric, picaresque heroes, from Don Quixote to Samuel Pickwick.[27] What these readers neglect to see—or at least to mention—is that Lavengro's libido is expressed through language and, in certain moments, is very much in evidence. The most extended episode of courtship, all of it conveyed through double entendres, appears in *The Romany Rye*, when Lavengro gives Belle a lesson in Armenian. Hovering between seduction and coercion, Lavengro's initiation of Belle into a language to which she is indifferent comes across as badgering and overbearing, but its sexual content is not in question. After telling her that he intends to give her the longest lesson she has yet had and will teach her to conjugate an Armenian verb, she protests that she cannot bear much more. "I wish to be gentle with you," he declares, and proceeds to teach her the verb *siriel* (to love), maneuvering her in the process to confess that she loves him. Not satisfied with extracting this admission, he also teases her unmercifully by pretending that the words they speak, which clearly have a personal meaning, must not be applied to their real lives. Finally reducing her to tears, he gives up the lesson and invites her to run off to America with him: "'To America together?' said Belle, looking full at me. 'Yes,' said I; 'where we will settle down in some forest, and conjugate the verb siriel conjugally'" (*RR* 92–95). Whether this amounts to foreplay or is, indeed, a substitute for sex, as A. S. Byatt has speculated, Belle apparently experiences this peculiar courtship as delay and leaves the Dingle because Lavengro has waited too long to ask her to marry him (RR 103–4).[28] Shortly after Belle's departure, which sends him into a state of morose brooding, he, too, leaves this pastoral paradise, an Adam leaving Eden without Eve.

Lavengro's pastoral never fulfills its promise, either as an interlude of romantic love or, as in Shakespearean pastoral, as a temporary retreat from society that fosters renewal and a fortified return to the world. Even the possibility of joining Jasper's people, of adopting Romany ways of living and working, proves unsatisfying, an inadequate, perhaps even a bogus, alternative to Lavengro's wandering. The plot of the family romance remains unresolved as well, by either Lavengro's discovering an authentic lineage—elevated or debased, Gypsy or otherwise—or his fathering a child.[29] It is at this point in Borrow's two texts that his hero's "freedom from desire"—from what Duncan calls "a complex and affective economy that . . . defines what are recognizably human relations"—becomes complete, or at least appears to have become so.[30] The formal manifestation of this ostensible absence of desire is a kind of breakdown of the narrative into episodic aimlessness, into the *picaro*'s meandering, a journey void of the dynamics of quest or pursuit.

Reversions and Departure

After Lavengro leaves Mumper's Dingle to go on the tramp, his adventures take him back to an older idiom and an older England. He stops at an "inn of times gone by," expatiates on the stagecoach-men of England, and offers a paean to the wonders of staying home and traveling in his native country rather than roaming abroad (RR 141, 151, 180). Ostlers, postillions, and "boots" populate this backward-looking version of coaching days, and Lavengro the word master and sometime blacksmith fades into a depressed silence. His melancholy self-effacement has the effect, however, of allowing him to gather and reproduce the stories of others: eccentrics and solitaries he meets along the way, "traversing England from west to east" (RR 180). In these encounters, he regains something of selfhood and sense of purpose.

The most significant characters he meets share one of two things with Lavengro, either unhappiness in love or obsession with language, and thus function as doubles for the wanderer, holding up to him a mirror of his own identity and submerged, although not wholly absent, longing. He reencounters a friend, Francis Ardry, from London days. Ardry, like Lavengro a would-be literary man, has been abandoned by his lover, Annette, and swears off love. In a moment of veiled self-reflection, Lavengro inquires of Ardry if perhaps he is responsible for the failure of his romance: "did you never treat her with coldness," he asks his friend, describing indirectly his own treatment of Belle, "and repay her marks of affectionate interest with strange fits of eccentric humor?" (*RR* 161). Another chance encounter introduces him to a hermit-like man who has made a thirty-five-year study of Chinese after learning the language from bits of crockery and paper that had been used to wrap tea. For ten years, he has labored to "undo the locks" of Chinese writing. Not only is the old man a fellow philologist, but he has become so because of disappointment in love:

> "I have no desire for literary distinction," said he; "no ambition. My original wish was to pass my life in easy, quiet obscurity, with her whom I loved. I was disappointed in my wish; she was removed, who constituted my only felicity in this life; desolation came to my heart, and misery to my head. To escape from the latter I had recourse to Chinese. By degrees the misery left my head, but the desolation of the heart yet remains." (*RR* 211)

Lavengro tries to comfort him by suggesting that affliction has led to learning and to the ability to offer hospitality to the likes of him. Sorrow produces knowledge, particularly knowledge of apparently undecipherable mysteries, and fellowship with kindred souls. The solitariness of Lavengro and the scholar of Chinese link them, perhaps paradoxically, to a world beyond England and their own culture.

Three more chance encounters, almost randomly represented, consolidate Lavengro's reemerging sense of self. First, he meets a Hungarian gentleman who has had extensive experience of Gypsies in a variety of lands. Not only does the Hungarian tell Lavengro that Gypsies, whether found in Hungary, Turkey, Russia, or England, "are alike in their ways and their language" (an idea that will soon become important), but he claims to recognize Lavengro as the Romany rye talked of by all the British Gypsies he has met on his travels (*RR* 246). Almost without his knowledge, the identity that Lavengro seeks has been established and recognized. Next, he rediscovers the Irishman, Murtagh, who taught him Irish—"the foundation of all my acquisitions in philology"—when he was a boy. "Without you," he tells his old teacher, "I should not have been what I am—Lavengro! which signifies a philologist" (*RR* 304). The encounter suggests that Lavengro need only reflect on the nature of his name, from which the essence of his identity unfolds, to understand his place in the world. Finally, in the episode that ends *The Romany Rye* and the narrative of Lavengro's life, the word master meets a recruiting officer, an East India man, who tries to sign him up to fight and make his fortune in India. Lavengro inquires about the people there, and the officer replies by describing them in derogatory terms, although he uses words from their own "gibberish." Struck momentarily dumb by the familiarity of the sounds, Lavengro stares at the officer and declares, "Why . . . this is the very language of Mr. Petulengro" (*RR* 309). Thinking him mad, the East India man recoils from Lavengro and rescinds his offer of a shilling and a soldier's post. The colonial recruiter decides not to recruit, but our hero, drawn not by the specter of wealth or warfare but by the promise of language and brotherhood, decides to leave for the East anyway.[31] It is not the mere exoticism of the language that attracts him but the idea of a language that, as the Hungarian gentleman had indicated, links all the Gypsies of the globe, unites the Gypsies with other peoples, and, further, seems to lend credence to the theory, tentatively offered by Lavengro, that Romani might "turn out to be the mother of all languages in the world" (L 267). The text ends with the words "I think I'll go there," signifying that England will not be a sufficient stage for Lavengro's travels after all and that the ending for a true wanderer is another beginning.

Language as Origin

By the end of *The Romany Rye*, Lavengro arrives at an understanding of what his life's narrative has implied all along: his identity, his fate, and even his origin are to be discovered in words. The desire that does survive intact the disintegration of both Lavengro's worldly ambition and his erotic longing is a compulsion to learn and use foreign languages, the more esoteric the better. Indeed, linguistic desire seems to replace all other forms, both as a substitute and as a more authentic, primary impulse. And it is through language that he experiences kinship and a sense of connection to the wider world. It takes him beyond the search for paternity and lineage—the stuff of family romance—to the discovery of fraternity, and beyond the search for home or homecoming to the discovery of arenas for adventure and knowledge outside England.

From the early episode of the Jewish peddler's visit to Norwich and his introduction to the child Lavengro, tracing Hebrew letters in the dust, Lavengro's attachment to words and to foreignness is clear. His name, given to him by the Petulengros, signals his primary identity—word master—and replaces his given name. In the course of *Lavengro* and *The Romany Rye*, he is never referred to as George, which, among other things, complicates the question of autobiography, although Murtaugh calls him Shorsha, presumably an Irish version of that name. He possesses no nominal identity other than "Lavengro." If the Gypsies name him, Murtagh, by teaching him Irish, vivifies the name. The learning of languages becomes the boy's sole pursuit. As it replaced his given name, it replaces a conventional career:

> I applied myself to the study of languages. By the acquisition of Irish . . . I had contracted a certain zest and inclination for the pursuit. Yet it is probable, that had I been launched about this time into some agreeable career, that of arms,

for example, . . . I might have thought nothing more of the acquisition of tongues of any kind; but, having nothing to do, I followed the only course suited to my genius which appeared open to me. (*L* 89)

Lavengro later realizes that living "at the commencement of a philological age, [when] everyone studies languages," gives license to his own predilections (*L* 269). Even the vague sense that his age recognizes philology as a legitimate vocation—or, at least, avocation—bolsters Lavengro's wish to devote himself to the acquisition of languages.

By referring to his own relationship to this "philological age," Borrow also alludes to the place held by Romani in nineteenth-century linguistic study. The Gypsies' language was not simply of random interest to Lavengro/Borrow or to philologists. In addition to its apparent ubiquity across the globe, which in itself fascinated early anthropologists, Romani claimed the attention of philologists because of its similarities to Indic languages. Late-eighteenth-century German philologists and their Victorian descendants, like Max Müller, regarded ancient Indian languages as central to their scholarly work, in part because of their newly perceived links to modern European languages and, more broadly, because comparative philology provided what J. W. Burrow calls "a model for different kinds of inquiry into the remote past, as an ethnological tool—a means of classifying racial families and perhaps even showing the single (or diverse) origin of the human race."[32] Philology, he continues, might prove to be "the Ariadne's thread into pre-history."[33] If Romani is an offshoot of an Indian language, as philologists had determined by the end of the eighteenth century, then it might provide clues to ancient history, the origin of humankind, and the links that still bound apparently disparate peoples.

The Gypsies' language is, indeed, the hook that draws Lavengro into his lifelong preoccupation: "Of all connected with them, . . . their language was doubtless that which exercised the greatest influence over my imagination" (*L* 107). As he moves through his narrative, Romani begins to appear to him as a "picklock, an open sesame" to other languages and to the relationships among them (*L* 196). Like the solitary man who has labored for years to "undo the locks" of Chinese writing and perhaps even like Freud, who sought the right "collection of picklocks" to open the case of Dora, Lavengro sees in a particular artifact of human culture or experience the means of entry into a vast web of connection and coherent meaning (*RR* 210).[34] Romani opens the mysteries of linguistic correspondences: "tanner" means "sixpence," the smallest of English coins, to the Cockney apple seller and "little child" to the Petulengros; "pannam," London street cant for "bread," is connected to the Latin *panis*, which Lavengro reckons must be linked by some unknown root word to the Romani *morro* or *manro* (*L* 196, 267). But Romani might also unlock the door to history. Like those nineteenth-century philologists who sought an ur-language or, at least, an "Ariadne's thread" leading back to the beginning of human civilization, Lavengro ultimately speculates that the "language of Mr. Petulengro" might "turn out to be the mother of all languages in the world" (*L* 267). Language, itself the origin of Lavengro's identity, has a parallel in Romani, the imagined originator or maternal forebear of all other languages. The history revealed is no less than that of all humankind, but it is also the individual history of Lavengro.

On the most personal level, Romani is meaningful to Lavengro as the "language of Mr. Petulengro"—that is, of his brother or, one might say, his brothers. For a man whose relations with others—his own family as well as his comrades and lovers—are hampered by reticence and even mutism (the Jewish peddler sees the boy writing, but fails to hear him speak), words themselves become agents of intimacy. It is not through speech, or the use of language as communication, that he forms connections to others, but through the knowledge and the contemplation of others' vocabularies. In his idiosyncratic wooing of Belle Berners, the *teaching* of language functions as erotic expression, at least for the instructor. The flirtatious Ursula, Jasper Petulengro's sister-in-law, is of little interest to Lavengro until she tells him a secret of the Romany tongue. When she divulges that the important word *patteran*, used to mean "trail," comes from Romani for "leaf" (leaves being the way to mark a trail in the forest), he finds her especially attractive: "'I think I never saw you look so pretty as you do now,'" he tells her (*RR* 74). Jasper understands that this love of words, which often overwhelms or masks other kinds of desire in Lavengro, binds the Romany rye to him:

> "I say, brother!"
> "Yes, Jasper."
> "What do you think of our women?"
> "They certainly have very singular names, Jasper."
> "Names! Lavengro! However, brother, if you had been as fond of things as of names, you would never have been a pal of ours." (*RR* 58)

If Lavengro had been like a normal man, preferring things to words, he never would have become Jasper's brother. Words serve him as both a substitute for and a source of feeling.

Language has a complicated relationship to the divine word in Lavengro/Borrow's universe. Clearly an ambivalent Christian, Lavengro enters a church once in the course of his story. He finds himself there almost accidentally, led by Jasper's wife, whose dreams of respectability draw her to Christian practice. A line from the liturgy—"I will arise, and go to my father"—evokes memories of his childhood, his parents, and his old church in Norwich. Transported back to the time when, as a child, he would fall asleep in the pews, he feels now that he has just awakened from one of those naps and that the intervening years have vanished. The power of the liturgy to erase the passage of time and the difference in place astonishes him, but he concludes that it was "the magic of the words which brought the dear enchanting past so powerfully before the mind of Lavengro . . . the words that were the same sonorous words of high import which had first made an impression on his childish ear in the old church" (*RR* 52). He is not moved by religious feeling or by a rhetoric of belief, but by a phrase that invokes "my father." The vexed relationship between father and son, which colors all the exchanges between them in the narrative, falls away. Words open memory and recast the past as consoling and calming.

In the appendix to *The Romany Rye*, Borrow meditates on the uncanny power of a text to relieve depressed spirits. A Welsh preacher, one of the recurring characters in Lavengro's tale, had been restored to equanimity in the following way:

> And here it will be as well for the reader to ponder upon the means by which the Welsh preacher is relieved from his mental misery: he is not relieved by a text from the Bible, by the words of consolation from his angel-minded wife, nor by the preaching of one yet more eloquent than himself; but by a quotation made by Lavengro from the life of Mary Flanders, cut-purse and prostitute, which life Lavengro had been in the habit of reading at the stall of his old friend the apple-woman, on London Bridge, who had herself been very much addicted to the perusal of it. (*RR* 315)

The secular—not to say, profane—words of Daniel Defoe, which have a special place in Lavengro's own life and bind him to the apple seller during his lonely stay in London, eventually work their incantatory magic on the preacher. Two of Defoe's books are important to Lavengro: *Robinson Crusoe* (1719–1720), whose illustrations he pores over in childhood, and *Moll Flanders* (1722), which the apple seller reads and rereads because it gives her hope that her daughter, a transported convict like Moll, will return home like Defoe's heroine (*L* 18–19, 194–95). A drawing of Crusoe's discovery of Friday's footprint on the island fills the child with "emotions strange and novel," as though he recognizes his future self in Defoe's hero, another exiled traveler and isolate who forms a bond with a non-white companion in his wanderings.[35] Although profane, Defoe's works are of great personal and spiritual meaning to Lavengro, and he believes that they may be the means through which God "accomplishes his purposes" (*RR* 315). Furthermore, he tells us, the balm that heals might be derived not in fashionable Albermarle Street, but in the "low society" of London Bridge and from the life of an outlaw. Lavengro's own life story—dependent on the companionship of Gypsies, a Cockney apple seller, and a woman born in a workhouse—clearly bears this out.

The antipathetic relationship between Lavengro and the peripatetic "man in black," the Catholic priest who keeps reappearing on horseback in the narrative, also hinges on contrasting views of the importance of words and texts. The man in black, a double for both Lavengro and Borrow as a solitary and celibate traveler and missionary, ridicules both Gypsies and philologists (L 486–87). The former are illiterate and ignorant; the latter, stupid and irrational. For his part, Lavengro detests what he regards as the idolatry of Catholicism, the kind of faith that the man in black preaches. At the beginning of *The Romany Rye*, they have a lengthy dispute about religion that can be described as an argument about word versus body. The priest argues that images of the body of Christ are sufficient and necessary to sustain belief. Without a visual image, a tangible and imaginable body, there can be no worship. Indeed, the priest goes on, even the worship of secular saints, like Shakespeare, depends on bowing before an image: "Shakespeare's works are not sufficient for you; no more are the Bible or the legend of Saint Anthony or Ignacio for us. . . . I tell you, Zingara [Italian for "Gypsy"], that no religion can exist long which rejects a good bodily image" (RR 11). For Lavengro, it is Shakespeare's words and works that make him an immortal and Moses's assault on idol worship that defines Christianity. He represents the priest's argument as ultimately an elitist one, a lack of confidence in the ability of the people, the masses, the uneducated to grasp religious faith through language. Protestantism opposes Catholicism in *The Romany Rye*, as elsewhere, as a democratic Christianity of the Book against a tyrannical Christianity of the dictate. Borrow's work for the British and Foreign Bible Society lies behind this dispute and behind his continuing vilification of Catholicism. As a distributor of the Bible, which the man in black refers to as "a vulgar book," Borrow believed himself to be the opponent of oppression—and of Roman Catholicism (RR 23). The popularity of *The Bible in Spain*, his most successful book, rested in part on its championing of English Protestantism and celebration of the Word: "Where the Scriptures were read, neither priestcraft nor tyranny could long exist and instanced the case of my own country, the cause of whose freedom and prosperity was the Bible, and that only, as the last persecutor of this book, the bloody and infamous Mary, was the last tyrant on the throne of England."[36] A book stands against not just ignorance but oppression and so has a political as well as a spiritual significance. Words have the power to liberate in a way that blurs the distinction between religious and secular, between the word of God and the words of Shakespeare and Defoe.

The identity of word master replaces both the surname that is never used in the narrative and the lineage that his parents themselves bequeath to him. It is worth emphasizing, however, that Lavengro never actually discovers a paternal or parental substitute or adopts an identity derived from any group or "race" to which he remains attracted—principally, of course, the Gypsies. Canny and honest enough to understand the distinction between playing at and becoming one of the Romany, he fleetingly and unsuccessfully aspires to initiate his own genealogy, with Belle as matriarch and America as land of Eden. The Oedipal drama stalls. He neither vanquishes the father, whose youthful pugilism and preference for Lavengro's brother cast him firmly in the role of opponent, nor wins the mother, who clearly, if weakly, favors her less conventional son: "it is the way of women," Lavengro's father admonishes her, comparing her with the biblical Rebecca, "always to side with the second-born" (*L* 87). What he does discover, however, is a tongue that may be the "mother of all languages" and an adoptive brother, Jasper Petulengro, who reflects Lavengro's own idiosyncrasies but possesses as well the physical strength to challenge the bullying father and rival the favored biological brother.

Lavengro's older brother, the fair-haired, visibly English son who recalls his father when he fought the dusky Big Ben, is displaced—at least in the Romany rye's affective universe—by Jasper and then dies prematurely. Perhaps the brother is vanquished in his father's place, as a surrogate object for Lavengro's Oedipal aggression. Nonetheless, this unresolved narrative of family romance or bildung seems consistent with the triumph of language and brotherhood as the particular ties that bind Lavengro to humankind. The vertical tensions of family romance are superseded by horizontal lines of association that emphasize neither inheritance nor reproduction. The masculine world of the picaresque tradition—of Don Quixote and Sancho Panza, of Samuel Pickwick and Sam Weller—celebrates fraternity and eschews heterosexual domesticity. Borrow's works follow this pattern, even by reproducing the cross-class nature of the *picaro*'s male companionship. As Herbert Sussman has pointed out in relation to the early Victorian "masculine plot," in which the embrace of male community and rejection of the feminine offer the hero an alternative to the marriage plot, "closure is often ambiguous."[37] The two end points of the Oedipal crisis, status (supplanting the father) and heterosexual union (finding a legitimate substitute for the mother), elude Lavengro. Instead, he ends by beginning to wander anew, propelled by the attraction of language and fraternity. His progeny will be more words and more languages; his kin, other brothers.

The Question of Ideology

The centenary of George Borrow's death was commemorated in the *Times Literary Supplement* in 1981 with a number of suggestive articles and reviews. Most striking among them was Andrew Motion's account of a lecture about Borrow delivered at the Cheltenham Literary Festival by Enoch Powell, the Tory politician who combined extreme erudition with virulent xenophobia.[38] Motion, intrigued by Powell's enthusiasm for the mostly forgotten writer, explained it in two ways. Predictably, Powell associated Borrow with the "pastoral past of

. . . England," a "golden age" that might never be discovered again, and with nostalgia for a rural and very English landscape. But Powell, born in 1912, also revealed that a revival of interest in Borrow had coincided with his youth and that he knew large chunks of the works by heart. "His enthusiasm," Motion writes, "was initially of his father's making: the family had caught the contemporary craze for walking expeditions—poking around the countryside 'in semi-vagrant guise'—on which Borrow was an ideal guide." A year later, Michael Mason, reviewing two recently published biographies of Borrow, did a brilliant job of identifying the contours of his intellectual obsessions and political stance: an abiding fascination with languages and Gypsies combined with an ambivalent and often apparently contradictory suspicion of political subversion, on the one hand, and strong anti-authoritarian impulses, on the other.[39] "There is more vacillation," Mason concludes, "more Arnoldian 'mental strife,' in George Borrow than in George Eliot." For Powell, Borrow's rebelliousness remains invisible and his attraction to Romany life a matter of masquerade. For Mason, back-to-the-land nostalgia misses the point, and Borrow's interest in Gypsies and their language bespeaks an unsettled and complex relationship to modern life.

These late-twentieth-century views of Borrow suggest the volatile nature of the history of his reception and make clear his contested status as both a deeply conservative and a radically unconventional character and writer. This history, which pivots on a late-nineteenth- and early-twentieth-century revival and re-creation of the early Victorian Borrow as a backward-looking and antimodern figure, also exemplifies the evolution of British literary and intellectual interest in Gypsies. Powell was born during this revival, generally a period of pastoral nostalgia, and as a child participated in its rituals of masquerade and playacting. The same rituals, however, were also associated with a sensibility of bohemian escapism and disdain for the strictures of bourgeois life—a sensibility shared, as we shall see, by members of the Gypsy Lore Society and antithetical to the socially and politically conservative views of the likes of the adult Enoch Powell. Projected onto the complicated figure of Borrow, a Gypsy scholar of an earlier era and a different stripe, these turn-of-the-century longings for a premodern England refashioned and distorted his work and his beliefs. He became a proxy for ideologically charged debates about what Englishness, or England's past, might really signify. By 1981, Powell's enthusiasm for Borrow had taken on yet another layer of nostalgia—for his own youth—and had purged Borrow of his fondness for just those aspects of Britishness that Powell reviled: cultural variation and eclecticism.

We arrive at a more complex and nuanced view of Borrow's peculiar political identity, a sense of his Arnoldian vacillation and "mental strife," through his attachment to the Gypsies and their language and his invention of the persona of the Romany rye. As with Walter Scott and Matthew Arnold, Borrow's psychic and aesthetic involvement with the Gypsies turns in large part on questions of change and changelessness, as well as on a sense of identification, however fleeting, with the Gypsies' marginality, homelessness, and sometimes willed, sometimes enforced wandering. What distinguishes Borrow's fascination with the Romany from Scott's, Arnold's, or even John Clare's, however, are his linguistic obsession and the greater intimacy with Gypsy life this affords him. He neither makes a fetish of their allegedly primitive way of life nor romanticizes their pristine associations with an older, rural Englishness. Like Scott, and like the Arnold of "Resignation," he recognizes that the Gypsies of his own historical moment—in his case the 1820s—have been subjected to the alterations of time and assimilation.

Lavengro comments on the frequency of marriages between "gorgios [non-Gypsies] and Romany chies [women]" and the mixed progeny, called "half and half," that are the result (*RR* 68). Jasper concedes that his wife is "fond of Frenchmen and French discourse" and aspires to the state of "gentility" that may ultimately destroy gypsyism for good (*RR* 79). Lavengro's interest in the Gypsies' language gives him another way of apprehending the transformation of their culture. Unlike the later Gypsy lorists, who would comb the north of England and Wales in search of "pure" Gypsies who spoke an unadulterated Romani, Lavengro places this myth of Gypsy purity many centuries in the past. His pastoralism is complicated, then, by a sense that the Gypsies are already a mixed group and an attenuated version of "the old stock" (*RR* 82). He speculates on the strangeness, peculiarity, vast knowledge of secrets, and "more perfect" language he might have encountered had he lived among Gypsies two or three centuries earlier. The myth of Gypsy changelessness, which, I have argued, finds its mid-nineteenth-century avatar in Arnold's "The Scholar-Gipsy," never seems credible in *Lavengro* and *The Romany Rye*. The railroad may be a threat to the survival of the Romany, but that is precisely because they are not outside history, not phantoms untouched by change.

The greatest threat to gypsyism, according to Borrow, is the press of gentility, by which he means the Englishman's aspiration to rise in society by parroting—in a manner that amounts to parody—the ways of a more privileged class. He anatomizes the foibles of each social class. The aristocracy, sometime admirers of the emperors of Austria and Russia, aspire to an imperial or military model of gentility, with "flaming epaulets, a cocked hat, and plumes." The middle classes mimic aristocratic ways. And the lower classes find their "beau ideal" in railroad contactors (*RR* 330–31). The end result of this tyranny of gentility will be the erasure of difference, distinctness of character, and authenticity, and its greatest casualties will be those religious and ethnic minorities whose idiosyncrasies make them especially appealing to Borrow/Lavengro: Gypsies, Jews, and Quakers. Wealthy Jews, he reports, already forsake the synagogue for the opera house, and they abandon their ancient texts—Mishnah, Gemara, and

Zohar—for silver-fork novels like Benjamin Disraeli's *The Young Duke* (1831) (*RR* 343). Gypsies, he continues, risk becoming the irresponsible people many already believe them to be: the women may indeed become harlots and the men, careless husbands and fathers. They will try to pass as Christians, spouting the accepted political and religious beliefs of the day, only to be ridiculed and rejected because of their poverty. Quakers, like Jews and Gypsies, will seek after intermarriage, conversion, and fakery and, because of their relative wealth and physical indistinctiveness, be accepted and absorbed by the genteel majority.

There is a Carlylean strain of antidandiacal fervor in Borrow's assault on gentility, but its purpose is quite different. In *Sartor Resartus* (1833–1834), Thomas Carlyle assaults the do-nothingism and lack of productivity of foppish aristocrats and their middle-class mimics, whereas Borrow particularly resents the homogenizing effects of a mock-aristocratic culture. In a twist unlikely to be found outside Borrow's profoundly anticlerical and anti-Catholic universe, he also associates the brand of gentility he reviles with Catholicism, Gothicism, and the priest of *Lavengro*, the "man in black." Into the mouth of the priest he inserts an expression of delight that the English, who have always prized a "plain and simple religion," might now quit Protestantism for the more genteel religion of Rome, "with which Templars, Hospitalers, mitres, abbots, Gothic abbeys, long-drawn aisles, golden censers, incense, et cetera, are connected" (*RR* 344). Whereas the antidandiacal Carlyle sees in the Gothic abbey a model of serious fellowship and communal labor, Borrow sees a symbol of Catholic opulence, sensuality, and mystification.

Often associated with Toryism because of his jaundiced view of modernity and his clear skepticism about Whiggery, Borrow's clearest political affinities are Radical and republican, and he expatiates quixotically and at some length on the "real Radicals" of the Cato Street Conspiracy: Arthur Thistlewood and James Ings. Enraged by the state's assault in 1819 on workingmen in Manchester at St. Peter's Fields and influenced by Jacobin ideas and other forms of republicanism, the Cato Street group plotted to overthrow the government and assassinate members of the cabinet.[40] To Borrow, these men, who were hanged for high treason in 1820, were true radicals, unlike the "humbugs" of a later time who only "jobbed and traded in Republicanism" (*RR* 378). "Oh, there was something in these fellows! honesty and courage," he writes of Ings and Thistlewood, despairing of finding any authentic facsimiles in his own day. Demonstrating once again that he was formed by, and perhaps stalled in, the 1820s, Borrow casts a critical eye on the reformers of 1832 and all the Whigs of the present moment. Although not a consistent or even an especially logical political thinker, Borrow was not the "staunch conservative" and rural escapist that George Saintsbury, Leslie Stephen, and Enoch Powell believed him to be.

Borrow's awareness that the British Romany he encountered were subject to change and the forces of history distinguishes him from those who persisted in regarding the Gypsies as frozen in time, an indelible reminder of a forgotten age. He is also able to express some skepticism about his own position as Gypsy fellow traveler and writes into the narrative of Lavengro an indication that he understands the limitations of the role. Powell's boyhood outings in the guise of a vagrant, a custom of the early decades of the twentieth century that his father enjoyed, suggests something of the morally suspect habit of identity masquerade. The taint of "slumming," of a patronizing appropriation of the garb and habits of a socially marginal and culturally distinct group, haunts the narrative of Lavengro even as it colors more thoroughly the holiday disguise of the Powells. Borrow signals his attentiveness to this pose at a number of points, certainly when Lavengro comments that it is easy to play at being a Gypsy and not so straightforward to become one and when he leaves his temporary Gypsy camp in Mumper's Dingle. But it is the episode of Mrs. Herne and the poisoned cake that most powerfully, if obliquely, communicates Borrow's critique of his protagonist's pose.

Mrs. Herne, the mother-in-law of Jasper, is alone among the Petulengro kin in taking a dislike to Lavengro and leaves for Yorkshire to get away from him (figure 13). "I hates the gorgio," she tells her daughter, "and would like, speaking Romanly, to mix a little poison with his waters." She would rather part from her family than remain near the Romany rye, she continues, so "to gain a bad brother, ye have lost a good mother" (L 108). But although she leaves, she plots against him. Many chapters later, a young Romany girl appears before Lavengro, dancing and singing seductively in a virtual caricature of a sexually enticing Gypsy woman, and feeds him a rich cake. After becoming deathly ill from the cake, Lavengro realizes that he has been poisoned, and Mrs. Herne arrives to tell him why she has plotted his death: "Halloo, tinker! you must introduce yourself into a quiet family and raise confusion. . . . *You must steal its language*, and, what was never done before, write it down Christianly" (L 389). Putting it more graphically some pages later, Mrs. Herne accuses Lavengro of stealing "the tongue out of her head" (L 397). Guilty not only of masquerade, Lavengro also commits the offense of the ethnologist or philologist. He appropriates the Romany's language, the very thing that attracts him to them most powerfully, and translates it into a "Christian" form. The story does not end here. Lavengro's ability to survive the poisoning, together with Mrs. Herne's conviction that his recovery has fulfilled a terrible dream of hers, sends the woman into deep despondency, and she hangs herself in despair. At this point, Jasper, who gained a brother at the expense of a mother-in-law, must demonstrate his loyalty to his kin and make a show of punishing Lavengro. The Gypsy challenges the *górgio* to a boxing match, recalling Lavengro's father's contest with Big Ben, and beats him handily, drawing Lavengro's blood but harming him very little. Now, this ritual of revenge and masculine rivalry out of the way, Lavengro can truly be embraced. Jasper offers Lavengro the hand of Ursula, his sister-in-law and Mrs. Herne's other daughter, and invites him to settle down with them. It is as though, after public acknowledgment of his

FIGURE 13 E. J. Sullivan, "Mrs. Herne." (From George Borrow, *Lavengro* [London: Macmillan, 1896])

transgressions, linguistic and otherwise, Lavengro can be accepted as a rye, with all the moral ambiguities that position implies.

The story of Mrs. Herne invites us to conclude that Lavengro's narrative is, in fact, about himself, rather than about the Gypsies to whom he is attracted. Because of their social marginality, their exotic language, and their associations with a pastoral way of life for which Lavengro longs, Gypsies enable George Borrow to tell the story of a marginal man whose identity and desire are constituted around language. Their habitual status as peripheral figures in the cultural imagination and in literary texts also suits Borrow's purposes in creating works of indeterminate form and inconclusive structure. As with most nineteenth-century writers who were drawn to the subject of Gypsies, however, Borrow's personal identification with the Romany is inseparable from his serious interest in their language, history, and global ubiquity. And if his identification verges on solipsism, it is accompanied by a commitment—both political and aesthetic—to the preservation of Gypsy identity, not for the sake of nostalgia or some notion of cultural purity but in the interests of cultural heterogeneity and multifarious Englishness. His lifelong interest in Gypsies was of a piece with his opposition to "gentility," the enemy of difference, and with his radical, if inconsistent, political sympathies.

4

"Marks of Race"

The Impossible Gypsy in George Eliot

T**HE STORIES**, novels, and poems of George Eliot are peppered with references to Gypsies, from Mr. Dempster's pet name for his "dark-eyed wife" in "Janet's Repentance" (1857) to Maggie Tulliver's escape to the Gypsy camp in *The Mill on the Floss* and, finally, to the principal subject of her book-length poem, *The Spanish Gypsy*.[1] Like Walter Scott and George Borrow, she was drawn to the fantasy of family romance and the theme of disinheritance. Like Borrow and, to some extent, Matthew Arnold, she saw the Gypsy as a figure who could signify gender heterodoxy—feminized masculinity and, for Eliot, unconventional femininity. In a general sense, she used the Gypsy as a way to mark the kind of individual to whom she returned again and again in her fiction: the alien or inexplicably aberrant member of a community that is otherwise homogeneous, organic, and traditional. Eliot's powerful interest in what Raymond Williams calls "knowable communities" is matched by and inseparable from her engagement with the individual who does not quite fit in and who struggles with the desire for both acceptance and escape.[2] Often, although not always, Eliot imagines this individual as a being marked by physical difference—an un-English swarthiness, foreignness that expresses itself in a bodily way, lameness, or deformity. The Gypsy, set apart by appearance and, ostensibly, by what the Victorians understood as race, suited Eliot well in her desire to represent difference and unassimilability.

Two movements are evident in Eliot's reliance on the Gypsy to indicate temperamental and physical difference in her characters. The first involves her initial use of "gypsiness" and foreignness generally as metaphors for other kinds of unconventionality and her ultimate turn to the actual alien as a character in exile. This first movement, or transition, might be described as a shift from the fantasy of family romance to the actualization of family romance and, beyond that, to the romance of nation. Although Maggie Tulliver harbors the suspicion that she was born to Gypsies and not to the Dodsons and Tullivers, Eliot emphasizes the ultimately delusional nature of her fantasy. In Eliot's book-length narrative poem, *The Spanish Gypsy*, however, the heroine, Fedalma, discovers that she was in fact born into a Gypsy tribe and is not a Spanish princess of uncertain birth, just as, in *Daniel Deronda*, Daniel learns that he is a Jew and not the illegitimate son of an English aristocrat. In both stories, then, the odd child turns out to be biologically other, and this "racial" difference leads naturally to the project of nationalism—a homeland for the Gypsies and for the Jews. The question of origin, with which the literary representation of Gypsies is almost always associated, is transferred from family to nation, from the identity of an individual to that of a people. Origin turns out to be not simply genetic but also geographic, however elusive and hypothetical that geography might be.

The second shift takes place within the transition from *The Spanish Gypsy* to *Daniel Deronda*. In both works, the protagonist discovers the secret of her or his birth and ends by leaving a country of exile for a country of origin. By the end of *The Spanish Gypsy*, Fedalma has inherited from her father, a Gypsy chieftain, the mission of leading her people to a homeland in Africa. Similarly, Deronda sets sail for the Levant, not, like Fedalma, with boatloads of his brethren but with his Jewish wife, Mirah. In this, her final novel, Eliot rewrote the story of a Gypsy woman in fifteenth-century Spain as the story of a Jewish man in late-nineteenth-century England. It is noteworthy that she repeated this plot so faithfully, the poem being in some respects a rehearsal for the novel, and that she chose to change the sex and "race" of her central character, as well as the time and place of her story of exile, in these particular ways. The success of Daniel Deronda's narrative sheds light on the failures of Fedalma's. Eliot's need to repeat Fedalma's plot so exactly—and yet with crucial differences of time, place, and protagonist—underscores the unresolved and highly problematic nature of the Spanish Gypsy's story.

I want to look at the changes that Eliot made in recasting her narrative of national identity in light of *The Spanish Gypsy*'s problematic conclusion, a vexed ending that hauntingly separates Fedalma from the traditional womanly fate of marriage, and in terms of the kind of nationalist vision that Eliot wished to represent. Why and how do a man and a Jew enable her to tell her story differently? And what does this successful revision say about Eliot's unresolved conflicts about femininity and the status of the Gypsy as a candidate for nationalism? Why did she turn from Gypsy to Jew in order to imagine a triumphant and, to her mind, fully modern resolution to the problem of the alien? Like many others in the nineteenth century, Eliot paired these two "others within," Gypsy and Jew, in her thinking about seemingly cohesive but stateless nations. In spite of Eliot's apprehension of the resemblance between the two groups, she ultimately saw the Jews as a people tied fortuitously to history and text and, therefore, as worthy creators of a modern state, while she regarded the Gypsies as tragically cut off from their past and tradition and thus unable to forge a salutary future. The Gypsy heroine Fedalma and the Jewish hero Deronda—the two end points, if you will, of Eliot's long meditation on the outsider—meet with very different personal and political fates. Fedalma's fate, as I have suggested by the title of this chapter, is an impossible one.

From Family Romance to the Romance of Nation

In trying to delineate George Eliot's passionate and long-standing commitment to representing the provincial communities of England's recent past, Raymond Williams uses the phrase "knowable communities."[3] The St. Oggs of *The Mill on the Floss*, Middlemarch, the Raveloe of *Silas Marner*, the Hayslope of *Adam Bede* (1859)—these are the fictional communities that drew Eliot's novelistic interest and constitute the great achievements of her sociological imagination. Each can be fully known because, in Steven Marcus's words, "the world [they] represent has already been defined and in some sense closed off; things in it . . . *have already happened*."[4] But these places are knowable as well because of the homogeneity, despite class differences, of the social experiences of their inhabitants and the presumed familiarity—the knowability—of each inhabitant to his or her neighbors. Williams locates the dramatic tension of Eliot's novels in the conflict between the knowable community and the "separated individual": "It is part of a crucial history in the development of the novel in which the knowable community . . . comes to be known primarily as a problem of ambivalent relationship: of how the separated individual, with a divided consciousness of belonging and not belonging, makes his own moral history."[5] Eliot's divided individual, who struggles against traditional ways of being and yearns for a modernity that frees individual desire, is often, but not always, a woman and often at risk of going beyond separateness to the condition of being a pariah. Williams argues that Eliot finds it nearly impossible to imagine or to represent a satisfying resolution to the conflict between traditional community and individual aspiration, and her heroines in particular, as Gillian Beer has noted, tend to suffer a kind of imprisonment or stagnation in their own ultimate typicality.[6]

In Eliot's fiction, the separated individual is often figured as disinherited, either literally or metaphorically: Will Ladislaw, object of a double disinheritance; Silas Marner, robbed of both love and wealth; Daniel Deronda, denied his Jewish inheritance; Dorothea Brooke, in danger of being written out of her husband's will; Tom and Maggie Tulliver, ejected from childhood happiness and economic stability, like Adam and Eve from Eden. Indeed, the theme of disinheritance informs a good deal of eighteenth- and nineteenth-century fiction, beginning but certainly not ending with *Tom Jones* (1749), *Jane Eyre*, and *David Copperfield* (1849–1850). The plight of the orphan, unanswered questions of origin, and the fantasy of noble or at least salutary birth—the family romance—are central to the development of the novel. But for Eliot, the phenomenon of disinheritance is always linked not only to relations between child and parents and to fortune or property, but also—and more important—to the individual's vexed relation to community and often to race or nation.

Critics like Michael Ragussis and Bernard Semmel have emphasized Eliot's extensive debt to Walter Scott, in whose works the theme of disinheritance is ubiquitous. Ragussis's focus on the question of Jews and conversion in English culture makes *Daniel Deronda* an obvious point of interest for him, but he also devotes attention to *The Spanish Gypsy*, which he discusses in relation to *Ivanhoe*. Semmel concentrates on both texts and identifies *The Spanish Gypsy* as an inversion of the kidnapping plot of *Guy Mannering*.[7] The debt to Scott is particularly instructive in trying to establish the contours of Eliot's interest in Gypsies and Jews—the disinherited ones—and use of these groups in her earlier work to evoke various kinds of marginality. If we look, for example, at *Ivanhoe*, we see that Scott has given the "Disinherited Knight," the novel's hero, a counterpart in the Jews, whom Isaac of York describes to his daughter, Rebecca, as "disinherited and wandering."[8] Scott had used this kind of analogous relation as well in *Guy Mannering*, in which, as we have seen, a disinherited Scottish laird is implicitly compared with a tribe of Gypsies banished from their home on the laird's property. Eliot takes up Scott's fascination with dispossessed groups, deepening the connection between estranged individual and disinherited nation, evoking characters metaphorically as marked by race, or, later in her career, giving them distinct but hidden racial identities.

Silas Marner (1861), a novel in which no racial or national group appears or is overtly mentioned, nonetheless offers an example of Eliot's metaphorical deployment of the alien to figure the outsider, the separated individual, or the pariah. The novel opens with a meditation on the displaced linen weavers, "emigrants from the town into the country," who make their way among the "brawny country-folk" looking like "the remnants of a disinherited race."[9] The author here sets the stage for the questions to be addressed by the novel as a whole: How will these peripheral, peripatetic men manage to attach themselves to a settled community, and will they ever reconcile their marginality with the demands and ethos of such a community? Moving from wanderer and stranger to settler, will these men become integrated or remain alien, unassimilable, "contract[ing] the eccentric habits which belong to a state of loneliness" (SM 6)? These weavers, of whom Silas Marner will emerge as one, are marked as a separate race, distinguished by a particular physicality—"pallid undersized men," "alien-looking"—and they exist in a "state of wandering."

The narrator uses the precise words—"disinherited" and "wandering"—to identify the likes of Silas that Scott's Isaac uses to describe the Jews in *Ivanhoe*, but Gypsies also come to mind. Both groups are peripatetic: they wander the globe in exile but live, always within view of settled community, as what Jonathan Boyarin calls "the other within."[10] But whereas the Jew usually is associated with urban plots and contexts in nineteenth-century literature, the Gypsy most often appears as an itinerant in the English countryside, a pastoral figure who wanders the roads or camps on the edge of town. Eliot underscores Silas's unstated connection to the Gypsies later in the novel when the community of Raveloe suspects that a swarthy peddler—with curly black hair, "a foreign complexion," and earrings—has stolen the miser's gold (SM 61–62, 75). Just as the superstitious inhabitants of Raveloe initially had suspected and shunned Silas, they now invent out of whole cloth another outsider, a peripatetic of a different sort and an ironic double for Silas, to blame for this crime. In the opening paragraph of the novel, the narrator also establishes one of the signal features of knowable community by stating that no one knew "where wandering men had their homes or their origin" or could account for such people, "unless you at least knew somebody who knew his father and mother" (SM 5). Eliot will return repeatedly to the trope of unknown origin and to the anxieties it creates both for the closed community and for the individual who feels out of place therein. In the world of Raveloe, the status of stranger might be tantamount to some form of tainted birth, blemished by miscegenation or illegitimacy.

Imagined as the remnant of a "disinherited race," a wanderer whose origin, home, and parentage are unknown to those among whom he comes to dwell, Silas himself is evoked only obliquely as an alien. Maggie Tulliver, however, is an outsider in the very community into which she was born, and she is evoked by the narrator, her family, and herself through persistent association with a racially distinct group. With *The Mill on the Floss* (1860), Eliot begins to deploy the myth of family romance—the possibility, although not the reality, of mysterious origin, kidnapping, and babies switched at birth. Maggie's parents lament her anomalous femininity—her dark complexion and straight, unruly hair, her tomboy ways and lack of decorousness—as a sign of insanity, genetic mutation, or racial otherness. In chapter 2 of *The Mill on the Floss*, Mrs. Tulliver frets about Maggie's resemblance to "a Bedlam creatur" and the "brown skin as makes her look like a mulatter," while Mr. Tulliver explains that his daughter's inheritance of his, rather than her mother's, mental and physical characteristics makes her a casualty of "the crossing o' breeds," a freak of nature like a "long-tailed sheep."[11] Her idiosyncrasies of appearance and temperament separate her not only from her family—and especially from the phalanx of Dodson women she fails to resemble—but also from the community of St. Oggs itself, the knowable community that insists on conformity to gender norms as well as to other forms of unexceptionable behavior.

Eliot marks Maggie's difference through metaphor as well as through a sense that she is physically, even genetically, eccentric. Even after she undergoes a metamorphosis from wild child to liquid-eyed, brown-cheeked, red-lipped beauty, she still draws the opprobrium of those Eliot refers to as the "world's wife," who see her "very physique . . . to be prophetic of harm" (MF 619, 621). This bodily difference, associated with her dark skin and hair, accounts both for Maggie's seductive powers as a young woman and for her ultimate romantic failures. Like the dark-haired heroines of Scott's fiction and the eponymous heroine of Madame de Staël's *Corinne, or Italy* (1807), with whom she feels a deep if frustrating affinity, Maggie is destined for unhappiness. Flinging de Staël's novel back at its owner, Philip Wakem, Maggie declares, "I'm determined to read no more books where the blond haired women carry away all the happiness. I should begin to have a prejudice against them—If you would give me some story, now, where the dark woman triumphs, it would restore the balance—I want to avenge Rebecca and Flora Mac-Ivor, and Minna and all the rest of the dark unhappy ones" (MF 433). Eliot places Maggie Tulliver within this literary tradition of paired heroines—one light, one dark—and, like Scott, overlays the pairing, at its most fundamental a contrast of good and evil or chaste and impure, with racial difference. Although Philip predicts that Maggie might avenge all the miserable dark women and steal the love from her cousin Lucy Deane, Maggie's own blond-haired nemesis, *The Mill on the Floss* does not substantially controvert de Staël's model of blond victory and brunette loss.

In childhood, Maggie and Lucy (named for Corinne's rival, Lucille) compete for the attention not of a lover but of Maggie's brother Tom. In a comic episode that nonetheless underscores the moral and racial drama of dark and light femininity, Maggie disgraces herself by pushing "poor little pink-and-white Lucy into the cow-trodden mud" with "a fierce thrust of her small brown arm" (MF 164). Wanting to punish Lucy for her much praised decorousness and for the charm that attracts Tom to her, Maggie tries to make her pastel-colored cousin as brown as she is by coating her with mud and dung. Disgraced and facing certain punishment, Maggie decides to run off to join the brown-skinned Gypsies, having been told so often that she is like a Gypsy and "half wild." Impulsively in search of her "unknown kindred," imagining herself a changeling, and fueled by motives of revenge, Maggie seeks her true parentage and people. The narrative of Maggie's brief escape to Dunlow Common, where she believes the Gypsies are camped, combines the poignant evocation of her discovery of another family—in particular, another mother—with gentle mockery of her arrogance and naïveté. Maggie's misguided expectations and selfish desires are exposed throughout the scene, beginning with her disappointment that the Gypsies have camped in a lane rather than on a common and continuing with her belief that this experience will be like a fairy tale, "just like a story."

Although she will discover that her fantasy of Gypsy life bears no resemblance to the reality she discovers in this Gypsy camp on the edge of St. Oggs, she does glimpse the face of a "gypsy-mother" who resembles her: "Maggie looked up in the new face rather tremblingly as it approached, and was reassured by the thought that . . . the rest were right when they called her a gypsy, for this face with the bright dark eyes and the long hair was really something like what she used to see in the glass before she cut her hair off" (*MF* 171–72). Maggie imagines—and sees—a new mother who, like a looking glass, reflects and thereby affirms what her own mother rejects. Something in Maggie remains unaccounted for and unabsorbed by her life in her own tribe, and something in her is reflected in the Gypsy woman's mien. This moment of recognition is eclipsed by Maggie's ultimate fear of the Gypsies and her desire to return home, the chastened child who has foolishly run away. But in the course of *The Mill on the Floss*, Maggie never does discover her true kin, either by childish escape or, more conventionally, by marriage. Although her waifishness turns into a dark and voluptuous beauty as she grows older, her racially marked body changing from freakish to exotic, Maggie's ability to attract the love of men fails utterly to ensure her happiness or even her survival. As she had run off, with unhappy results, to the Gypsies, she later disappears, with even more disastrous consequences, in the company of her cousin's fiancé, a man she can never marry. Her routes of escape are fully blocked; she resumes the status of pariah, this time irrevocably; and she is "rescued" from a life of isolation, disgrace, and celibacy by regression and death. The fantasy of family romance dictates that the dream of alternative parentage be just that—an illusion—and Maggie's imagined tie to the alien Gypsies provides her with neither family nor home. Hers is an exile with no possibility of repatriation.

Although published after *The Spanish Gypsy*, Eliot's novel *Middlemarch* (1871–1872) includes a figure whose foreignness, or foreign ancestry, serves as a transition from the largely figurative strangeness of Maggie Tulliver—and Silas Marner before her—to the actual, although hidden, foreign origins of both Fedalma and Daniel Deronda.[12] The identity of Will Ladislaw, Dorothea Brooke's lover and second husband, is never separable from the foreignness of his ancestry, his surname, and his appearance. Neither are his foreign ancestry and name separable from his bohemianism, his artistic interests, his reformist politics, and his heterodox masculinity. The nephew of Dorothea's punitive and dry-as-dust first husband, Casaubon, Will is descended from a Polish grandfather—a patriot and musician—on one side and a pawnbroker and his high-spirited actress daughter on the other: "You see," he tells Dorothea, "I come of rebellious blood on both sides."[13] On both sides, as I have indicated, he has been disinherited: his paternal grandmother had been disowned after running off with the Pole, Ladislaw, and his mother ostensibly had forfeited the inheritance from her father after going on the stage.

Although Will's Polish ancestry remains his only real claim to foreignness, numerous characters in the novel allude to him as an alien of various sorts. His peripatetic ways, uninhibited manner, and social promiscuity inspire Lydgate, an outsider of a different kind, to refer to Ladislaw as "a sort of gypsy" (M 436).[14] The narrator repeats Lydgate's comment a number of pages later and corroborates that Will "rather enjoy[s] the sense of belonging to no class" and has a "feeling of romance in his position, and a pleasant consciousness of creating a little surprise wherever he went" (M 461–62). The narrator, continuing to emphasize the benign aspects of Will's unconventional behavior, remarks on his delight in taking the town's children "on a gypsy excursion to Halsell Wood at nutting time" and on his habit of stretching out full length on the floor of the homes of those he visits. But the narrator sounds a more ominous note by referring to the way in which this recumbent posture confirms for other visitors "the notions of his dangerously mixed blood" (M 463). When rumors begin to circulate in Middlemarch about the possibility of a love match between Dorothea and her late husband's nephew, the epithets directed at Will begin to accrue and intensify in their distastefulness. No longer just a Pole or a Gypsy, he becomes, in the words of his detractors, an "Italian with white mice," then the possessor of "any cursed alien blood, Jew, Corsican, or Gypsy," and, finally, when news of his maternal grandfather's occupation becomes a matter of common knowledge, "the grandson of a thieving Jew pawnbroker" (M 490, 719, 772).

Although critics have disagreed about whether Eliot intended to suggest that Will's grandfather was, indeed, a Jew and whether Will is, therefore, an early version of Daniel Deronda, the novelist's point seems to be that Will's status as an outsider is both salutary and an incitement to the bigotry of those around him in the knowable community to which he has attached himself.[15] He is an ideal husband for Dorothea, the novel suggests, because of his foreignness, which is inseparable from his artistic spirit, political liberalism, and lack of social snobbery. But his identity is also a flashpoint for the insularity and narrow-mindedness of Middlemarchers, a way of exposing the liabilities of existence in a community that insists on homogeneity, or at least on its appearance. Dorothea's friends and relations imagine Ladislaw's "bad origin"—as Sir James Chettam, Dorothea's brother-in-law, refers to his birth—to be inextricably connected to the lack of principle and "light character" they attribute to him (M 816). But the resolution of Dorothea and Will's story suggests that this persistent prejudice is only a minor impediment to happiness and success. Will, we learn, "became an ardent public man, working well in those times when reforms were begun with a young hopefulness," and his marriage to Dorothea is loving and reproductive. Dorothea may be prevented from becoming a new Saint Theresa or an Antigone because of the "imperfect social state" into which she was born, but her happiness is not marred by the convictions of others that her marriage is a mistake (M 836, 838). The doubly disinherited outsider, Will Ladislaw, prospers and finds his place in a changing England.

With Fedalma and Daniel Deronda, Eliot's "separated individual" moves from pariah to exile. No mere metaphoric aliens or foreigners capable of a satisfactory, if resigned, integration into English society, these characters are members of disinherited and displaced nations and implicit exiles from homes or places of origin to which they will ultimately try to return. Although it would be a mistake to attribute an absolute teleology in Eliot's fiction from disinherited individual to disinherited nation, it seems that, by the latter part of her career, she was attracted to the idea of permanent separateness—or separation—as a solution to the problem of the outcast. The mechanism for this imagined solution is "racial" difference, not as a metaphor for temperamental difference or tenuous social position, but as a total and irreducible identity. Racial or national identity is offered as the reason, perhaps the occasion, for severing ties to a seemingly temporary home, a natal country that becomes a diaspora. Furthermore, identity in both *The Spanish Gypsy* and *Daniel Deronda* is a hidden reality, a secret fact of birth to be discovered by the protagonist. Maggie Tulliver may imagine that she is a foundling, but, with Fedalma and Daniel Deronda, this daydream—or nightmare—comes true. The Freudian fantasy of family romance becomes the plot of family romance, and the discovery of true parentage brings with it the confirmation and reification of difference. The trauma of disinheritance and ostracism is ostensibly to be overcome by inheriting an unknown lineage and a distant land. The disaffected child is a changeling after all.

Influenced by mid-nineteenth-century discussions of nationalism and inspired by the unification of Italy, Eliot valued the persistence and cultivation of national identities.[16] In her essay "The Modern Hep! Hep! Hep!" published as part of *Impressions of Theophrastus Such*, Eliot, through her alter-ego narrator Such, laments a current tendency toward the "fusion of races" and counsels "moderation" in the "effacement of those national traditions and customs which are the language of the national genius":

> Such moderating and guidance of inevitable movement is worthy of all effort. And it is in this sense that the modern insistence on the idea of Nationalities has value. *That any people at once distinct and coherent enough to form a state should be held in subjection by an alien antipathetic government has been becoming more and more a ground of sympathetic indignation;* and, in virtue of this, at least one great State has been added to European councils.[17]

Nationalism is valued not only because Such/Eliot wishes to safeguard cultural traditions but also because national, religious, or (as we would say) ethnic groups suffer oppression, or "subjection," in societies like Britain. Using biological metaphors, Such ruminates about the "national life" that dwells "in our veins" and about the powerful role played by memory in establishing group identity. But he seems to suggest as well that certain groups have stronger "spirit[s] of separateness" than others and singles out the Jews, an "expatriated, denationalised race," as one such people ("MH" 348, 338). It is not simply, then, that he prizes the Jews' survival as a distinct group with a set of traditions, rituals, and cultural characteristics but that he regards the Jews as exiles awaiting return to "a native country, the birthplace of common memories and habits of mind, *existing like a parental hearth quitted but loved*" ("MH" 338 [emphasis added]).[18] Like the Italians, the Jews merit a state of their own, and the state is imagined as the wellspring, the "parent," of group identity. In *Daniel Deronda*, the visionary Mordecai, who acts as Daniel's spiritual and political guide, speaks of reviving the Jews' "organic centre," a community that will, like Italy, be a "republic" and the realization of a people's connection to its ancient land.[19] Using the metaphor of the parental hearth in "The Modern Hep! Hep! Hep!" Eliot brings into relief what her fictions imply: that individual inheritance and identity find their analogue, perhaps their extension, in the contours and vicissitudes of national identity, that the familial home and the national home are images of each other.

The knowable communities that form the heart of Eliot's fiction constrain and yet hold most of the individuals—separated, marginal, outcast—who find themselves in a struggle with convention and tradition. Fedalma and Daniel Deronda, however, outsiders who discover that their separateness derives from a biological tie to an alien group, leave their countries of exile—Spain and England, respectively—to seek a homeland. Both outcasts begin not in knowable communities, but in a hostile, incommodious land in one case and in a modern England where community is at best elusive in the other. Both places offer little in the way of redemptive social or national life, making urgent the need for a radical resolution to the protagonist's marginality. Nationalism provides an answer to the separated individual's conflict with a radically inhospitable and not merely knowable community. Difference that is both temperamental and racial can be transcended through the creation of a community of fellow outsiders, in which difference itself constitutes the basis for citizenship. Eliot's sympathy with subject groups and her desire to invent at least a novelistic solution to their oppression coalesce, one imagines, with her own fantasy of an alternative community that is both knowable and hospitable to the alien and the outcast.[20]

The partly idealized and partly oppressive knowable community, then, gives way to what Benedict Anderson calls the "imagined community." For Anderson, nationalist passion is fueled by the longing for a hypothetical homeland and the desire to live with strangers as fellow citizens. It is based on a fantasy of nation and an "image of communion."[21] As Mordecai declares, "Community was felt before it was called good," even before it was imagined in the form of nation

(*DD* 594). Anderson also emphasizes the way the state, in a nationalist imagination, "loom[s] out of an immemorial past, . . . and glide[s] into a limitless future."[22] He sounds a note very similar to Eliot's account of the role of memory in "The Modern Hep! Hep! Hep!" In both Eliot and Anderson, the individual's memory ties him to something that he cannot himself remember but locates in a very distant, primordial past and takes as the basis of identity, as well as fate. "It is the magic of nationalism to turn chance [the chance of birth] into destiny," writes Anderson, crafting a line that could stand as the synopsis of both *The Spanish Gypsy* and *Daniel Deronda*.[23] These works add another meaning to "imagined community" by refusing to represent—how could they?—the homelands toward which they merely gesture at narrative's end. The reader, as Irene Tucker has suggested, is left to do the imagining.[24]

Exiles: The Difference of Gender

As I have suggested in my brief discussions of *Silas Marner, The Mill on the Floss,* and *Middlemarch,* Eliot's pariah-heroes fare better than her pariah-heroines. Some twenty-five years ago, in the heyday of feminist literary criticism, Gillian Beer offered an observation about Eliot's heroines whose accuracy and poignancy have, to my mind, not been surpassed. "Eliot chose always," she wrote, "to imprison her most favored women. . . . She does not allow them to share her own extraordinary flight from St. Oggs and from Middlemarch. She needs them to endure their own typicality."[25] Those female characters associated with foreignness and racial difference, Maggie Tulliver and Fedalma, the heroine of *The Spanish Gypsy,* are no exceptions to this rule, and yet they suffer radically different sorts of imprisonment. Maggie, as Beer remarks, can never escape St. Oggs. Fedalma, though, rises above typicality and becomes the leader of her people— a Moses destined to deliver them from bondage into freedom in a new land. But both women, as we shall see, are denied the recompense of love. Eliot's deep ambivalence about the freedom of women and the need to weigh it against the demands of community and the kind of national identity that she endorses in "The Modern Hep! Hep! Hep!" make her finally unable to reconcile female heroism and romantic love.

The male characters tainted by foreignness in Eliot's novels not only achieve a kind of social integration and acceptance but, perhaps more significant, secure for themselves—or are blessed with—procreative futures. Will Ladislaw, although still suspect in the eyes of some hidebound Middlemarchers, realizes his political ambitions as an English reformer and produces a family with Dorothea Brooke. Even Silas Marner becomes a father, not through marriage and biological paternity but through the fortuitous adoption of Eppie.[26] His fatherhood helps not only to redeem him as a moral being but also to bind him to his community. Maggie Tulliver—mulatto, Bedlamite, Gypsy—perishes, barred from marriage because of her romantic failures and destined for a premature death as an estranged member of her community. Her male counterpart in the novel, Philip Wakem—who, as a hunchback, is bodily although not racially marked—survives but remains celibate. Maggie's victory, if she can be said to have one, is in the grave, where both her lovers in life come to visit and mourn her and where she is permanently reunited with her brother, Tom. Nonetheless, her sex, which makes her vulnerable to public disgrace, precludes both procreativity and survival.

What, then, of Fedalma, the Spanish Gypsy? Eliot's long dramatic poem, set in Spain during the time of the Inquisition, has attracted attention of late from critics interested in issues of race, conversion, and nationalism in Eliot's fiction. The most cogent way of identifying the philosophical debate in the poem would employ the terms that Bernard Semmel uses to analyze much of Eliot's work. Eliot struggles between two powerful and competing beliefs: on the one hand, the Comtean imperative that the individual sacrifice his will to the "general good" and, on the other, the liberal individualist critique of Comte, best represented by John Stuart Mill—and, not incidentally, by George Henry Lewes, Eliot's mate—that emphasizes the paramount importance of individual liberty.[27] In *The Spanish Gypsy* (1868), Eliot dramatizes this struggle in the heroine, Fedalma, raised as a Spanish princess and torn between her love for the Castilian knight Duke Silva, to whom she is betrothed, and her duty to the people, the Gypsies or Zincali, she discovers to be her own. Her father, Zarca, leader of a tribe of Zincali who have been brutally captured by the Spanish and are destined for annihilation by Silva's uncle, the vicious Prior, demands of Fedalma that she become his second-in-command, "the angel of a homeless tribe":

> To help me bless a race taught by no prophet
> And make their name, now but a badge of scorn
>
> I'll guide my brethren forth to their new land,
> Where they shall plant and sow and reap their own,
>
> Where we may kindle our first altar-fire
> From settled hearths, *and call our Holy Place*
> *The hearth that binds us in one family.*
> That land awaits them: they await their chief—
> Me, who am imprisoned. All depends on you.[28]

Fedalma must dedicate herself to a project of nationalism, imagined in *The Spanish Gypsy* much as it is in *Theophrastus Such*, as an effort to build a "birthplace of common memories and habits of mind, existing like a parental hearth."

Duke Silva, Fedalma's lover and, by association, the inevitable enemy of her people, argues for the Millite position: the primitive tie of blood and the call of birth must not be given primacy. "Love comes to cancel all ancestral hate," Silva proclaims, "[s]ubdues all heritage, proves that in mankind / Union is deeper than division" (SG 288). The freedom to choose one's destiny is crucial to Silva, and so he decides to join the Zincali, to become a Gypsy, so he can marry Fedalma and support her people's just cause. Eliot stages what amounts to a refutation of Silva's belief in individual liberty, however, when the Zincali hang his uncle, the Prior, and Silva, feeling betrayed and enraged by the people with whom he has chosen to ally himself, murders Zarca, the father of his beloved Fedalma. This act establishes a permanent enmity between the lovers, demonstrates the impossibility of choosing identity and ignoring birth, and bestows the leadership of Fedalma's people wholly on her. Obliged to take her father's place, she haltingly but dutifully proceeds to set sail with her people for an unknown homeland in Africa. Not dead like Maggie Tulliver, her sacrifice is only partial: she will keep faith with her father's dream and "plant / His sacred hope within the sanctuary," but will die a "priestess," a "hoary [white-haired] woman on the altar-step" who has become the "funeral urn," the "temple" of her father's remains (SG 370). Heroic but celibate, she will not achieve the synthesis of personal happiness and vocational success that Will Ladislaw enjoys or even the surrogate parenthood and communal integration of Silas Marner.

Fedalma is linked to the other "imprisoned" heroines of Eliot's works not because of her typicality or her ties to a knowable community, but because she is denied individual liberty and the fulfillment of personal desire, as a result of her dedication to the imagined community of nation. Gender, then, complicates the philosophical debate that informs *The Spanish Gypsy*. For women, the two poles of individual liberty and devotion to the general good seem farther apart than they ever do for men in Eliot's fiction; indeed, for the likes of Maggie, Dorothea, and Fedalma, they seem always to be at odds. What has confounded readers and critics of *The Spanish Gypsy*, however, is that the general good and allegiance to community for the heroine are aligned with a heroic, public, and distinctly political role rather than with fealty to the customs of St. Oggs and the imperative to marry and procreate.

When Eliot was planning her narrative poem *The Spanish Gypsy*, she noted the image that had inspired its plot and helped explain her thinking about the relationship between tragedy and the origin of individual destiny. In Venice, viewing a painting of the Annunciation attributed to Titian, she thought of the Virgin as a figure of tragedy, as a woman precluded from sharing in "the ordinary lot of womanhood" because it is "suddenly announced to her that she is chosen to fulfill a great destiny."[29] Mary, like Fedalma, cannot choose her own fate but is herself a chosen one, "not by any momentary arbitrariness, but as a result of foregoing hereditary conditions." In order to tell a tale about the power of biological inheritance to overcome individual will, Eliot writes that she "required the opposition of race." And at this point, she imagines the stigmas of heredity as inextricably linked to femininity: "Now, what is the fact about our individual lots? A woman, say, finds herself on earth with an inherited organisation [Eliot appears to mean a physiological "organisation"]: she may be lame, she may inherit a disease, or what is tantamount to a disease: she may be a negress, or have other marks of race repulsive to the community where she is born, etc, etc."[30] While we inevitably stumble over Eliot's equation of disease with the fact of being a "negress," the degree to which she likens unconventional—indeed, heroic—femininity to physical deformity and racial otherness is also worth noting. The woman who is different, chosen, destined for a fate beyond "the ordinary lot of womanhood," inherits this destiny as she would a bodily stigma. As a result, she resigns herself to what Eliot calls the "general" and the "inevitable," which in regard to woman amounts, paradoxically, to a physical fact—whether pregnancy, lameness, or race.[31] Eliot settles on race—or what she calls a "hereditary condition"—to pry her heroine loose from love, marriage, and desire. That she means the circumstances of female heroism and celibacy to inspire ambivalence is clear: "It is the individual with whom we sympathise," she continues in the journal, "and the general of which we recognize the irresistible power."[32] It is this ambivalence that current readers of the poem find difficult to grasp.

Michael Ragussis places Fedalma, along with the daughter heroines of Edward Bulwer-Lytton's *Leila, or, The Siege of Granada* (1838) and Grace Aguilar's *The Vale of Cedars; or the Martyr* (1850), in the literary tradition of Walter Scott's Rebecca.[33] These heroines of what Ragussis calls "racial plots" (as opposed to marriage plots) are paired with apparently widowed fathers who try to prohibit their marriages to *górgios* or Gentiles. Fedalma, Ragussis writes, faces "an exile based in the sacrifice of the erotic," and her body "becomes no more than a kind of grave for the memorialization of the dead father."[34] Although Ragussis concedes that Fedalma's dismal fate does not override what he calls "the central ideology of the text," the poem's rejection of assimilation or "conversion," he emphasizes the cruelty of the daughter's sacrifice to the father's will. If Ragussis stresses the denial of individual desire—or liberty—in his reading of the poem, Alicia Carroll finds in Fedalma's acquiescence to the needs of the "general" a decidedly sanguine meaning. Far from seeing Fedalma as sacrificial or the conclusion of the poem as funereal, she argues that Fedalma represents "a technically chaste maternal subjectivity that nonetheless resonates with erotic meaning."[35] Carroll finds in Fedalma a type of queenly presence that, combined with her elevated role as mother to her people, makes her a triumphant and resplendent figure.

It may be difficult to reconcile these two views: a young woman denied an erotic and procreative future, on the one hand, and a leader of her people whose symbolic motherhood has an erotic tinge, on the other. But it is not, I think, difficult to see that these contradictory readings are the result of the mixed signals that Eliot leaves at the poem's end. Although the association that Eliot herself makes between the Virgin Mary and Fedalma might tend to support Carroll's interpretation, it also seems clear from the poem's imagery—"I am but the funeral urn that bears the ashes of a leader," "A hoary woman on the altar-step"—that Fedalma faces celibacy and sterility and has been masculinized at her father's bidding. Before Zarca dies, he refers to his daughter—now wearing a turban and Moorish dress, and bearing a dagger—as "my younger self" (SG 272). Earlier, Zarca had dared Fedalma to deny her Gypsy inheritance by using language that conflates an exaggerated femininity with "passing" as a Spanish Christian:

> Unmake yourself, then, from a Zincala—
> Unmake yourself from being a child of mine!
> Take holy water, cross your dark skin white;
> Round your proud eyes to foolish kitten looks;
> Walk mincingly, and smirk, and twitch your robe;
> Unmake yourself—doff all the eagle plumes
> And be a parrot. (SG 157)

To remain a Spanish princess is to remain inauthentic and to be a coquette. To be what she really is—a Gypsy—is to strip herself of both Christian and feminine pretenses, to leave behind what Zarca calls "the petty round of circumstance . . . [t]hat makes a woman's lot." Fedalma must defeminize herself to become a leader of her people. The poem also suggests that the nationalist project that Fedalma is about to undertake is likely doomed:

> . . . her father's hope,
> Which she must plant and see it wither only—
> Wither and die. She saw the end begun. (SG 360)

Without the "invisible passion" of Zarca, the "great force" who held the Zincali together, the voyage from Spain takes on a melancholy, enervated air. And Fedalma is just as "resigned" to her fate as the celibate leader of her people as other of Eliot's heroines are to their lives of typicality and conventional domesticity. As Ragussis implies, the grimness of the poem's conclusion makes it difficult for the reader to muster enthusiasm for what ought to be Fedalma's heroic mission, and yet this mission is endorsed by the poem as the means of the Gypsies' survival and as Fedalma's incontrovertible destiny.

There is a moment much earlier in the poem that dramatically prefigures Fedalma's role as leader of her people and expresses her genuine yearning for community and the experience of collective identity. Before she learns the secret of her birth, she ventures into the Plaça Santiago and is swept up in the joy of the crowd. She dances before the common people in the square, tambourine in hand. But this is not simply a frivolous moment of pleasure. Fedalma, as Eliot describes her,

> [m]oves as, in dance religious, Miriam,
> When, on the Red Sea shore she raised her voice
> And led the chorus of the people's joy. (SG 64)

The poem evokes Fedalma as a type of Miriam, the sister of Moses, who helped lead the Israelites out of exile in Egypt to journey to the Promised Land. Later, Fedalma will lead the Zincali in just this way, although by then she will combine the role of Miriam with that of Aaron, the brother of Moses, who brought the people into Canaan after their great leader's death.[36] At this point, the poem celebrates, through prefiguration and biblical allusion, the full and transcendent meaning of Fedalma's role in the Zincali's exodus. When Duke Silva admonishes her, shocked that she would display herself by dancing in a public square, Fedalma argues that the dance, far from separating her from the crowd as a spectacle to be gawked at, brought her into communion with the people:

> I seemed new-waked
> To life in unison with a multitude—
> Feeling my soul upbourne by all their souls. . . . Soon I lost
> All sense of separateness. (SG 92)

Merging with the general will and with communal purpose takes on a joyous and spiritually uplifting cast. That this feeling should almost wholly evaporate by the end of the poem, replacing joy with sacrifice and devotion to community with the apparent suppression of individual desire, perplexes the reader and confounds easy interpretation. What does seem clear, however, is that this poem, like Eliot's novels, cannot find a way to reconcile public heroism with an acceptable feminine destiny, the leadership of community with domesticity and "a woman's lot." When Eliot tries a second time to write the story of hidden parentage, alien identity, and nationalist idealism, she makes her protagonist a man.

It might be said that when George Eliot wrote *Daniel Deronda* (1874–1876), her last novel, she rewrote the figure of Fedalma by dispersing her qualities among at least three characters, two of whom are women and one of whom is a man. Eliot transforms the Rebecca figure—the beautiful, nubile young woman who at the end of the narrative is unmarried and bereft of the man she has loved—into an Englishwoman, Gwendolen Harleth. As the Jewish Rebecca loses Ivanhoe to the golden-haired Rowena, the golden-haired Gwendolen loses Daniel Deronda to the Jewish, raven-haired Mirah. Gwendolen, then, is the "imprisoned" heroine, although she is imprisoned, like Fedalma, in celibacy rather than, like Dorothea, in domesticity. Eliot restages the conflict that Fedalma faces between faithfulness to her people and personal desire in the history of the Alcharisi, Daniel's mother, a Jewish woman who gave up her son and hid her identity in order to practice her art and escape the moral strictures and obligations of her religion. Judaism to her is simply "bondage," obedience to the ideals of Jewish womanhood "slavery" (*DD* 689, 694). Unlike Fedalma, the Alcharisi chose desire over community, and, through the perspective and grief of her abandoned son, she is vilified. The power that racial inheritance holds for Eliot helps to explain why this woman, who pursued her vocation and her longing for "the wide world" in a manner that strikes the modern reader as understandable and, in some respects, admirable, receives such brutal treatment in the novel.[37]

Fedalma's most important double, however, is Deronda himself. Like Fedalma, he discovers the secret of his birth and ends by leaving his erstwhile homeland to explore a national home for his people, to become, *avant la lettre*, a Zionist. Deronda, however, leaves England in an aura of hopefulness, idealism, and nobility and with a Jewish wife, Mirah. Further, Daniel fulfills the dream of the scholarly and gentle Mordecai, Mirah's brother, who, more than anyone else, blesses Daniel's marriage, while Fedalma is tied to the legacy of an exigent father who stands in determined opposition to the person she loves. Put simply, love and mission merge for Deronda, while they split disastrously for Fedalma. The impasse of *The Spanish Gypsy*—a heroine too bereft and too uncertain to embrace with passion the mission she nonetheless accepts—may have given Eliot the impetus to reimagine her story differently. Crucial to this reimagining are the question of choice and the evolution, rather than the imposition, of identity.

The narrative traces the gradual process by which Deronda *becomes* a Jew, even before he discovers the religion (or "race") of his parents, and makes clear that, once he learns the truth of his ancestry, he chooses an identity with the full exercise of his will. Unlike Fedalma—and more like Maggie Tulliver—Deronda feels certain that his birth was an anomalous one, and his psychology, about which Eliot is quite precise, develops from that feeling:

> The sense of an entailed disadvantage—the deformed foot doubtfully hidden by the shoe, makes a restlessly active spiritual yeast, and easily turns a self-centered, unloving nature into an Ishmaelite. But in the rarer sort, who presently see their own frustrated claim as one among a myriad, the inexorable sorrow takes the form of fellowship and makes the imagination tender. . . . [I]t had given a bias to his conscience, a sympathy with certain ills, and a tension of resolve in certain directions. (*DD* 215)

Although Deronda did not become an Ishmaelite as a result of his childhood anguish and insecurities, he developed sympathy for other "Hagars and . . . Ishmaels," for those who, like himself, had been disinherited (*DD* 489). A descendant not of Abraham's rejected son but, somewhat paradoxically, of Isaac, the favored one, Deronda will become a Jew and a friend to the outcast—especially to outcast women like Mrs. Glasher and, ultimately, Gwendolen. This instinct of rescue draws him to a Jewish love object, Mirah, who, because Deronda is what we might call an evolving Jew, does not have to share the celibate fate of Scott's Rebecca.

Refusing the path of a conventional English gentleman, Deronda wanders abroad, not knowing precisely what he is looking for (although he is ostensibly seeking news of Mirah's lost mother and brother), and enters a synagogue in Frankfurt. There a stranger stops him and asks about his parentage, thereby causing Deronda to form an inchoate and largely unconscious association between his unknown origin and the experience of Jewishness. Looking for Mirah's brother in the East End of London, he encounters Mordecai, who takes Deronda under his tutelage and decides to regard him as a Jew for his own quixotic reasons. By the time Deronda meets his mother and learns the story of his birth, then, he is primed to be a Jew: a Jewish sensibility, we are to understand, has naturally taken root within him. As if to emphasize that he actively chooses, as well as inherits, Jewishness and does not, like Fedalma, simply regard it as a worthy although inescapable duty, he declares, "I shall call myself a Jew. . . . But I will not say that I shall profess to believe exactly as my fathers have believed" (*DD* 792). Unlike Deronda, Fedalma resists the full implications of her Gypsyhood and, most important, is never allowed the luxury of choice: "being of the blood you are—my blood," Zarca tells her, "you have no right to choose" (*SG* 155). Instead of chafing at the prospect of his Jewish identity and all its attendant responsibilities, Deronda embraces his Jewishness easily—because he has already become a Jew.[38]

The identity of difference, of otherness, that Fedalma briefly senses and revels in during her dance in the town square ultimately becomes her burden, her legacy of responsibility. Although the moment in the square suggests the possibility of a Deronda-like evolution of identity, it is not fulfilled, in part because the poem places her national inheritance and her lover irrevocably at odds. So, unlike Deronda, she does not choose her fate or discover a nearly perfect congruence of temperament and revealed identity, nor does she enjoy a perfect synthesis of love and mission, of personal desire and devotion to community. In *Daniel Deronda*, Eliot is not interested in staging a struggle between the individual will and the "general," and, for this reason among others, she shifts to a male protagonist who does not face the conflict, habitual to women in Eliot's fiction and Eliot's time, between private and public desire. Women's ability to choose their destinies in Eliot's works tends to be suppressed: their will remains subject to the demand that they fulfill, first and foremost, a woman's lot and the will of the community. Fedalma's obligation to the community dictates that she embrace a life of political heroism and romantic denial. Indeed, she all but ceases to be a woman at the poem's end, as if to underscore the necessarily masculine nature of a political leader's public role and its irreconcilability with conventional femininity.

The discussion of *The Spanish Gypsy* makes clear, I hope, that escape from typicality, from knowable to imagined community, nullifies the heroine's sexuality and femininity. The strictures of imagined community turn out to be just as confining, in their own way, as the demands of knowable community: each inhibits female choice and exacts a price for woman's expression of desire. Imagined community offers Daniel Deronda refuge and transcendence, as it might be expected to do for Fedalma, who, as a Gypsy during the period of the Inquisition, would be denied a life of liberty in Spain, or perhaps a life at all. Fedalma's return from exile turns out, however, to be a highly equivocal fate. The heroine's difference of race in *The Spanish Gypsy* acts much as does the sexual transgression attributed to Maggie Tulliver in *The Mill on the Floss*: as bodily stigma, as a physical marking that short-circuits the resolution of the marriage plot. In her notes on *The Spanish Gypsy*, Eliot, as we have seen, defines the "inherited organisation" that would necessarily prevent a woman from attaining personal happiness: lameness, disease, or "marks of race." But, we might ask at this point, does "race" mark the male body, as it does the female? Does anomalous masculinity carry with it a bodily stigma similar to Maggie's embodied sexual sinfulness and Fedalma's dark skin? And if favored men, to use Gillian Beer's language, are also marked, are they also always imprisoned?

Anomalous masculinity expressed as foreignness, as with Will Ladislaw, or as actual "racial" difference, as with Daniel Deronda, does not bar Eliot's heroes from private satisfactions and public efficaciousness. But do such men carry an enduring mark, a physical sign of difference? And, if so, can they compensate for bodily stigma or, perhaps, obscure it in some way that enables them to mask their alien identities? In *The Mill on the Floss*, Eliot represents Philip Wakem's difference of temperament and sensibility as a literal physical deformity. She associates his crippled frame with his sensitivity and acute ability to understand the most complicated motives of others. But his marked body is also associated with his femininity. The narrator repeatedly refers to Philip, who blushes more often than any other character in the novel, as being or looking like a girl. This is true not only in his childhood, but in his young adulthood as well. At the very moment that Philip declares his love for Maggie and she hesitantly but hopefully reciprocates, we read: "Maggie smiled . . . and then stooped her tall head to kiss the low pale face that was full of pleading, timid love—like a woman's" (MF 438). Even before Maggie runs off with another man and her death precludes the possibility that she and Philip will marry, we know that this union will not happen. In the erotic economy of Victorian romance, Philip's girlishness and vulnerability make him an object of pity and tenderness but not of heterosexual love. Philip's curved spine, like the wound of Philoctetes, with whom the text aligns him, makes the young man a pariah.[39] The narrator's last words about Philip describe him as "always solitary," a being whose "great companionship" after Maggie's death remains the trees among which they walked. Philip survives while Maggie perishes, but he is destined for celibacy and noble isolation.

Daniel Deronda's stigma — his wound — is a more complicated and more hidden business. Inevitably, critics have been fascinated by the question of circumcision in a novel about a young Jewish man who cannot tell that he is a Jew. If, in the nineteenth century, all Jewish boys were circumcised and non-Jews were not, then Deronda had only to look at his own body and compare it with those of his fellow students at Eton and Cambridge to know his identity.[40] It is possible that Deronda's mother contrived not to have her baby circumcised because she was determined that he not be raised a Jew. Her devout father died before Daniel's birth, and Daniel's father was entirely subject to his wife's will ("he went against his conscience for me," she says of him), so she may have been able to avoid this most basic of Jewish rituals. I would argue that Eliot leaves this matter obscure out of necessity — in all likelihood, she could not mention circumcision in her text — but refers to it a number of times obliquely in the novel.

I have quoted the passage in which Deronda thinks of the stigma of his "hidden birth" as "the *deformed foot doubtfully hidden by the shoe*" (*DD* 215 [emphasis added]). Unlike Philip Wakem's wound (which is also displaced to the foot in the comparison with Philoctetes), Deronda's can be covered and temporarily obscured: he can pass as an Englishman, at least up to a point. Toward the end of the novel, the Alcharisi, Daniel's mother, also equates Jewishness with bodily stigma. "I rid myself of the Jewish tatters and gibberish that make people nudge each other at sight of us," she tells her son, "as if we were *tattooed under our clothes, though our faces are as whole as theirs*" (*DD* 698 [emphasis added]). The tattoo, like the deformed foot and like circumcision, is both a literal and a metaphorical sign of difference. The body is invisibly marked, cut beneath clothing, and yet the mark is somehow visible, a sign of something that appears to be but is not "whole." Eliot was fascinated by the Jews' status as both visible and invisible aliens. In her research notes for *The Spanish Gypsy*, she comments at length on the persecution of the Jews by the Inquisition and the fate of the Nuevos Christianos [*sic*]," the converts who tried to hide their Jewish identities in order to avoid immolation. She recorded a series of questions that would have been used to detect the secret of a Jew's true religious faith: "Does he wear clean linen on a Saturday? Does he reject suet and fat? Does he wash his meat & get rid of the blood? Does he observe the Jewish fasts . . . ? . . . Has he given his children a Hebrew name? . . . Has he . . . invited his relatives or friends to supper before a journey?"[41] These practices, many of which involve the Jew's body and what he ingests, can be hidden: he can be invisible and yet always in danger of exposure under the pressure of discrimination or even persecution. Clearly, as shown by the Alcharisi and Jewish women under the Inquisition in Spain, this phenomenon of unseen but ever-present stigma is not merely a gendered one. But it is difficult not to see the Alcharisi's mention of the hidden tattoo and Daniel's consciousness of the "deformed foot" as oblique references to circumcision, the concealed but crucial and ultimately unavoidable indicator of Jewishness that men alone bear. Deronda's hidden circumcision, like the undergarments or dietary practices of the Spanish *conversos*, is also a "mark of race."

For Eliot, then, the body of the alien, anomalous, and, to some degree, feminized male is also marked. And, as with Fedalma, race joins a profound physical difference to an unconventional destiny. Deronda's body is marked, however, in a way that allows him to marry Mirah or, put slightly differently, that allows him to marry *only* Mirah. He proves able to survive the physical sign of difference in a way that is unavailable to Eliot's favored but doomed women. His stigmatized body must be matched with that of a woman of his kind, whereas Philip Wakem's deformity seems to preclude coupling. Both men prevail, however, by means denied to their female counterparts. The wound to Philip's masculinity might lead to a solitary life, but the wound to Maggie's femininity—a bodily difference that is understood as bodily taint—dooms her to an early death. Deronda's wound, whether actual circumcision or metaphoric marking, exiles him but allows him a bride, whereas Fedalma's injury—her racial difference—blights her femininity irrevocably. In Eliot's universe, a wound to masculinity is endurable, while a wound to femininity is not. For the chosen women, to return to the language of Eliot's notes on *The Spanish Gypsy*, "foregoing hereditary conditions" cannot be reconciled with a bridegroom (this is Eliot's point) or even with the attainment of equanimity and satisfactory resignation. The racialized and unsexed woman ceases to be a woman at all, whereas the man whose masculinity is diminished because of race or other (bodily) difference is still a man. Eliot finds in Daniel Deronda—and in his gender—a resolution to the impasses of Fedalma's grim unsexing and self-sacrifice.

Exiles: The Difference of History

Like Walter Scott, George Eliot was drawn to the figures of Gypsy and Jew by her interest in disinheritance and national difference. These two stateless and wandering peoples, residents but not citizens of many nations, seemed twinned subjects for the novelists' working out of themes of individual and racial marginality. But for Eliot in *The Spanish Gypsy*, in part because she was intent on the narrative of nation and return from exile, Gypsies proved inadequate, or at least problematic, for her literary purposes. The subdued, not to say, defeatist, rhetoric of the end of the poem reflects a difference of history as well as a difference of gender. Throughout the work, as we shall see, Eliot touches on the problems inherent in what she imagines to be the Gypsies' relationship to their own past, and she repeatedly falls back on a mythic or literary tradition as her source for Gypsy history and identity. The very illusion under which Maggie Tulliver mistakenly operates—that her sojourn with the Gypsies on Dunlow Common will be "just like a story"—also hampers Eliot's ability to represent Gypsies as historical and, ultimately, literary subjects. We can better understand the limitations that Eliot faced in *The Spanish Gypsy* through a consideration of her rather different engagement with Jews in *Daniel Deronda*. These limitations were partly the result of Eliot's conception of Gypsy life and her projection, much like Maggie's, of her own psychic drama onto the Gypsy heroine, but they also derived from the general cultural habit of what Katie Trumpener calls "the conflation of literary traditions with living people," of seeing the Gypsy as an intractably ahistorical and symbolic figure.[42] It is much more problematic, although unavoidable, to conclude as well that this impulse to imagine the Gypsy in a purely literary context was also due to the paucity of historical and textual sources beyond either the fictional or the philological.

Eliot wrote in her notes on *The Spanish Gypsy* that when she began to meditate on the theme of a young female prohibited from experiencing "ordinary womanhood" because "chosen to fulfil a great destiny," her thoughts fixed on the setting of fifteenth-century Spain:

> My reflections brought me nothing that would serve me except that moment in Spanish history when the struggle with the Moors was attaining its climax, and when there was the gypsy race present under such conditions as would enable me to get my heroine and the hereditary claim on her among the gypsies. . . . I could not use the Jews or the Moors, because the facts of their history were too conspicuously opposed to the working out of my catastrophe.[43]

What Eliot had in mind is somewhat unclear, but it is likely that she believed that she could not use other persecuted groups in Spain—Jews or Moors—because their fates were disastrous and she wanted a "working out," rather than a recapitulation, of catastrophe. This resolution took the form, of course, of exodus from persecution and embarkation on the search for a homeland. Eliot seems to imply that since her audience would know that this outcome was not consistent with the histories of Moors or Jews in this period, she could not employ it in relation to them. If this is indeed her meaning (and it is, admittedly, hard to tell), it is not clear why she reckoned her readers would accept such a fanciful resolution to the suffering of the Zincali, other than that her readers would consider them an essentially fictive people.

The idea of a Gypsy homeland in Africa seems to have been Eliot's alone, although Bernard Semmel suggests that she may have been influenced by Bulwer-Lytton's novel *Leila*, in which a Spanish Jew of the late fifteenth century envisions a return to Palestine as the only redemption for his people.[44] It seems likely, however, that Eliot felt free to invent this turn of narrative because she was uninhibited by a known historical record. Her readers might simply not know the "facts of [the Gypsies'] history," and we can wonder how much Eliot knew of it herself.[45] She apparently relied on George Borrow's *The Zincali*, the German philologist August Friedrich Pott's *Die Zigeuner in Europe und Asien* (1844–1845), and a variety of literary texts, among them Miguel de Cervantes's *La gitanilla* (1613), but her notes are strikingly empty of references to sources or readings on the subject.[46] In Eliot's version of the Gypsies' fate under the Inquisition, the Zincali are treated as slaves and beasts of burden, "fit for the hardest tasks," although one character remarks that some believe the queen should have exiled the Gypsies with the Jews (SG 47). The argument against banishment of the Gypsies is their pure physical usefulness to the Spaniards. Zarca's band, allies of the Moors, have been captured so that Duke Silva can employ them as laborers. Zarca himself is known to be a practitioner of "fallacious alchemy" (SG 49). The Gypsy chieftain's rebelliousness, refusal to do the duke's bidding, and rage at his daughter's abduction and his wife's murder by Spanish Christians make him an enemy and a danger to the court. Eliot fashions a Gypsy leader as proud nationalist and exacting patriarch.

It is, above all, Zarca himself who articulates the difference between his own people and the others—Jews but also Moors—who suffer in Spain, and it is a difference of religion and, more important, of history:

> Yes: wanderers whom no God took knowledge of
> To give them laws, to fight for them, or blight
> Another race to make them ampler room;
> Who have no Whence or Whither in their souls,
> No dimmest love of glorious ancestors
> To make a common hearth for piety. (SG 142)

Not the "chosen people," the Zincali lack a divine protector, a text of laws, and a sense of either past or destiny: "no Whence or Whither." Their lack of memory robs them of a desire for the "common hearth for piety," a phrase reminiscent of Eliot's evocation of a homeland longed for by exiles in "The Modern Hep! Hep! Hep!": "a native country, the birthplace of common memories and habits of mind, existing like a parental hearth quitted but loved" ("MH" 338). Neither God nor memory primes them for nationalist ambition.

The only faith they have derives from their loyalty to one another, and this loyalty is dictated by their "beating hearts" rather than by a priest or a prophet (SG 145). For this reason—and Zarca is quite explicit about this—he must be not just their leader but also their memory and their godhead. He has learned from Jew and Moor "the rich heritage, the milder life, / Of nations fathered by a mighty Past" and concludes that he must provide the bond that makes his people into a nation (SG 143):

> The Zincali have no god
> Who speaks to them and calls them his, unless
> I, Zarca, carry living in my frame
> The power divine that chooses them and saves. (SG 325)

If there is no God to choose the Zincali, as the God of the Hebrew Bible chose the Jews, Zarca will be both hero and divinity, the one who chooses. With this, Eliot sounds a note of caution: not only does this hubris preclude the possibility of choice for Fedalma, but it ensures that, once Zarca dies, the Spanish Gypsies will lose their way.

The highly equivocal conclusion of *The Spanish Gypsy*, then, can be traced to problems of history, collective memory, and origin, as well as to those of gender. The contrast between Gypsies and Jews established in the poem by Zarca suggests that Eliot had begun to imagine her way out of the impasse of this first version of the nationalist narrative. Semmel observes that certain strains of thought in the poem indicate that Jews were already on Eliot's mind, and her notes for the poem, replete with lengthy discussions of *conversos*, bear this out.[47] The Jews, she believed, had a clear past and, as a consequence, a clear destiny. They had both an established link to a specific homeland and the beginnings of a modern ideology of return.[48] Unlike the rootless Gwendolen Harleth, Daniel Deronda inherits a tradition and a hearth.[49] Possessed of a written record and what Eliot refers to in "The Modern Hep! Hep! Hep!" as "a sense of separateness unique in its intensity," the Jews enjoyed "an organized memory of a national consciousness" that was inseparable from their religion and its holy texts ("MH" 140, 153). And as Mordecai declares, "the effect of . . . separateness will not be completed and have its highest transformation unless [the] race takes on again the character of a nationality" (DD 594). Aligned with the new Italy and the "great North American nation," a Jewish homeland will assume the contours of a modern state with an enlightened political vision (DD 597).

Because Eliot regarded the Gypsies as a people lacking home, tradition, and memory of their past, she could not render them as a people with a future or, to put it differently, with a modern identity. Stuck in representational limbo, a literary or mythic place unconnected to history or geography, the Gypsies remained in some fundamental way primitive or atavistic. Needless to say,

Eliot was not alone in this characterization, and yet it is striking to consider her sense of the Jews' radical difference from the Gypsies, even in the context of her belief in the deep connections between these two peoples. Part of the project of *Daniel Deronda* is precisely to establish the modernity of the Jews, their candidacy for nationhood, and their fitness to contribute a political vision to the other nations of the world. Mordecai insists that the "history and literature" of his coreligionists are not dead, that they are as alive as those of Greece and Rome, "which have inspired revolutions, enkindled the thought of Europe, and made the unrighteous tremble." Not only do ancient texts inform the present and animate the future but, in the case of Judaism, the memory of these texts and their meanings have never wholly gone underground. The inheritance of the great civilizations of Greece and Rome was "dug from the tomb," while the inheritance of the Jews has "never ceased to quiver in millions of human frames" (*DD* 596).

Daniel Deronda must learn that Jewishness, which he initially assumes to be hopelessly archaic, has a modern incarnation that is vibrant and generative. His original view of Judaism does not differ tremendously from the view of the Gypsies that plagues Eliot's poem: he regards it as "a sort of eccentric fossilized form," unworthy of study or contemporary scholarship. It is through his encounters with Mirah that he comes to see Judaism as "still something throbbing in human lives, still making for them the only conceivable vesture of the world" (*DD* 411). It is important to Eliot's revision of *The Spanish Gypsy* that Deronda's journey of individual identity bring him a revelation of Jewish modernity through empathy for a loved one. The intellectual and the affective are fused in a way that makes his discovery of origin ennobling and redemptive rather than, as with Fedalma, constricting, isolating, and preclusive of love. For the Gypsy woman, heroism comes at the cost of what Eliot calls "the ordinary lot of womanhood," and gender, as well as archaicism, freeze her in an impossible mythic present linked to neither living history nor future.

5

"The Last Romance"

Scholarship and Nostalgia in the Gypsy Lore Society

I N NOVEMBER 1931, John Sampson, linguist, librarian of the University of
Liverpool, and author of the monumental study *The Dialect of the Gypsies
of Wales*, received a proper Gypsy funeral.[1] The executor of his estate, not
his widow or one of his children but Dora Esther Yates, his protégée in Gypsy
scholarship, arranged for a procession, complete with harps and fiddles, to walk
up the peak of Foel Goch in Wales to scatter Sampson's ashes (figure 14). In her
memoir, *My Gypsy Days*, Yates records that after Sampson's cremation, Ithal
Lee, one of his local Gypsy friends and informants, walked ten miles to tell her
that many Romany had promised to scatter the ashes of the Rai (as they called
him) and were determined to do so. A collection of family members, professors
and university officials, English and Welsh Gypsies, and fellow Gypsy lorists like
Augustus John attended the ceremony. Journalists and photographers appeared
as well to record the event for the popular press. Margaret Sampson, John's
widow, tried to prevent the attendance of other women at the event, perhaps,
as her grandson Anthony Sampson speculates, to avoid "a parade of the Rai's
old girlfriends."[2] Augustus John read the funeral oration and recited a poem in
Romani that Sampson himself had composed on the occasion of the death of
another lorist, Francis Hindes Groome (GD 120).

This scene—curious, solemn, comical, authentic, and yet tinged with affecta-
tion—affords a glimpse into the strange world of the Gypsy Lore Society, founded
in 1888 and still going, albeit with a number of fits and starts, in 1930.[3] Many of its
salient features are visible in this drama: the close contact between many lorists
and the Gypsies whose language and culture they studied, an aura of theatricality, the central and largely unacknowledged role of Yates in keeping alive the
society and tending to its business and members, tensions between the bohemian

FIGURE 14 Gypsies at John Sampson's funeral. (Gypsy Lore Collection [SMGC Gypsy Photo Album 1.8.14]. Reproduced by courtesy of the University of Liverpool)

lorists and the bourgeois families they sought to elude, the sexual adventurism of some male lorists, and a persistent mix of serious scholarship and nostalgia for customs and rituals that seemed to defy modernity. The equivocal sexual politics of the group was deeply connected to its efforts to stave off the modern era's ostensible threats to a richer and older world—the world of the Romany and of a preindustrial England. Like the Edwardian revivers of George Borrow, the Gypsy lorists mourned an age that was passing and imagined the Gypsies as a lasting but endangered remnant of that age. Their fantasy of an Edenic Romany existence, the result of projection and an ultimately self-regarding nostalgia, often limited their ability to acknowledge the Gypsies as independent beings subject to change and possessed of a complex history At the same time, however, the fantasies to which they clung were undermined by their dedication to serious scholarship and their impressive knowledge of Gypsy language and life, and their romanticizing impulses were matched by a championing of Gypsy existence that served to sustain a reviled and harassed minority.

In order to get at the complex significance of the Gypsy Lore Society, I place it within the larger context of folklore and philological scholarship undertaken in the last decades of the nineteenth century. During this period, interest in Gypsy life entered a new phase: the "Romany ryes" ceased to be largely literary men and sought to render their knowledge of the language and customs of British Gypsies in what appeared to them to be a scientific, scholarly form. The mainly literary renderings of Borrow and the novelists and poets I have written about in this book had an enormous influence on the Gypsy lorists, but many of these new gypsiologists aspired to a level of philological and theoretical sophistication that would gain them academic respectability, if not university positions. Their efforts coincided with—and were influenced by—an enormous broadening of research and writing in mythology and cultural and social anthropology. Max Müller prepared the way for comparative mythologists with his philological research, focused on India, in the 1850s and 1860s; the Folk-Lore Society was founded in London in 1878; Andrew Lang espoused his theories of cultural evolution in a number of studies published in the 1880s and beyond; and volume 1 of Sir James Frazer's *The Golden Bough* appeared in 1890.[4] The efforts of the Gypsy Lore Society addressed many of the questions posed by work in other, contiguous disciplines: Does the primitive have a place in modern society? Why do certain cultural patterns—stories, practices, words—appear in both ancient and modern civilizations, in different cultures across the globe, in metropole and empire alike? How are resemblances among disparate cultures to be explained, and were there sites of origin that can be identified? And what is the role of the folklorist, anthropologist, or scholar of mythology in gathering, examining, and preserving these artifacts of culture? George Lawrence Gomme, president of the Folk-Lore Society in the early 1890s, put the aim of the folklorists succinctly: "I should like it to be settled once for all that folk-lore is a science."[5]

As these questions immediately suggest, knotty and controversial issues related to race, ideas of primitivism, Western assumptions of cultural superiority, and exploitative relations between social scientists and their objects of study were associated with the scholarly enterprises of anthropology at the end of the nineteenth century, and the Gypsy lorists have come in for their share of stringent criticism. In addition to being dismissed or ridiculed as bohemian amateurs fond of masquerading as Gypsies and of traveling about in caravans, lorists have been accused of perpetuating naïve and potentially racist ideas about the "purity" of certain English and, especially, Welsh Gypsies and of clinging to false beliefs about their cohesive identity and Indian origins.[6] They have also been criticized for ignoring the political implications of their work and eschewing social activism. Most disturbing of all, their detractors have linked their research to the persecution and slaughter of Gypsies during the Holocaust.[7] It is important to highlight the contradictory nature of their theories and assertions but to keep in mind the potentially distorting powers of the lens of retrospect, especially when the lens is inevitably shaped by the horrors of World War II. The lorists had demonstrable ties to larger, more visible intellectual movements of the late nineteenth century and thus their work reflected both the excitement and enterprise of this scholarship and the moral ambiguity of new efforts in social science. The crucial first decades of the society occupied a specific historical moment, wedged between the romanticizing impulse of Victorian letters (its members *were* the scholar-gypsies of Matthew Arnold's poem) and the lethal racist discourses and policies of the twentieth century.

The Lorists: Victorian Roots, Fin-de-siècle Influences

In one of his lectures, John Sampson declaimed that he "rate[d] it as fair a thing to be a Romani Rai as others a poet or Christian" (figure 15). He sometimes marveled, he went on, "like a numismatic who collected Greek coins, that all the world is not for our own pastime" (quoted in GD 12). He signaled in this speech that being a lorist was an obsession and an entire identity, both an external activity that involved the "collection" of artifacts and an internal, apparently spiritual state. Lorists often described their first encounter with Gypsies as a religious experience, even an experience of conversion. When Sampson introduced Dora Yates and another female protégée to the inhabitants of a Gypsy camp in 1903, Yates felt "almost the thrill of a novitiate who first beholds with his own eyes the object of his worship" (GD 15). In this regard, Sampson, Yates, and other lorists were heirs of George Borrow's Lavengro, even of Joseph Glanvill's and Matthew Arnold's dropout scholars.[8] Reading Borrow first sparked Yates's interest in Gypsies. She writes in her memoir that she was "soaked in the atmosphere of *Lavengro*, and *The Romany Rye, The Bible in Spain*, and the *Zincali*" and entered the University of Liverpool at age sixteen expecting—naïvely—to make the Romany her primary subject of study (GD 11). When Sampson discovered an extended family of Gypsies in Wales who spoke not the semi-jargon of Anglo-Romani, which he was used to hearing, but what he considered the "ancient Romani tongue," he felt that "Borrow's dream was fulfilled in my own person."[9] He named his Gypsy anthology *The Wind on the Heath*, a phrase from Borrow's *Lavengro*.[10] The prolific American lorist Charles Leland, author (under the pseudonym Hans Breitmann) of a series of dialect ballads burlesquing German Americans, knew Borrow, claimed to owe his love of "gypsying" to him, and fancied himself Borrow's successor (G 177–78).

FIGURE 15 Augustus John, *A caricature of John Sampson, the Gypsy Scholar.* (Reproduced by courtesy of the Liverpool Art Gallery and Collections)

The lorists took from Borrow the pose of the misfit and wanderer, the marginal man who identifies with Gypsies and yet occupies a position of distinction among them because of his canny knowledge of their language. "Then it was widely rumored," writes Leland in his *Memoirs*, "that the Coopers [a local Gypsy clan] had got a *rye*, or master, who spoke Romany, . . . so that in due time there was hardly a wanderer of gypsy kind in Southern England who had not heard of me."[11] The lorists were Borrow's heirs as lovers, learners, and recorders of Gypsy speech. Sampson's *The Dialect of the Gypsies of Wales* is considered by late-twentieth-century Gypsy scholars to be one of the most important Romani dictionaries ever compiled.[12] Not unlike Borrow, Sampson was what Thomas Acton calls a "young auto-didact linguist," yet his scholarship, unlike Borrow's, was rigorous and apparently reliable. Both Sampson and Francis Hindes Groome were well aware of the deficiencies of Borrow's knowledge of Romani; Borrow was "a great but careless linguist," Sampson wrote in an introduction to *The Romany Rye,* but "assuredly no philologist." And they were influenced by contemporary linguists on the Continent whose own philological studies of the Gypsies' language far surpassed Borrow's efforts.[13] Leland studied Romani after arriving in England in 1870 and produced *The English Gipsies and Their Language* (1873). Despite his profession of affection for Borrow, Leland's book competed with and clearly outdid the dictionary, called *Romano Lavo-Lil* (1874), that Borrow published late in his life. The lorists took Borrow as a model but strove for an accuracy in their work that they associated with professional philologists rather than with the amateur efforts of the "word master."

The lorists hovered between amateurism and semiprofessional aspirations, a pattern common to a variety of late-nineteenth-century scholars whose work took place outside academic institutions. The founding of learned and highly specialized societies was not new to this period, but groups like the Gypsy Lore Society sought a kind of scholarly legitimacy that distinguished them from the likes of the Pickwick Club and its prototypes. Their passion for proselytizing about the significance and fragility of the Gypsies' way of life only partly accounts for their decision to start a journal in 1888, the year the society itself was founded; they also regarded the journal as a way to claim intellectual and professional authority for their efforts. With the journal they extended their sphere beyond Britain, publishing articles on the Gypsies of contemporary Turkey, Brazil, Catalonia, and Germany, as well as on Gypsies of the European past. They included contributions by Continental colleagues and brief glossaries of Gypsy dialects from other lands. The journal covered music, dance, and folktales, again in a comparative context, and combined philological and anthropological interests. The *Journal of the Gypsy Lore Society,* John Sampson asserted, was "the medium through which eminent scholars from every part of the globe communicated their collections, discoveries, and theories to the learned world."[14]

Some of the society's finest work appeared in the journal during the first decades of the twentieth century, when Yates and others carried out extensive research on Continental Gypsy groups that appeared in Britain as a result of intensified harassment in their own countries.[15] Through excellent language skills and painstaking fieldwork methods, lorists like Yates, Sampson, and Groome produced reputable scholarship, even as they maintained their celebrity among and identification with local Gypsies (figure 16). The *Journal of the Gypsy Lore Society* has served as a link between late-nineteenth-century Romany ryes and late-twentieth-century university scholars, such as Walter Starkie, and scholar-activists, like Donald Kenrick and Thomas Acton. Yates, who kept the journal going after the deaths of a couple of generations of male lorists, first urged Kenrick to submit work for publication in the 1960s. Starkie, who became president of the Gypsy Lore Society in 1965 and whose career ultimately took him to a number of visiting professorships at American universities from the

FIGURE 16 Members of the Gypsy Lore Society with Oliver Lee. (Gypsy Lore Collection [SMGC Gypsiologist photographs; Ferguson.5]. Reproduced by courtesy of the University of Liverpool)

1950s until his death in 1976, remembered hearing of Sampson and his two female assistants (one of whom was Yates) in 1909, as a boy wandering around Shrewsbury and looking for Gypsies.[16]

If the lorists' scholarship occupied a transitional space between dilettantism and academic professionalism, their "gypsying" crossed from Borrovian fellow traveling to what Angus Fraser has called "Open Road" bohemianism.[17] John Clare and George Borrow were eccentrics who chose to spend time among the Gypsies, but they hardly fit the bohemian mold. Indeed, the British fascination with Gypsies in the early and mid-nineteenth century differed significantly from the French in just this way. Whereas in France, Gypsies—called bohémiens— were elided with artistic figures and associated with a way of life antithetical to bourgeois complacency and constraint as early as the 1830s and 1840s, in England this connection became overt only toward the end of the nineteenth century.[18] Arnold's scholar-gypsy drops out of society not to pursue artistic or sexual freedom but to free his mind, escape from time, and live a pastoral exis- tence. In vivid contrast to the solitary, apparently celibate scholar-gypsy and Lavengro, many of the lorists made ostentatious heterosexuality a mark of their countercultural identities. The quintessential British rye, whether sexualized or not, is a figure attracted to rural life, whereas the French bohemian-Gypsy is largely an urban type who leans toward, rather than away from, the modernity of the metropolis. Charles Dickens claimed that the "true modern bohemian" resembled the models of neither Borrow nor Victor Hugo, but belonged to the world of the café and the Quartier Latin.[19] As Lisa Tickner, writing about Augustus John, suggests, the *flânerie* of the urban bohemian has its pastoral analogue in the "tramping" or caravanning of the Gypsy lorist[20]

The bohemianism of the lorists was apparent in their sexual heterodoxy, the self-conscious unconventionality of their personal styles, and their taste for caravanning. In *The Gypsies*, Leland bids farewell to the worn, brown velveteen coat in which he has been traveling the English roads: "a true Bohemian thou hast ever been, and as a right Bohemian thou wilt die, the garment of a roving Romany" (G 170). The most self-consciously literary of the lorists, Leland makes overt the association between artist and Gypsy, or between the vagabond literary man and the lover of Gypsy lore. Augustus John signaled similar connections in his paintings and in comments about his own identity and class position. After an encounter with Russian Gypsies in Cherbourg in the early years of the twentieth century, he wrote to a friend, "We spoke together in their language—wonderful people with everyone's hand against them—like artists in a world of petits bourgeois."[21] In 1908, inspired by his friendship with Sampson and other members of the Gypsy Lore Society, he took off with his family, a canary-yellow caravan, six horses, a tent, and "a stray boy 'for washing up'" and traveled into Surrey, Cambridgeshire, and East Anglia.[22] In 1935, Yates, having reached a safely respectable fifty-six, bought herself a "gaily-painted, barrel-topped caravan" (figure 17) for £10 and a horse for another £10 and traveled about her home in the countryside (GD 176). The sexual self-fashioning of some of the male lorists, to which I will return, cannot be separated from their intellectual avocations. The philandering of Sampson and John was deeply associated with their "gypsying," and the marriage of Francis Hindes Groome to a stunning and talented Gypsy, Esmeralda Lock, became a subject of scandal in the press and a legend among British lorists.[23]

Origins: Purity and the "True Eden-life"

The rhetoric of many Gypsy lorists reflected an urgency about the need to salvage what was left of a people and a culture that were gradually disappearing. In a latter-day version of John Clare's anxiety that enclosure would destroy the Gypsies' way of life, they imagined modernity overwhelming and thereby erasing something primal and essential in British culture. As a very young woman, Dora Yates heard Sir James Frazer lecture at the University of Liverpool, and, according to family legend, she was set on her lorist path when he "urged his audience to discover a living folk-lore among the fast-disappearing Gypsies."[24] John Clare and the Matthew Arnold of "Resignation" worry that the law and

FIGURE 17 Dora Yates in front of her caravan. (Gypsy Lore Collection [SMGC Gypsy Photo Album 2.3.8]. Reproduced by courtesy of the University of Liverpool)

pinched circumstances will reduce and cramp Gypsies' lives, but, in the later part of the nineteenth century, lorists seem to have believed that modernity and a losing battle with time would actually wipe them out entirely—or would, at least, wipe out the true Gypsies. Whether actually threatened with extinction or not, Gypsies appeared to lorists as a redoubt against a vapid, conformist, and mechanistic modern world. This rhetoric of threatened disappearance circulated repeatedly throughout the nineteenth century, associated not only with Gypsies, but with rural life, preurban innocence, village customs, horse-and-carriage travel, and the like. Patrick Brantlinger, writing largely about imperial subjects, uses the term "proleptic elegy" to refer to the tendency to mourn lost groups of ostensibly primitive peoples before they are actually lost. He regards this habit of premature lamentation as "a primary motivation for the funereal but very modern science of anthropology."[25] Among the lorists, this discourse of extinction incorporated a preoccupation with purity—purity of language and of "race"—and an obsession with origin that should by now be familiar. Some invoked the distant moment of genesis before the Gypsies and their language had been compromised and defiled as a golden age, or, as John Sampson, quoting George Borrow, put it, the "true Eden-life."[26]

When Sampson published *The Dialect of the Gypsies of Wales* (1926), he placed an epigraph from Borrow on the first page. In this long passage from *The Romany Rye*, the word master meditates on what it would have been like to know the Gypsies of three hundred years earlier: they would have been stranger than at present, possessed of greater knowledge and many more arcane secrets, and their language would have been "more perfect." "What might I not have done with that language," he speculates, "had I known it in its purity?"[27] Lavengro imagines an Edenic moment that predates—by centuries—the Eden that he nonetheless has found among the British Gypsies, and the focus of this fantasy of "purity" is, as we would expect of him, language and not "race" or blood. Sampson begins with this fancy because he wants to claim that he actually discovered the ur-Romani of which Borrow only dreamed. Believing that Romani had become debased, "little more than the debris of a once stately and beautifully constructed language," he went in search of some remnant of the primal idiom (*DGW* vii). And in 1894, while on a "caravan tour" of northern Wales, he came upon just that: near Bala, the "ancient Romani tongue" had been preserved by descendants of Abram Wood, erstwhile king of the Gypsies, who was born toward the end of the seventeenth century. Sampson apparently fulfilled Borrow's dream—or so he claimed.

In his preface to the dictionary, Sampson admits, however, that "decay has already begun to set in" and that the pure Romani of the Wood clan might not last beyond the next couple of generations (*DGW* xi). He discovered something pure and original, but he also wants to sound the alarm of decline and degeneration. As we shall see, this kind of contradiction characterizes—and, indeed, is central to—much lorist writing. The gypsiologists wanted to claim both scientific importance and urgency for their efforts; they not only sought acknowledgment for having made extraordinary discoveries and for working diligently at the preservation of a way of life that was about to become wholly beyond anyone's reach, but also reflected the tendency of their time to lament the cultural disintegration that modernity had visited on contemporary life and the need to prove this decline by producing the shards of a golden age.

Crucial, too, to the lorists' project was the explanation that Sampson offered for the decay of Romani among the Wood clan. The Woods had failed to be "prolific" and so were dying out. What lay behind this lack of fecundity was probably, according to Sampson, their inbreeding and "intermarriage" with

Welsh non-Gypsies and hybrid English Gypsies (*DGW* xi). Fascinated by genealogy and by tracing the history of Gypsy clans in a relatively isolated part of the
United Kingdom, the lorists repeatedly fell back on the idea that pure language
and pure "race" went together. Intermarriage between Gypsies and *górgios* wore
away at pristine Gypsy culture and at "deep" Romani, as the lorists liked to call
it, which Sampson believed he had nonetheless uncovered. David Mayall, who
sharply criticizes the lorists' theories about race and language, puts it this way:
"Scientific tools such as genealogy and philology were applied with vigour and
despite the existence of contradictory evidence, the lorists discovered the race
they had set out to find." Mayall's general perspective on the British Gypsies
favors the theory that patterns of intermarriage started soon after the arrival of
the Gypsies in Britain in the early sixteenth century and continued to the nineteenth century, when lorists claimed that the Wood family and certain others
had kept themselves relatively aloof from the rest of the population. Mayall con-
ceives of the Gypsies as a group defined over time by their means of subsistence
and minimizes the idea that they continued to possess any group integrity as
descendants of Indian migrants to Britain. Furthermore, he contends, the argu-
ments made by the lorists about racial and linguistic purity could be used to
justify persecution and worse.[28]

The lorists' obsession with purity is difficult to separate from their quarrel
with modernity and their habitual search for origins. Charles Leland's picaresque narrative, *The Gypsies*, combines a heavy dose of nostalgia for an older,
preindustrial England with a detective story that culminates in his discovery
of the "real gypsies of India" (G 337). The detective plot has a decidedly fictive quality, and the key-to-all-mythologies conclusion it reaches was never
taken up with any seriousness by other lorists. Leland's source for this secret
but essential knowledge is a man he comes across one day on the Marylebone
Road, one John Nano, an Indian "Rom," who tells him of his people in India,
the "Trablūs" (G 338). Not only has Leland found irrefutable evidence that the
Gypsies originated in India, but he has discovered that these Indian "Rom" still
live in their homeland and share a language with the British Romany he knows.
His chance encounter with Nano and his instant recognition of the man as a
Gypsy—"I met a very dark man, poorly clad, . . . his eyes had the very expression of the purest blood of the oldest families"—overshadow his theorizing and
mark the real interest of Leland's narrative. He writes in a mode that is akin to
earlier nineteenth-century writing—the nostalgic Romantic essay or sketch, for
example—and the encounter itself is proof to the author that an older form of
social intercourse can still exist in late-nineteenth-century London, intercourse
that might connect him not merely to an older England but to an ancient
moment and site.

Like many other lorists, Leland sounds an alarm about the disappearance of
the Gypsy—"the child was born who would see the last gypsy"—and, for him,

this certain extinction is symptomatic of a waning rural culture (G 26). Just as sensitivity to nature is in decline, so are the Gypsy and the village festivals and holidays—"burlesque pageant and splendid procession"—that epitomize the spirit of old England. Natural beauty, the picturesque, county fairs, country dances, even "sensuous, naïve womanhood" form a nexus of endangered phenomena that can be summed up in the shorthand of Gypsy life: "Gypsies are the human types of this vanishing, direct love of nature, of this mute sense of rural romance, and of *al fresco* life" (G 13). More disturbing and more significant than talk of "purest blood" in Leland is his reduction of the Gypsy to a type and, ultimately, to a creature indistinguishable from animals and inanimate objects. He refers to himself as "a collector of human bric-a-brac," for whom the Gypsies have special value as the most antique and quaintest of finds (G 189). "The day is coming," he warns, "when there will be no more wild parrots nor wild wanderers, no wild nature, and certainly no gypsies. . . . [T]he people of self-conscious culture and the mart and factory are banishing the wilder sort" (G 26). For Leland, modern society and what he calls the "house-world" are responsible for destroying or, perhaps, taming the wild things, of which the Gypsies are but one species.

Like George Borrow in the appendix to *The Romany Rye*, Leland laments the conformity—Borrow calls it "gentility" and Leland "advancing republicanism"—that robs groups of their distinctiveness and idiosyncrasies (G 135).[29] But the difference between them is meaningful. In Borrow's critique, England's minorities—Gypsies, Quakers, Jews—are forced to lose the characteristics that enable them to preserve their own histories and, at the same time, the free and multicultural nature of Britain. For Leland, however, the loss is aesthetic and solipsistic. His Gypsies are part of the scenery, a gorgeous bric-a-brac, a beautiful parrot for his own delectation. His regrets amount to a self-indulgent nostalgia; Borrow's, to a longing for a variegated and eclectic citizenry.

Dora Yates and other lorists were fond of quoting an essay by the critic and poet Arthur Symons that articulates succinctly and passionately the view that "the freedom of the Gypsy is like a lesson against civilisation." His paean to "the last romance left in the world" is called "In Praise of Gypsies," an echo of titles like Charles Lamb's "The Praise of Chimney-Sweepers."[30] Symons's rhapsodic tone barely masks the solipsism, similar to Leland's but greatly elaborated, that lies at the heart of his essay. He represents the Gypsies as a people moved by pure instinct: they live by "rote and by faith and by tradition," and they remain unchanged and untouched by history or by "us." The piece sounds an orientalist note—"they are our only link with the East"—and mystifies the Gypsies' access to secret knowledge and magic. Symons also tries to elevate them by dehumanizing them, commenting that the Gypsies are "nearer to the animals than any race known to us in Europe." It is not only, I would argue, that Symons is eager to cast the Gypsies as lower—although somehow privileged—forms of being that makes his views repugnant. He also wants to use the Gypsies as a trope to represent and justify as natural his own dissent from the community of the "civilized."[31]

Unlike Leland's, his image of the Gypsies smacks not so much of condescension as of pure projection: "They are the symbol of our aspirations, and we do not know it; they . . . stand . . . for all in us that is a protest against progress. Progress is a heavy wheel, turned backward upon us. . . . He does what we dream. . . . That is the curse of all civilization, it is a tyranny, *it is the force of repression.* To try to repress the Gypsies is to fight against instinct, to try to cut out of humanity its rarest impulse."[32] Civilization will not repress the Gypsy or, by extension, the bohemian lorist, no matter how great the effort. Predictably, this Edwardian protest against repression is accompanied by a screed against the smoke-filled, noisy cities, "degraded into the likeness of a vast machine."[33] Symons asserts that the Gypsies turn their backs on the urban world, an assertion that is, by the way, undermined by the lorists—for example, Yates—who regret the Gypsies' increasing need to gather at the edge of cities in order to survive (GD 28). But this imagined opposition between Gypsy and city-as-machine is crucial to Symons's vision and to what amounts ultimately to a defense of his own social and cultural stance as a man prominently associated with the decadent movement and French symbolism. He concludes his essay with what appears at first to be a change of gears but, at second glance, makes obvious the self-referential thrust of his piece. There is so much talk, he complains, of degeneracy and decadence in the world of letters and in the cult of individuality. "But it is," he concludes, "the millionaire, the merchant, the money-maker, the sweater, who are the degenerates of civilization." His praise of Gypsies is a defense of self and, more precisely, an assault on agents of modernity, onto whom he wishes to deflect accusations of dissoluteness and corruption.

Symons's protest against the encroachments of modern life is less a dream of the "true Eden-life" or of a quaint, bucolic England or even of a pristine language and race than a fantasy of the Gypsy-as-primitive to bolster middle-class bohemianism. Still, he uses a rhetoric of pastoralism, of antiurbanism, that, in varying forms, characterizes many of the lorists' representations of Gypsy life. It is no accident that the Gypsy Lore Society grew up around Liverpool, with its urban intensity and its proximity to sparsely settled countryside. Yates, who lived in Liverpool her entire life and whose career would have been unimaginable without the city's cultural and professional possibilities, was a devoted naturalist, hiker, and lover of the open road.[34] When she gave up her caravan, she wrote with regret that she would never again be able to "gaze at the stars from bed, or listen to the curlews calling, or through its half-open door watch a string of geese fly, honking overhead."[35] Hers was a pastoralism of the true city dweller besotted with the experience of nature. Her survival into the eighth decade of the twentieth century adds an element of poignancy to her enduring ability to be sustained by the sight of a Gypsy encampment. She ends her memoir with a latter-day, prosaic version of John Clare's Gypsy poems:

> When one passes from the sordid streets and mean hovels of a city into a country lane, or over a wind-swept moor, or even onto a cinder-swept piece of waste ground, and smells the good smell of food cooked in the open, and sees the blue smoke curling up from the Gypsies' wood fires, do these stir the imagination less because to-day they may burn before a luxurious motor trailer instead of a horse-drawn caravan? These good things I actually saw and smelled in the June of this year of grace 1952. (GD 181)

Neither modern life in the form of a trailer nor a wasteland setting diminishes the real pastoral power or sensory pleasures of the Gypsy camp.

The Folklore Movement: Diffusion and Empiricism

Although the leading lorists began as students of philology, it was their devotion to the collection and interpretation of Gypsy folktales that qualified them as representative members of the folklore movement of their day. This movement, which flourished in the last quarter of the nineteenth century and continued up until World War I, was the result of a confluence of intellectual currents: antiquarianism, the study of Sanskrit, linguistics, ethnology, anthropology, mythology, and evolutionary theory.[36] Mary Beard has tried to account for the impact of James Frazer's The Golden Bough, a major text for the folklore movement, and, in so doing, has observed that Frazer managed to unite the study of the "foreign Other" with inquiries into both the classical past and British rural folklore.[37] The same linking of cultural patterns separated by vast differences in language, time, and place characterized the contributions of many British folklorists, whose passion lay in finding the repetition of cultural forms in myths of antiquity, European fairy tales, local British lore, and stories gleaned in the outposts of empire. For the Gypsy lorists, the foreign other and British rural folklore were merged in the single figure of the Gypsy, whose Asian origin, global ubiquity, and special association with the British rural past made him an apparently ideal subject for studying the relationship between the primitive—so-called—and the modern.

When Beard speaks of the "foreign Other," she gestures to an imperial context and to Europeans' encounters with colonized peoples. Frazer understood, she believes, that questions raised by the experience of empire were inseparable from what she calls "the changing face of British traditions in the face of growing industrialisation," and he implicitly invited comparison between the peoples of empire and those of rural England.[38] Yoking together through sheer association, as Christopher Herbert has pointed out, cultural practices from disparate and remote parts of the world and from similarly unrelated moments in history, Frazer asserted an "essential similarity" among peoples.[39] Ignoring the question of causation—how to account for this similarity—Frazer suggested that time and place had nothing to do with the "magical" resemblances observable between cultures that sometimes were separated by oceans or centuries. The beliefs, customs, and stories of contemporary Scottish peasants, for example, might mimic those found in ancient societies.[40] Crucial to these parallels was the uniformity of "primitive thinking," which, according to Frazer, "remains everywhere and at all times alike."[41] This phrase recalls Heinrich Grellman's and John Hoyland's early assertions that, despite their wanderings, the Gypsies had remained essentially the same over the centuries and in all parts of the globe. In some respects, then, Gypsies appeared to be an observable form of enduring primitivism and an extant link between ancient tribes—whose homeland was the very center of the modern British Empire, no less—and the rural nomads of contemporary England.

Frazer may not have wanted to theorize about what accounted for repeated patterns in disparate cultures, but many folklorists did. The question of causation—what could explain the multiple existence of folktales across cultures—was widely disputed among folklorists; indeed, it became the issue that distinguished the two competing camps in the last decades of the nineteenth century. On one side were the diffusionists, scholars influenced by the philological research of Max Müller and committed to the comparative study of mythology.[42] They believed that certain prototypical stories and myths had spread from culture to culture as a result of the migration and circulation of peoples. Diffusionists might debate whether the tales had one or many points of origin, but Müller's argument for the common Aryan stock of all Indo-European languages gave weight to the notion of a single originary source. The diffusionists' beliefs were largely consistent with the theory of monogenesis, which held that all peoples had descended from a single seed.[43]

On the other side were the evolutionists, scholars more influenced by Darwinism, anthropology, and psychology than by philology, who believed in a kind of cultural evolution. Foremost among them was Andrew Lang, who argued that modern humans had inherited cultural and psychological elements from their savage ancestors and that, because this pattern of inheritance was universal and human psychology was everywhere the same, groups across the globe would share much—including folktales, customs, and beliefs. Especially interested in the appearance of totemism, animism, and fetishism in myths and fairy tales, Lang believed that these elements "hark[ed] back to the stage of culture when men did not sharply distinguish between the human and the natural world."[44] "Savagery" and magical thinking survived, to some extent, in modern societies, and folktales contained the remnants of primitive cultures. Furthermore, evolutionists claimed that they could detect in the customs of contemporary "primitives" analogues for seemingly defunct cultural patterns.[45]

Francis Hindes Groome, the chief link between the Gypsy lorists and the larger community of scholars associated with the Folk-Lore Society, was a vocal diffusionist. Not only did he support the hypothesis that migrating groups had disseminated folktales from one culture to another, but he ventured the theory that Gypsies had been the very itinerant storytellers responsible for carrying tales from place to place (GT 169).[46] If the diffusionists believed that some agent or agents of distribution had acted in the distant past to connect disparate and far-flung cultures, then why look further for the identity of this agent than a group of people—the Romany—who had an Indian ancestry and whose very history consisted of migration, nomadism, and settlement over the centuries and throughout the world?[47] If, as Müller and others had suggested, many European tales were traceable to Indian sources, then perhaps Europe owed at least a portion of its folklore to the Gypsies, a logical conduit for diffusion. Groome saw a parallel between folkloric and philological patterns of correspondence—that is, between the similarities in Indian and European tales and the shared vocabularies of Hindustani and Romani.[48]

In the introduction to his collection *Gypsy Folk-Tales*, Groome discusses and argues against Lang's evolutionary position, making clear not only that larger theoretical debates within the folklore movement were relevant to Gypsy studies, but that Gypsy studies might well provide the actual resolution to these far-reaching debates. He goes on to point out that examining English and Welsh Gypsy tales collected by members of the Gypsy Lore Society and comparing them with German, Gaelic, or other European tales support the credibility of the diffusion theory. Beyond this, he argues, Gypsies have long been great practitioners of the art of storytelling and probably lent and gathered tales as they traveled:

> The Gypsies quitted India at an unknown date, probably taking with them some scores of Indian folk-tales, as they certainly took with them many hundreds of Indian words. By way of Persia and Armenia, they arrived in the Greek-speaking Balkan Peninsula, and tarried there for several centuries, probably disseminating their Indian folk-tales, and themselves picking up Greek folk-tales, as they certainly gave Greek the Romani word *bakht*, "fortune," and borrowed from it *paramísi*, "story," and about a hundred more terms. From the Balkan Peninsula they have spread since 1417, or possibly earlier, to Siberia, Norway, Scotland, Wales, Spain, Brazil, and the countries between, everywhere disseminating the folk-tales they started with and those they picked up by the way, and everywhere probably adding to their store. Thus, I take it, they picked up the complete Rhampsinitus story in the Balkan Peninsula, and carried it thence to Roumania and Scotland; in Scotland, if John MacDonald was any sort of a Gypsy, they seem to have picked up "Osean after the Feen."[49]

Summing up his grand theory, Groome borrows a phrase from Charles Leland to refer to the Gypsies as the "Colporteurs [peddlers] of Folklore."

Clearly, Groome wanted to elevate the work of Gypsy lorists by entering into the diffusion–evolution debate and to enhance the prestige of the Gypsies, as Richard Dorson points out, by advancing the "colporteur" theory. But it must be said, too, that Groome's discussion of the role of the Gypsies in the dissemination of folktales in Europe forcefully and convincingly challenged the assumptions of the evolutionists: "these colporteurs of popular fictions," Dorson writes, "distributing tales found in the Grimms, in the *Gesta Romanorum*, in distant India, must be reckoned another thorn in the side of the evolutionists."[50] Groome was neither dogmatic nor absolute in proposing his ideas about the Gypsies' role, and he never claimed that Gypsies were necessarily the ultimate source of tales or their only disseminators.[51] He clearly fit within the tradition of nineteenth-century Gypsy scholars in associating the Gypsies with the origins of civilization and did not simply relegate them to the position of contemporary "primitives." Indeed, he cast them among the heroic propagators of culture.

Of all the Gypsy lorists, Groome was the most serious and rigorous scholar of folklore, in part because he believed in and practiced the empiricism that characterized the folklore movement. Folklorists enthusiastically collected tales of all kinds, both from literary sources and in the field, wherever that might be. In his comprehensive history of the British folklore movement, Dorson describes the common enterprise of colonials and folklorists. In India, for instance, as well as in other parts of the British Empire, an interest in folklore inspired missionaries, traders, civil servants, military men, and some of their wives and daughters to collect, record, and even publish indigenous folktales.[52] The *ayahs* who cared for British children and colonial households were a frequent source of stories and folktales. This impulse to seek out and record local lore was at the heart of the folklore movement, the first step in a scientific rendering, comparing, and analyzing of material. Not only did the *Journal of the Gypsy Lore Society* print tales from around the globe, but the Gypsy lorists produced compendia of folklore as well as Romani dictionaries; Charles Leland collected Gypsy songs and published a group of them in Romani with English translations, including one by Alfred Tennyson, in 1875; Groome published *Gypsy Folk-Tales* in 1899; and Dora Yates waited until 1948 to bring out her *Book of Gypsy Folktales*, with stories that she had culled and translated from eleven countries.

The work that Yates did as John Sampson's protégée offers a good example of lorist methods. Sampson recruited her to collect Gypsy lore in 1900, when she was twenty-one, because of her skill with languages. He trained her and another young woman, Agnes Marston, to speak Romani, introduced them to the Gypsy families he knew around Liverpool, and sent them into the field to do research.

Like anthropologists, they sought out subjects at horse fairs, annual festivals, and other casual gathering places and worked to gain the confidence of their interlocutors.[53] The Gypsies who came to trust and welcome them called the dark-haired Yates "I Kawli Yek" (the black one) and fair-complexioned Agnes "I Porni Yek" (the white one). Sampson's method for recording dialects and tales with accuracy required two witnesses, both of whom would take down the same utterances or stories. Yates's proficiently developed ear made her a useful researcher, scribe, and interpreter, and her talents were employed not only by scholars like Sampson, but also by local police confronted with Gypsy groups newly arrived from the Continent (GD 87). She was able to compare the dialects of Welsh and British Gypsies with those of German, Romanian, and Greek Gypsies, and she collected family lore that allowed her to reconstruct genealogies and patterns of migration.

The lorists' empiricism extended beyond the collection of words, tales, customs, and testimonies to the perusal of parish registers and the compilation of family trees (GD 65). Yates did this assiduously in her search for the Wood family, the key to the "ancient Romani tongue," which Sampson claimed to have discovered in northern Wales (GD 60). Together with Henry Crofton, a Lancashire historian who published his own *Dialect of the English Gipsies* (1875), Yates, Sampson, and Groome could account for three major Gypsy families—the Boswells, Lowells, and Woods—over a number of generations. Of particular interest to them was the degree of intermarriage with *górgios* in each family over the decades. In *In Gipsy Tents*, Groome comments on the extraordinary frequency of intermarriage in the Wood family—a rate far greater than that in either of the other two major clans. The result, he concludes, is a mish-mash of Gypsy and *górgio* characteristics:

> The offspring of such mixed marriages are sometimes górgios . . . and sometimes Gipsies. . . . By górgios, I mean that they have not the Romani look, language, habits, and modes of thought; by Gipsies, that they retain these distinguishing marks *in a greater or less degree*. These marks may co-exist in one and the same person, e.g. in Silvanus, a full-blood Gipsy, whose face is of a thoroughly un-English type, whole sentences of whose *Romanes* would be quite intelligible to Turkish Tchinghianés, who was born in a tent and hopes to die in one, whose heart is as Romani as his face is brown. John [a grandson of Abram Wood], on the other hand, has for years been a house-dweller, and bears few traces of the Romani blood, yet speaks the language with a far greater purity than Silvanus, and is a storehouse of old Gipsy beliefs. . . . Are we to pronounce him a górgio, because he lives between four walls, and is not so dark as several of his own sons? Or the Crink down the lane a Gipsy on the score of his scattered tent? Assuredly not. . . . *[T]hese three cases illustrate the difficulty of drawing a hard and fast line between Gipsies and non-Gipsies*. (GT 252 [emphasis added])

Still in need of a "satisfactory test," however, Groome concludes that it is language alone that characterizes a true Gypsy: ignorance of Romani must always be a disqualifier (*GT* 253).

Groome's account of the uneven results of intermarriage and assimilation does not square with the Gypsy lorists' ostensible belief in the myth of the "pure" Gypsy. He takes the very example—the Wood family—that Sampson has offered as evidence of the link between racial and linguistic purity and concedes that there is little purity to be found in its lineage. If we return to David Mayall's indictment of the lorists' fetishizing of racial purity, we can see that he is not wholly accurate—or, at least, comprehensive—in the way he represents the lorists' refusal to acknowledge the implications of their own research.[54] What we find in Groome, I think, is a clear awareness that evidence contradicts theory, that observation and research belie a romanticizing but impossible desire to discover something original and pristine. Yates insists on referring to "pure-blooded families" and, at the same, offers the example of Dora Boswell, of "mixed ancestry" and yet proficient in ancient Gypsy lore, as evidence of the irrelevance of such a concept (*GD* 31). Groome tries to cling to the sine qua non of language but gets into trouble even here: knowledge of Romani, he asserts, is the mark of a real Gypsy, but many who speak the language, he admits, are not Gypsies at all. The lorists occupied a position between scholarship and mystification, between a serious, empirical attempt to uncover the nature of Gypsy culture and language and an insistence, born of the lorists' own need to find remnants of a golden age, that the chimera of the wholly authentic Gypsy was real. As with many a late-nineteenth-century folklorist, philologist, or anthropologist, "science" and fantasy naturally coexisted.

Gender Stories

If the archetypal Gypsy for Matthew Arnold and George Borrow was a feminized man and for Walter Scott and George Eliot a masculinized woman, the quintessential Gypsy for the lorists was a sexualized and seductive woman. The atypical gender identities of the scholar-gypsy, Meg Merrilies, Lavengro, Fedalma, and even Maggie Tulliver gave way to the boilerplate sultriness and hypersexual femininity of numerous minor female figures in male lorists' writings and fantasies. In *The Wind on the Heath*, John Sampson's collection of literary allusions to Gypsies, an entire section, "The Romany Chye," is devoted to Gypsy women, with no analogous part for Romany chals, or Gypsy men. Among the entries are passages from fellow lorist Theodore Watts-Dunton's *Aylwin* and *The Coming of Love*, works of the late 1890s that include memorable descriptions of two such Gypsy beauties: Sinfi Lovell and Rhona Boswell. Watts-Dunton remarks that "between Englishmen of a certain type and gypsy women there is an extraordinary physical attraction," but adds that this attraction did not exist for Borrow, who loved (chastely) "a splendid East-Anglian road-girl."[55] Although nowhere near as powerfully imagined as Scott's Meg Merrilies, these late-nineteenth-century figures became the signifiers of Gypsy femininity — exotic, musical, sexually desirable, and stunningly beautiful. Esmeralda Lock, the Romany wife of Francis Hindes Groome, assumed legendary status among both lorists and the public. Her image was frequently reproduced. Dante Gabriel Rossetti, introduced to her by Watts-Dunton, drew her often as a dancing Gypsy girl and, according to lorists, painted her as Victor Hugo's Esmeralda on the steps of Notre Dame. In the portrait by Rossetti and the imaginations of Gypsy lorists, the eroticized Gypsy woman of French letters met the lush beauty of Pre-Raphaelite iconography (GD 105).[56]

The writings of male lorists habitually include descriptions of female Gypsies that highlight their "Oriental" and exotic looks, their animal natures, and their potential for explosive and potentially dangerous sexuality. Almost all such descriptions tend to be static portraits. These figures never play a role in the narrator's experience or function as active characters in the narrative; they barely move and never speak; they are evoked purely as images, as objects to be taken in with the eye. For Arthur Symons, Gypsy women appear the same in all places, "wherever one travels, east or west": a girl of fifteen in Belgrade leans languidly against a wall, "haughty, magnetic, indifferent; a swift animal, like a strung bow, bringing all the East with her, and a shy wildness which is the Gypsy's only."[57] There is a suggestion in this depiction of powerful energy coiled (a word that appears frequently in these descriptions) and ready to strike, a dormant but nonetheless readily apparent erotic aggression. Charles Leland portrays one Gypsy girl as "pantherine, with diabolesque charm," and another "wild beauty" as a "damsel . . . with devil's gunpowder in her . . . of a figure suggestive of leaping hedges; and [with] . . . white teeth and burning black eyes, there was a hint of biting, too, about her" (G 190, 176). Again and again, eyes and teeth are emphasized, as are languorousness and its opposite, passion. Groome quotes a passage from the *Illustrated London News* that underscores a Gypsy beauty's "veiled fire," "serpent-like power," "filmy languor," and "latent fascination" (GT 324). The Englishman lorist safely projects sexual desire onto these canvases: the women promise sexual adventure but, still and subordinate, never pose a threat. Wordless and motionless, they possess the erotic power of the odalisque.

Gypsy women appear in lorists' imaginations not only as sirens, but also as mothers. Popular imagery of the last few decades of the nineteenth century features Gypsy women with children, sometimes in groups and often in Madonna–child dyads. Hubert von Herkomer's engraving "A Gipsy Encampment on Putney Common" features a group of Gypsies engaged in a variety of activities (figure 18). On the left, two men sit on the ground, one inside and the other in front of their tent, and weave baskets. On the right, a couple of children play in a wagon near what looks like a donkey. But in the very center, and towering above the others, is a Gypsy mother looking lovingly and sadly at the baby wrapped in a shawl worn as a sling on her chest.[58] Such sentimentalized images highlight not the ragtag crowding of Gypsy families or the semidressed urchins of later photographs, but the maternal solicitude of the impoverished and burdened Gypsy woman. Babies often appear at a mother's breast or tied to her back.[59] In a brilliant discussion of Augustus John's drawings of Gypsy women and portraits of his extended family imagined as Gypsies, Lisa Tickner analyzes his unfinished painting, *Lyric Fantasy* (or *Blue Lake*, as it was later called), in relation to his other Gypsy works and his feelings of loss and longing for a golden age. In *Lyric Fantasy*, five women (four of them recognizable as mothers of John's children) and five children (all identifiable as his offspring) dance, play musical instruments, and frolic, some of them in Gypsy dress, in a stylized landscape reminiscent of that in Renaissance painting (figure 19). Tickner describes the scene as a "lost Arcadia" that reflects John's mourning for a child and one of these wives, as well as for the mother he lost in early childhood. An "imaginary proliferation of mothers," she writes, "is shored against loss, and John as the motherless, provincial orphan becomes at once a gypsy patriarch and the living heir to the Renaissance tradition: an heroic progenitor of paintings and children."[60]

This powerful example of John's private iconography reflects the representation of the female Gypsy in popular imagery and in the writings of other lorists, in which the Gypsy is identified with the related phenomena of a golden age, fin-de-siècle nostalgia for a preindustrialized England, and the idealized and objectified woman. Tickner hypothesizes that the "lyric fantasy of a golden age is always a dream of the restored plenitude of the maternal body," and certainly the representation of a particular mode of femininity offers reassurance and the promise of transcendence in the face of an exigent modernity. A new era and new forms of femininity threatened masculine self-regard, whereas the fantasy of woman as maternal presence or erotic promise is comforting and suggestive of renewal. Charles Leland makes these associations clear:

> The child and the gypsy have no words in which to express their sense of nature and its charm, but they have this sense, and there are very, very few who, acquiring culture, retain it. And it is gradually disappearing from the world, *just as the old delicately sensuous, naïve, picturesque type of woman's beauty—the perfection of natural beauty—is rapidly vanishing in every country, and being replaced by the mingled real and unreal attractiveness of "cleverness," intellect, and fashion.* (G 12–13 [emphasis added])

Passive female beauty, to be savored as a landscape or village scene, to be taken in by the rambler or spectator, is part of an age that is "vanishing," just as the

FIGURE 18 Hubert von Herkomer, "A Gipsy Encampment on Putney Common." (From *The Graphic: An Illustrated Weekly Newspaper*, June 18, 1870)

FIGURE 19 Augustus John, *Lyric Fantasy*, ca. 1913–1914. (Tate Gallery, London. Art Resource, New York)

Gypsy and "old England" are disappearing. The Gypsy woman is allied with nature: if women are conceived of as generally more "natural" than men, then Gypsy women outdo their male counterparts in their closeness to both the spirit and the physicality of the natural world. In Watts-Dunton's *The Coming of Love*, the force that the poet calls "Natura Benigna" expresses itself through the Gypsy beauty Rhona Boswell.[61] Leland seems fairly precise about what threatens this form of femininity in modern life. In place of the picturesque beauty, the age has produced a New Woman, clever, up-to-date, and, unlike the child or Gypsy of Leland's imagining, articulate.

Although the sexual unconventionality of John's domestic arrangements had no exact parallel among the other lorists, Francis Groome, the son of the archdeacon of Suffolk, did run off to the Continent with Esmeralda Lock, and John Sampson, called by Arthur Symons the "Rabelais-rai," spent a good deal of time away from his wife and fathered a child with one of his protégées, Gladys Imlach.[62] The lorists' masculinist bohemianism and golden age fantasies of available but unthreatening female sexuality constitute, however, only one of the gender stories of the Gypsy Lore Society. The other salient narrative involves one of those women of cleverness and intellect to whom Leland opposes the phantasmal Gypsy woman. Sampson's role as mentor to a number of young women in the early years of the twentieth century was double-edged: his relationship to them had both a sexual and an intellectual dimension and, in one case at least, he helped nurture a scholar and leader of the Gypsy Lore Society. Dora Yates, who may have been in love with Sampson and certainly never got her due from the society as the stalwart who kept it going, nonetheless found a personal and professional identity through the scholarship of linguistics and folklore and the fellowship of Gypsies and lorists.[63]

Dora Esther Yates, born into the large Anglo-Jewish family that produced Herbert Samuel, Liberal politician and the first British High Commissioner to Palestine, as well as the molecular biologist Rosalind Franklin, entered the University of Liverpool in 1895 (at the age of sixteen), when only seventy of the six hundred full-time students were women.[64] She studied literature and languages and went on to earn a master's degree in 1900. After a stint as teacher in a girls' school, she returned to the university in 1906 as a tutor in English literature and worked as lecturer, librarian, and curator there until 1945. She held a kind of legendary status at Liverpool and was known for her work with refugees from Hitler's Europe as well as for her Gypsy scholarship and serendipitous professional life.[65] After retirement and until her death in 1974, she maintained an office in the university library as curator of the Scott Macfie Collection of Books on Gypsy Lore. Macfie was the lorist who had trained her to edit the *Journal of the Gypsy Lore Society*, which she did unofficially after his death in 1935 and officially beginning in 1955, when she was seventy-six. It might go without saying that of the 144 members of the society as revived in 1907, Yates was the last survivor.[66]

When Sampson recruited Yates for Gypsy research, oversaw her study of Romani, and sent her into the field as his research assistant, he enabled her to create a vocation and identity for herself outside both marriage and, strictly speaking, the confines of professional life. Just as Sampson and other male lorists gained recognition, scholarly respectability, and some social status from their knowledge of Romani and Gypsy lore and their creation of a learned society, so did Yates craft a life of independence and gain a modicum of celebrity through her stewardship of the Gypsy Lore Society and her scholarly pursuits beyond the university. The society provided her with social ties and a substitute family. She represents her mother and father as "harsh Victorian parents," and it is likely that her rebellion against them was considerably eased by the company of other like-minded rebels (GD 42). She recounts one semicomic episode in 1906 when she and Agnes Marston returned late at night from a trip to Blackpool, where they had gone to "collect specimens of foreign dialect" from some German Gypsies camped there, and discovered that both their families had locked them out of their homes: "we each found the door barred against us." Agnes spent the night in Edge-Hill railway station; Dora, in the garden of her parents' house. As a woman in her late twenties, on her way to being a spinster, Yates occupied a social position in limbo: neither dependent child nor wholly self-sufficient career woman. Sleeping in the garden seems a fit metaphor for her liminal role.

The new "science" of folklore afforded women opportunities to work as collectors and editors. In his history of British folklorists, Richard Dorson mentions, without commenting on the phenomenon, a considerable number of women who figured in the movement: Alice Gomme, Charlotte Burne, Mary Kingsley, Lady Isabella Persse Gregory, Mary Frere, Maive Stokes, and Rachel Busk, to name a few. As with anthropology, also a field with a disproportionate number of women pioneers, the newness of the enterprise and its largely extra-institutional setting made folklore hospitable to women. And like the female charity visitors and rent collectors, who in the London of the 1880s helped create the profession of social work, these collectors of folklore may have had or may have been assumed to have had the ability to approach and communicate with people outside the realm of middle-class life, with social inferiors or foreigners at home and abroad. They were allowed to act as intermediaries of a sort between acknowledged male professionals and objects of study or charity.

In "My Romani Sisters," a chapter in her memoir, Yates talks about her relationship with two of the Gypsy women to whom she was closest: Esmeralda Lock Groome and Rosie Griffiths. The latter, a devout Roman Catholic, worked as a hawker to support her family, nursed John Sampson in his final illness, and helped Yates collect stories for her Book of Gypsy Folk-Tales (GD 112). Yates reckons Griffith a Romany heroine for her vehement dedication to opposing false representations of Gypsy life in any form of popular culture:

FIGURE 20 Esmeralda Lock Groome. (Gypsy Lore Collection [SMGC Gypsy Families A–M. Groome.3]. Reproduced by courtesy of the University of Liverpool)

Dora Yates chose to include this photograph of Esmeralda Groome in *My Gypsy Days* (1953).

> Rosie's wrath was a scorching fire, and on one occasion I remember she actually put a stop to a picture that was being shown in a large cinema hall in Liverpool. [The film depicted a Gypsy bride and groom cutting their wrists to exchange blood during their marriage ceremony.] . . . With the courage of a lioness this small Gypsy woman rose in her seat and shouted out to a crowded audience: "It's a lie! It's a lie! You're paying your sixpences for looking at a hoax." . . . The manager was forced to ring the curtain down to save a disturbance. (GD 113)

If Yates saw Griffiths as a "sister" engaged, like her, in exposing the falsity of prevailing myths about Gypsy existence, she regarded Groome not as the femme fatale of West End music halls, where she had performed in the 1870s, but as a rich source of Gypsy lore and genealogies (GD 104) (figure 20). But she also acknowledged this woman, twice married to and twice separated from English

Gypsy lorists, as a canny ethnographer in her own right, her subjects the class of men—the "line of *tacho* [true] *Romano Rais*"—who had moved through her life (GD 106). For Rossetti, who painted her as Victor Hugo's Gypsy, Esmeralda, Groome was the timeless and fiery Romany beauty. For consumers of sensation, she was the seductress who weakened the resolve of more than one Englishman. But for Yates, she was the "born rebel" who "fearlessly wrested from life anything and everything she wanted" and commanded attention not just with her looks but with her unforgettable voice (GD 99–100). Not only was Yates one of the most important and certainly the most unsung Gypsy lorist, but she understood and represented Gypsy women in a way that rescued them from the imagery of bohemian adventure.[67]

The Question of Racism

The Gypsy lorists' fascination with authenticity, nostalgia for a golden age, and anxieties about the impending disappearance of a pastoral, preindustrial way of life—of which the Gypsies seemed symbolic—led them to fetishize a notion of racial purity and to romanticize the primitive. They have been represented by critics as anti-assimilationist and as indifferent to the need for either reform or political action to improve conditions of Romany existence.[68] If lorists believed that it was desirable, above all, to preserve the "purity" of Gypsy culture and to protect the pure-blooded Gypsies who best exemplified it, then they would want to promote separation between Gypsy and non-Gypsy and to magnify distinctions between, for instance, speakers of "deep" Romani and those of a hybrid slang, the latter of mixed inheritance. But the lorists' commitment to the idea of the genuine Gypsy was blatantly undercut by their own research and experience—for example, on the effect of intermarriage on authenticity of language and degree of assimilation—and a number of them conceded this contradiction from time to time.[69] Did the Gypsy lorists' obsession with purity set the stage for a more virulent form of racism? How similar was their concept of race to that of Continental theorists of the Gypsy question? And what were the implications of the lorists' work for state policies and practices?

Historians of Gypsies and of their treatment under the law in nineteenth- and twentieth-century Britain have focused their attention on the legislative campaign of George Smith of Coalville, the leading Victorian "reformist" on Gypsy matters.[70] Briefly put, Smith believed that civilization had left the Gypsies far behind and that it was up to Parliament to enforce stability, cleanliness, education, and morality in their lives. On almost a yearly basis, from 1885 until his death in 1895, Smith promoted, without success, a bill that would have mandated the education of Romany children; registration of movable dwellings; regulation of sleeping arrangements with regard to space and sex; inspection of dwellings for health, sanitary, and moral irregularities; and encouragement of permanent settlement.[71] The bill failed repeatedly, in part because many saw it as unenforceable or redundant (there were already laws on the books that in theory prevented Gypsies from camping on certain public grounds, for example). Others opposed Smith's law because it was harsh, invasive, unnecessary, or an infringement of individual rights.[72] In *In Gipsy Tents*, Francis Groome devotes almost an entire chapter to Smith and lambastes him on two counts. First, Smith lumps all itinerant groups, not bothering to distinguish between real Gypsies and the common vagrants who often impersonate them (GT 231). Second, he fails to understand that the Gypsies are victims and not perpetrators of crime. "Why, having 'no heart to feel,'" he writes with bitter irony, "I hitherto had foolishly contrasted the scores of English Gipsies murderously hanged, with the one English Gipsy ever hanged for murder; I had deemed it rather creditable . . . that so few of them had ever been imprisoned for heavier crimes than fortune-telling or stopping in the midst of sticks and grass. Bah! It takes philanthropy to know that this keeping out of gaol implies incendiarism" (GT 242).

Because Smith was the contemporary of late-nineteenth-century lorists, his view of the Gypsies and his activities have habitually been considered in tandem with theirs. Clearly, as Groome's comments suggest, the lorists themselves took note of the proposals that Smith offered, as well as of the image of the Gypsies that he propagated. It is striking, however, that historians like David Mayall and sociologists like Thomas Acton not only equate the assimilationist Smith and the anti-assimilationist lorists, but, in some instances, find the lorists wanting by comparison. Mayall sees an investment in racial purity—the effort to distinguish between pure and mixed Gypsies—as the essential similarity between the lorists and Smith. Both blamed the mixed Gypsies, he asserts, for the worst offenses, criminal and otherwise, and Smith's followers often exempted the true Gypsies from their demands for assimilation.[73] Acton, focusing on Groome's reaction to Smith in *In Gipsy Tents*, remarks that the "ironic Oxford drop-out [Groome]" could never himself have led any kind of crusade and never considered the Gypsies capable of "pressure-group activity or self-organisation." Nevertheless, Smith and Groome fundamentally concurred in regarding the Gypsies as a people without agency, "a people to be done unto rather than to do." Acton ultimately claims that Smith regarded the Gypsies as equals, "possessed of the same rights and duties and possibilities as himself," whereas the lorists viewed them as "congenitally primitive" and nearer to the animals than to any other Europeans.[74] As the phrases of Charles Leland confirm, some, although certainly not all, lorists represented Romany in a dehumanizing and degrading way (whatever their conscious motives), but whether Smith viewed them as his equals is, at the very least, debatable.

Acton's desire to credit Smith with human sympathy, "despite his own propaganda," leads him to ignore the lorists' accomplishments as researchers, scholars, and defenders of Romany integrity. Their project was one of recovery, collection, and preservation. Despite their romanticizing rhetoric and contradictory statements about purity and authenticity, they stood against the persecution of the Romany and acquired serious knowledge of language and customs through their close contact with British and Welsh Gypsies. Acton concedes that "for a picture of Gypsy life in the period," one must go to Groome, Borrow, and others.[75] Mayall, intent on seeing British attitudes toward Gypsies in this period as monolithic, distorts the picture. He exaggerates the lorists' antipathy to what he calls "half-bred Gypsies," ignoring their frequent acknowledgments of the complexity of Gypsy lineage and its relation to the persistence of Gypsy culture. He also overestimates the degree to which Smith cared about differences among Gypsies and ultimately concedes that he was not much concerned with "subtleties of distinction."[76] Indeed, Groome's charge that Smith fails to distinguish between Gypsies and other travelers, tinkers, and itinerants is valid. Here the question of the equivocal moral value of searching for authentic Romany culture comes into play: there is clearly an insidious side to even the rhetoric of the "pure" Gypsy, but the lorists' insistence on distinguishing between Gypsies and non-Gypsies also serves to acknowledge Romany as an identity and a culture worth recognizing, studying, and preserving.

In his discussion of Smith's campaign and the Gypsy lorists' lack of interest in "Romani self-assertion," Acton makes the point that, nonetheless, Gypsies in turn-of-the-century Britain "escaped . . . the kind of regulation and state interference which was imposed on French Gypsies at about the same time, and on Scandinavian and east European Gypsies after the Second World War."[77] English attitudes—however ambivalent, hostile, or racist—had consequences for the Gypsies less oppressive and less destructive than the treatment they endured in nations on the Continent. The increasing harassment of Gypsies in other European countries beginning in 1900 can be inferred from Dora Yates's memoir. She describes three Gypsy migrations from the Continent to Britain between 1906 and 1934 and her consequent encounters with "foreign nomads" in and around Liverpool. One, in 1906, involved the group of German Gypsies who camped in Blackpool. In 1911, a band of relatively prosperous coppersmiths from Romania arrived in Liverpool by way of Marseilles, and in 1934 a Greek contingent appeared, having already traveled to Australia and back to Europe. English authorities reacted slightly differently to each influx, twice calling on Yates to act as interpreter, and, although constables evicted some of these groups from certain sites, did not deport the foreign-born Gypsies (GD 41). Mayall remarks that British antipathy to Gypsies increased during the period of foreign migration, from 1886 to 1911, the result ultimately of dramatically inhospitable circumstances in the countries from which they came.[78] Yates's responses to the immigrants varied. She clearly admired the handsome and resourceful Romanians and found the Greeks crude, "low-caste," and untrustworthy (feeling their "nimble fingers" as they searched her anatomy for coins), but she filled her "collector's bag" with lore from every new wave from the Continent (GD 125–29).

Angus Fraser, in his brief history of the Gypsy Lore Society, observes that the work of German and Austrian gypsiologists had taken on an insidious cast by the turn of the twentieth century. Criminology had played a part in Gypsy studies in Germany from the mid-nineteenth century, but, in the last decades of the nineteenth and the first of the twentieth, criminologists in Germany began to create institutions that would identify, classify, and help weed out large numbers of individual Gypsies.[79] In 1899, the German government established the Gypsy Information Agency to enforce the registration of all Gypsies. The director of the agency, Alfred Dillman, then published a register of all Gypsies as his *Zegeuner-Buch*, a document that emphasized criminal tendencies and warned especially against "mixed-race" Gypsies. It is likely that, as Fraser believes, these activities were "the first steps in the direction of the Final Solution," but they also suggest an approach alien to the English lorists.[80] This kind of racial science is reflected, too, in an article clipped by Gypsy lorist Henry Crofton for his scrapbook of Gypsy news from around the world. It reports on A. Weisbach, chief physician at the Austro-Hungarian Hospital in Constantinople, who sorted Gypsies, Jews, Patagonians, Maoris, and others according to various measurements: pulse, height, head circumference, length and breadth of nose, and width of chest.[81] Crofton underlined the "Zingari" measurements, which may indicate his interest in and even openness to the approach, but these methods never did figure in British gypsiology.

When the Gypsy Lore Society and its journal were revived in 1907, the new honorary secretary, Andrew Scott Macfie, made certain gestures toward repudiating the criminological and overtly racist strands of European Gypsy research.[82] The British Gypsy lorists' resistance to these strains in the study of Gypsies before the world wars certainly had something to do with the aggressive racism of the Germans' approach, but it also had to do with the lorists' dedication to the preservation, rather than the eradication, of Gypsies. Their belief, however shaky, in the difference between pure and "mongrel" Romany culture appeared to trigger no impulse to criminalize or censure Gypsy life and certainly not to expunge it. The Nazis' posture toward the "purity" of Gypsies shifted altogether, from an intention to spare pure Gypsies to a policy, whether ultimately carried out or not, of sparing individuals of mixed origin. They first deemed Gypsies undesirable on racial grounds, because they were not Aryans, but then placed them in the category of "a-socials" when their Aryan origins could no longer be denied. When their "race"—Aryan—was considered an asset, the pure Gypsies were not marked for extermination; when purity ceased to mean anything and the Gypsies' social and behavioral characteristics became paramount, lack of purity and a dose of German blood became virtues.[83] Where there was a will to exterminate, there was a way, and the discourse of purity was but a pretext.

The distance between the Victorians' Gypsy lorism and the Nazis' annihilation of more than 500,000 Gypsies seems vast, and yet the horror of genocide makes unavoidable the question of the lorists' brand of racialist thinking. The discourse of racial purity joins these two eras uncomfortably, but not, I have tried to suggest, definitively. In the end, it was the lorists' enduring conviction that the Romany represented a pristine and Edenic way of life that creates a kind of dissonance in the context of the Holocaust and its aftermath. Dora Yates and Augustus John were among the few early lorists who lived through World War II. In *Chiaroscuro*, his collection of autobiographical essays, John comments bitterly on Hitler's success in wiping out "as far as possible" the Gypsies of Germany and Poland. In England, he continues, persecution is less drastic but just as effective: we kill the Gypsies' spirit through "the present drive in the cause of uniformity, subservience and the sedentary life," so "before long there will be no dark and friendly strangers encamped in the green lane, and . . . our children will be the poorer."[84] John's concerns, genuine though they may have been, come across as blindly self-referential. British Gypsies may still be alive, he concedes, but they are no longer so easily observed by us, no longer figures in the set piece of rural life to be watched and savored by non-Gypsy lovers of Gypsy life.

Yates's agitated response to the attempted annihilation of European Gypsies was more serious and more urgent than John's lament, perhaps because, as a Jew, she could imagine herself in their position. In an article written in 1949 for American Jews, she informs her readers about the Nazi persecution of the Gypsies and appeals to them as Jews, another "isolated race" that has experienced "miraculous survivals."[85] Information about the extermination of Gypsies during the war was still hard to come by, and Yates marshaled evidence from informants, letters, and articles in the *Journal of the Gypsy Lore Society* to document the atrocities that the Sinti and Roma had suffered at the hands of the Nazis. After presenting her stark and gruesome case about what had happened in Birkenau and Buchenwald, Yates pleads with her American readers to treat the Gypsies among them with "decency and respect" and, above all, protect them from extinction through assimilation. "Since peace came to the world," she writes, "many hidebound government officials seem to regard the Gypsies as an 'anachronism.' There are protection societies for wild birds, wild flowers, and other rarities—but there is no protection, even in America, for wild Gypsies."[86] In the original version of her article, Yates follows this plea with a quotation from Arthur Symons, an often used passage from his essay "In Praise of Gypsies": "The Gypsy represents Nature before Civilization. He is the wanderer whom all of us who are poets or love the wind are summed up in. He does what we dream. He is the last romance left in the world. His is the only free race."[87] We cannot be sure whether Yates's editor excised these lines because of space constraints or because Symons's words are jarring, to say the least, in 1949, in an article about the slaughter of more than 500,000 Gypsies. Yates seems wholly oblivious to the cruel irony of the last line. That this aging lorist could still think of freedom as the distinguishing feature of Romany existence speaks to the power of this late-nineteenth-century fantasy and, in the end, to the limits of lorists' identification with the people they studied and whose cause they championed.

The Gypsy lorists' discourse of purity did not open the door to virulent racism or persecution, but it did help foster a relationship of separateness rather than identification between British lorist and British Gypsy. Walter Scott's intimation that the Gypsies of Scotland were a hybrid people and his invention of the ur-mother Meg Merrilies blurred the absolute distinction between self and other, non-Gypsy and Gypsy, in *Guy Mannering*. John Clare and Matthew Arnold cast the Gypsy as an object of emulation and empathy, and both poets represented the Gypsy as subject to the shifts and vicissitudes of history. George Eliot's inability finally to imagine the Gypsy as a modern figure grew, paradoxically, out of her intense identification with the pariah-Gypsy. Arnold and George Borrow conjured the scholar-gypsy, the observer who nonetheless becomes what he studies. The Arnold of "The Scholar-Gipsy"—as opposed to the Arnold of "Resignation"—began to imagine the Gypsy as changeless and as the antithesis of and antidote to modern life. Following closely this notion of the pristine and Edenic Romany world, the lorists projected their quarrel with modernity onto the Gypsies and saw them as both primitive and pure. Persisting in the need to oppose Gypsy "Nature" to British "Civilization," they obscured the humanity of those whose language, culture, and customs they wished to save.

6

The Phantom Gypsy

Invisibility, Writing, and History

I N MATTHEW ARNOLD'S "The Scholar-Gipsy," the "wild brotherhood" of
wanderers that welcomes the sometime Oxford student into its ranks never
appears. The Gypsies of the Cumner Hills are represented in the poem
only by the image of their "smoked tents," glimpsed from afar and taken as
the metonymic confirmation of their presence. The scholar, himself a ghostly
figure who mediates between poet and invisible Gypsies, serves as the latter's
surrogate, his "gipsy-lore" and mysterious immortality proof of the Gypsies'
existence and influence. He is the only link to the evanescent Gypsies, whose
identity is, as a result, greatly attenuated in the poem. The phantasmal nature
of Arnold's Gypsies presaged a thoroughgoing elision of Gypsy experience in
favor of mythic or literary representation in British culture by the last decades
of the nineteenth century.[1] Emptied of reference to personal observation or contemporary social realities, the literary representation of Gypsies came to rely
increasingly on two-dimensional caricatures, intertextual allusions, shorthand
tropes, and simple fantasy. Even the most sympathetic chroniclers, even those
who had firsthand knowledge of Gypsy life, clung to certain comforting and
yet wholly indefensible myths, like Dora Yates's post-Holocaust dream of the
"only free race," the "last romance." Their powerful need to see the Gypsies as
a restorative antidote to modern life—an idea that is also traceable to Arnold's
poem—eclipsed the complexity of Gypsies' lived experience and, in part, the
distinctiveness and humanity of British Gypsies.

Four texts, taken together, trace the movement from a tendency to obscure
Gypsy experience to an acknowledgment of the need to accommodate Gypsy
subjectivity. The iconic or symbolic use of Gypsies certainly did not end with
the twentieth century (it surely survives even in contemporary literary texts), but

there was a discernible retreat from the easy deployment of Gypsy stereotype and caricature.[2] In Arthur Conan Doyle's story "The Adventure of the Speckled Band," the Gypsies who are central to both the title and the resolution of the mystery never appear, while D. H. Lawrence's novella *The Virgin and the Gipsy* both exploits and debunks the cultural myths of Gypsies' elemental passion, association with nature, anonymity, and inarticulateness. The voices of Gypsies themselves are heard in the autobiography of Gordon Boswell, a British Gypsy, and the reflections of John Megel, an American Gypsy. The two literary narratives, Conan Doyle's and Lawrence's, rewrite in obvious and striking ways Walter Scott's *Guy Mannering* and George Eliot's *The Mill on the Floss*, respectively, and thereby illustrate the deeply literary and allusive nature of Gypsy representation. The last three texts—Lawrence's, Boswell's, and Megel's—comment either directly or obliquely on the issue of Gypsy literacy and imagine it as the pivot of self-expression and self-consciousness. Megel's piece makes a link not only between trauma and history but between writing and history and, beyond that, between knowing the past and possibilities for the future. He strives to recast Romany identity and subjectivity through the claiming of history and the illumination of the past.

Metonymic Representation

Reputed to be Arthur Conan Doyle's best loved story among ordinary readers and Sherlock Holmes aficionados alike, "The Adventure of the Speckled Band" (1891) turns on an erroneous theory and invisible murder suspects.[3] Holmes, called on by a young woman, Helen Stoner, to investigate the strange death of her twin sister at the estate of their dissolute stepfather, Dr. Roylott, initially concentrates his suspicions on the "wandering gypsies" who camp on the doctor's grounds and serve as his sometime companions. Roylott, descended from a long line of degenerate and profligate aristocrats, managed to obtain a medical degree and went on to practice medicine, ultimately quite successfully, in India. A scandal involving the doctor's fatal beating of a manservant and his subsequent incarceration for the crime sent him back to England, where he lives, now a widower, with his two stepdaughters in the ancestral home of Stoke Moran. While the young women remain unmarried and under his roof, the doctor benefits from his wife's—their mother's—considerable wealth through an annuity; when they marry, as Helen's dead sister was about to do, he will no longer receive the allowance.

Given the criminal history and obvious financial motive of the doctor (Helen is also about to marry and fears for her safety), Holmes's suspicions might well have fallen immediately on Roylott, but Conan Doyle throws a red herring Holmes's way. When Helen discovered her sister close to death, the stricken woman called out, "Oh, my God! Helen! It was the band! The speckled band!"[4] Holmes probes the meaning of this cryptic phrase and asks Helen if the Gypsies were in the area at that time. Yes, she replies; she, too, had wondered if the word "band" refers to the Gypsies. It might describe not only the group, but the spotted kerchiefs worn by the Gypsies on their heads: they both constitute and wear a speckled band. Holmes concludes that the Gypsies, Roylott's companions, may have acted as his surrogates in doing away with his stepdaughter. Holmes and Watson pursue this line of reasoning in their investigation, which now takes them to the scene of the crime, Stoke Moran, although each man sees "many objections to any such theory" (356). The objections remain obscure, and the reader, typically, has no idea what Holmes is thinking as he goes through the ingenious process of discovering the mode and perpetrator of the murder.

The murderer turns out, of course, to be Roylott himself or, rather, the Indian puff adder—the "speckled band"—he unleashed in his stepdaughter's room through a vent. Holmes catches him in the act of trying to repeat the assault, this time on Helen Stoner, and is able to reverse the adder's course so that it poisons the doctor. They find Roylott dead in his room, the spotted snake wrapped around his forehead in a gruesome parody of the Gypsies' reputed headgear. As John A. Hodgson has pointed out, the phrase "speckled band" is rhetorically misleading, "a false scent," but the visual image of the coiled adder redeems—indeed, proves partially true—Holmes's initial hypothesis (342).

As a term referring to both a scarf-like headdress and a cluster or an assembly of wanderers, "band" functioned commonly as a metonym for Gypsies. Like caravans, wood fires, gold earrings, swarthy skin, Arnold's "smoked tents," and tinkering, the word "band" conjures up the Gypsy without the need for any explanation or substantiation of the actual link between individuals and the accoutrements with which they are automatically associated. George Eliot makes comic use of this metonymic way of evoking the Gypsy in *Silas Marner*, when the folks of Raveloe wish to invent a suspect for the theft of Silas's gold and spin the tale of a peddler who wears gold earrings and has curly black hair. Kenneth Grahame deploys a broader kind of comedy in his Edwardian elegy for a pastoral England, *The Wind in the Willows*, when Toad becomes smitten with a gypsy caravan "shining with newness, painted a canary-yellow picked out with green, and red wheels." "There's real life for you," Toad exclaims, "embodied in that little cart. The open road, the dusty highway, the heath, the common, the hedgerows, the rolling downs! Camps, villages, towns, cities! Here to-day, up and off to somewhere else to-morrow!"[5] Grahame lampoons the early-twentieth-century craze for caravanning by launching, through Toad, a laundry list of images and tropes associated with Gypsy life, all of them inspired by the appearance of a caravan. And in *The Wind in the Willows*, as in *Silas Marner*, there is not a Gypsy in sight. Eliot's Gypsy is apocryphal; Grahame's, simply unnecessary. It is striking, although not surprising, then, that Gypsies never actually appear in "The Speckled Band."

The story's metonymic use of the phrase "speckled band" is underscored by the absence of Gypsies in the narrative. Helen Stoner's initial account to Holmes includes the salient feature of the Gypsies' presence on the family estate; her stepfather gives "these vagabonds leave to encamp upon the few acres of bramble-covered land . . . and would accept in return the hospitality of their tents, wandering away with them sometimes for weeks on end" (350). Aside from the dying sister's words and Holmes's articulation of the theory of Gypsy guilt, there is no further mention of the Gypsies and there is never a rendering of them that is not secondhand. Holmes does not see them in his journey to the estate, nor does anyone glimpse them from the window of the women's bedrooms at Stoke Moran. How, then, does the story sustain the possibility—even the likelihood—of the Gypsies' guilt when a more obvious suspect exists in Roylott, when we are told that Holmes himself has doubts about his theory, and when we are shown no actual Gypsies to imagine as the perpetrators? There is no evidence to link them to the crime, and the absent Gypsies can exhibit no suspicious behavior for detective or reader to observe.

Conan Doyle's story depends on its ability to divert attention from the true solution, and so, of course, it requires a red herring. But what interests me here is why Gypsies—even invisible ones—serve as an ideal "false scent," the "band" an easy shorthand by which to conjure criminal suspects. The story is able to rely on a reader's knowledge of the iconography associated with Gypsies, both because of the stereotypes at large in the culture and because of literary precedent and allusion. Gypsies appear as likely companions to the dissolute Dr. Roylott, given their bands' mythic role as a haven for dropouts, bohemians, and those generally in retreat from respectability. As two critics have put it, Roylott's friendship with the Gypsies is indicative of his degeneracy and "presented as simultaneously *self-explanatory* and suspicious."[6] Although Gypsies were not indeed much associated with murder, they were linked to criminality, especially theft and cheating, and to base, semihuman impulses. When Helen Stoner tells Holmes about her stepfather's odd taste for the company of Gypsies, she follows this comment directly with the information that he also "has a passion for Indian animals . . . and has at this moment a cheetah and a baboon, which wander freely over his grounds" (350). The doctor is a collector of both Gypsies and animals—exotic species out of place on a gentleman's grounds, creatures that, whether human or not, can be mentioned in the same breath and conflated as signifiers of Roylott's immorality and decadence.

Readers of "The Speckled Band" might also be expected to recognize, either consciously or not, that the story rewrites Walter Scott's *Guy Mannering* or, at least, relies on it as a precursor in the representation of Gypsies and in their handy use for the purposes of a mystery plot. In Scott's novel, a Gypsy band makes its home on the estate of a laird and is suspected of perpetrating a crime: the kidnapping of the laird's young son. Scott exploits the common association of Gypsies with the abduction of non-Gypsy children in order to set his plot in motion and, like Conan Doyle after him, establish a red herring. Just as Conan Doyle's Gypsies prove to be innocent, so are the Gypsies of *Guy Mannering*. The ultimate culprit in both stories is not a reviled "race" of wanderers, but the lord of the manor, although in Scott's novel, of course, the "lord" is an arriviste and not a faded aristocrat. *Guy Mannering* also establishes and makes use of an implicit link between Gypsies and the experience of empire or, more specifically, India, the Gypsies' presumed place of origin, and "The Speckled Band" follows suit. The astrologer Guy Mannering spends many years as a soldier in India before returning to Ellangowan, the scene of his earlier predictions, and Harry Bertram, the kidnapped heir, finds his way to India as well. Dr. Roylott, too, has spent a period of his life in India, and both he and Mannering return from empire after killing—or apparently killing—someone. Mannering believes that he killed a young man named Brown—really Harry Bertram—in a duel over his wife, and Roylott murdered a butler. The Gypsies on Roylott's estate are likened implicitly to the exotic animals that the doctor imported from India—a comparison made possible in part by assumptions about the Gypsies' homeland.[7] In *Guy Mannering*, it is through Meg Merrilies's appearance that Scott establishes the Gypsy tie to India: when Brown/Bertram sees her again after an absence of many years, he recognizes her, either from a dream, as he says, or from his "recollection . . . of the strange figures I have seen in our Indian pagodas."[8] Both Scott and Conan Doyle capitalize on the whiff of scandal that can hover over those who return from empire and yoke the plot of empire to the mysteries of landed estates at home through the figure of the Gypsy.

If Conan Doyle's readers knew *Guy Mannering* or even its cultural legacy (remember that the novel and, especially, its best known character, Meg Merrilies, were enormously popular), they knew enough to read the signs of potential Gypsy culpability in "The Speckled Band." They also were primed for the ultimate exoneration of the Gypsies, although, this time, had no investment in the Gypsies' innocence. Here the contrast with Scott's novel is telling. Not only does Scott give us the colorful and charismatic Meg Merrilies, the larger-than-life Gypsy sibyl who helps raise and rescue Harry Bertram, but he includes in his narrative the history of the Scottish Gypsies and the drama of their expulsion from the laird's estate. In so doing, he creates considerable sympathy for the novel's Gypsies, despite their quick disappearance from the scene and Meg's convenient death. Harry's childhood attachment to Meg and identification as wanderer and exile further heighten the sense that the novel mounts a subtle criticism of the dispossession of the Gypsies and the unfair suspicions that plague them. "The Speckled Band," however, offers no actual Gypsies with whom to sympathize or identify. The reader's reaction to the discovery of their innocence is likely to be an intellectual appreciation of a mystery cleverly solved and a false lead effectively deployed rather than any pleasure or relief associated with the Gypsies themselves. Further, to the extent that the story or its more sympathetic characters express any attitude toward the generic Gypsy, it is one of dismissiveness and callous indifference. Helen Stoner's words conflate the Stoke Moran Gypsies and her stepfather's Indian animals, and she implicitly condemns the former as Roylott's companions in dissoluteness. The weight of cultural prejudice, combined with a well-established tradition of literary evocation, makes possible Conan Doyle's metonymic representation of the Gypsies in the story. This method of characterization does not invite the reader to regard the suspect Gypsies as either human or individuated: it is simply a device, and a highly successful one, for putting the reader off the scent. "The Speckled Band" hinges on the Gypsy as a literary referent that has been wholly drained of historical or even contemporary social meaning.

Six years after the publication of "The Adventure of the Speckled Band," Bram Stoker appears to have taken inspiration from its use of Gypsies for the early chapters of *Dracula* (1897). Jonathan Harker, held prisoner in the count's castle, seizes on the possibility of using a "band of Szgany [east European Gypsies] . . . encamped in the courtyard" to convey some letters to friends in England. Harker has noted that these particular Transylvanians, "allied to the ordinary gipsies all over the world," tend to "attach themselves to some great noble"—like Roylott or the laird of Ellangowan—and are both fearless and godless.[9] Failing to heed the import of his own research, he allows himself to be tricked by the Szgany, who deliver his letters right into the hands of the count and then transport him in his coffin away from the castle. Although, unlike Conan Doyle's Gypsies, Stoker's Szgany both appear and speak, they resemble the Gypsies of Stoke Moran in their loyalty to an evil landlord, their lawlessness, and their wholly fictional genealogy.

Naming and Writing

The eponymous Gypsy in D. H. Lawrence's novella *The Virgin and the Gipsy* (1930) also wears a band, but his yellow-and-red silk kerchief is tied around his neck. Indeed, the virgin Yvette Saywell's first glimpse of him in the narrative draws on a number of visual clichés of Gypsy representation. Driving a cart and horse next to the automobile that Yvette and her smart set of "young people" occupy, he is a "black, loose-bodied, handsome" Gypsy with a "thin black moustache," a "dark face under his dark-green cap," a flamboyant scarf, and "loose, light shoulders."[10] The pairing of cart and car immediately suggests the warring relationship between nature and modernity that occupies Lawrence both in this and in other works and for which the trope of the Gypsy, as we have seen, has often been enlisted. The Gypsy's insouciance and compelling physical presence have a predictable effect on Yvette. When she sees him, her "heart [gives] a jump," and, as her eyes meet his, "something [takes] fire in her breast" (33–34). The language of Lawrentian passion coalesces with the metaphorical baggage that had attached itself to the Gypsy over decades. Just as Conan Doyle did not have to elaborate on—or even produce—the Gypsy suspects in "The Speckled Band," Lawrence can signal with considerable economy the sexual appeal of the virgin's Gypsy. Lawrence's is not the lawless Gypsy stereotype of the Holmes story, but a male version of the objectified erotic beauty and passive seductress favored by Gypsy lorists and others. A first incarnation of the gamekeeper Mellors in *Lady Chatterley's Lover* (1928), this Gypsy initially appears in Lawrence's novella as a sexual object and remains that way for much of the narrative in the mind and desires of Yvette Saywell.[11] What interests me is the way Lawrence milks this virtually ready-made imagery of charismatic, socially marginal masculinity throughout the narrative, only to expose it as cliché and fantasy in the end.[12]

Lawrence's story proceeds according to an apparent opposition of forces that vie for Yvette's psychic allegiance and future. On one side is her mother, referred to throughout most of the novella as "she-who-was-Cynthia," a free-spirited woman who left her vicar husband and two very young daughters to run off with a "young and penniless man." The scandal of her mother's disappearance haunts Yvette both as a source of guilt (the sisters think she left "because their mother found them negligible") and as a temptation. The mother, dangerous and selfish but also glamorous and vivid, paved a path that the daughter might follow, and the Gypsy whom Yvette glimpses on the road appears as the likely means of the daughter's replication of the mother's abandonment of respectable life.

On the other side is respectability itself: the smothering domestic world over which her aggrieved father, pious aunt, and, above all, pinched and life-denying Granny preside. The rectory as locus of stultifying and decaying life is crucial to Lawrence's evocation of this oppressive familial domain. Yvette, lying on her bed and thinking that she would like to be a Gypsy, considers that wandering in a caravan and sleeping in a camp, with a man who "never lived in a house," would be preferable to remaining in the rectory, against which her heart turned "hard with repugnance":

> She loathed these houses with their indoor sanitation and their bathrooms, and their extraordinary repulsiveness. She hated the rectory, and everything it implied. The whole stagnant, sewerage sort of life, where sewerage is never mentioned, but where it seems to smell from the centre of every two-legged inmate, from Granny to the servants, was foul. If gypsies had no bathrooms, at least they had no sewerage. There was fresh air. In the rectory there was *never* fresh air. And in the souls of the people, the air was stale till it stank. (52)

Indoor plumbing becomes emblematic of both psychic putrefaction and hypocrisy. The fresh air of a Gypsy encampment might remove the actual smells and moral contradictions of civilized life. At the heart of her settled, housebound world, Yvette thinks, is the domesticated sewer, placing filth in the center of things but hiding, never acknowledging, its presence.

Which of these lives will claim her? The choice that confronts her is familiar, and its literary and folkloric antecedents are clearly alluded to in the story. The narrative compares her longing for escape explicitly with the Lady of Shalott's and implicitly with Maggie Tulliver's. Like the lady, Yvette is trapped in her home, staring out the window (albeit not through a reflection) and "imag[ining] that someone would come along singing *Tirra-lirra!* or something equally intelligent, by the river" (62).[13] Like Maggie, she contemplates running off with the Gypsies to flee her stultifying home and feels herself more akin to the vagabonds that live on the periphery of settled society than to her own family. As critics have remarked, the novella's debt to George Eliot's novel is most apparent in the flood that concludes each narrative.[14] Although the flood in *The Mill on the Floss* can be understood to represent the rush of female desire—Maggie's desire for her brother and for a return to childhood unity— her childish Gypsy fantasies have little to do with sexual longing. The elements that Lawrence takes from both Tennyson's poem and Eliot's novel were also readily gleaned from the well-known Irish folk song "The Raggle Taggle Gypsy," in which a lord's bride runs off with a wandering Gypsy. When the aggrieved husband tracks down his wife in a "wide open field," he demands of her why she left her house, her land, her money, her comfortable bed, and her wedded lord, and she responds:

> Yerra what do I care for a goose feather bed
> what do I care for your blankets
> For tonight I'll lie in a wide open field
> In the arms of my raggle taggle Gypsy-O.[15]

Lawrence's motif, in which a respectable woman contemplates running off with a sexually compelling Gypsy and accepting a life of vagabondage over one of privilege, derives as much from folk legend as from literary precursors. With this folk narrative embedded in the consciousness of his readers, Lawrence can signal easily its likely conclusion—some form of consummation between the Gypsy and the lady—and then, as we will see, subvert and revise this predictable outcome.

The story's revision of the Gypsy myth coincides with its complication of the apparent duality of forces—open-road bohemianism and suffocating domesticity—that compete for Yvette's allegiance. Indeed, it is through Yvette's eyes that we see the Gypsy as the scandalous alternative to the stifling world of the rectory, the potential reprise of the "young and penniless man" who rescued—or stole—her mother. Through free indirect discourse, the narrative portrays Yvette's Gypsy as the dark, brooding, sexually potent man who has designs on her virginity, but when the story provides a different view of him, the easy dichotomy of raw and cooked, nature and civilization, begins to break down (70). Major Eastwood, the blond, Nordic companion of the wealthy, spoiled "Jewess" who encounters Yvette as she is about to enter the Gypsy's cart, had previous experience of the Gypsy that casts him in a role far removed from caravan and fortune-telling. A groom in Eastwood's artillery regiment during World War I, the Gypsy suddenly becomes, in the major's telling, a man of skill and mastery, with an institutional identity and a history. So successfully does this shifted angle of vision remake the Gypsy's character that Lawrence would repeat the fact of a military past for Mellors in *Lady Chatterley*.[16] Eastwood describes the Gypsy not only as "the best man we had, with horses," but as a man whose toughness enabled him to defeat death: "Nearly died of pneumonia. I thought he *was* dead. He's a resurrected man to me. I'm a resurrected man myself. . . . I was buried for twenty hours under snow" (107). No longer only an object of desire or an agent of liberatory feeling, the Gypsy is now seen to be as resilient as the major himself and to possess powers of rebirth and renewal.

It is ultimately the Gypsy's power to revivify and not his sexual potency that redeems Yvette. In the story's climactic flood, a harbinger of spring like the snowdrops that dot the landscape and the Gypsies' imminent departure from their winter camp, the Gypsy saves Yvette's life and brings renewal to her family. Although some readers have understood the flood and the attendant physical intimacy between Yvette and the Gypsy as a sexual climax, it seems clear that what transpires between them is not the sexual consummation that the narrative has led us to expect. The events of the flood defy expectations, both because the couple's coming together fails to result in sexual union and because the Gypsy saves Yvette not by rescuing her from her home but by leading her toward its very center—the chimney, the hearth. When the floodwater begins to invade the Saywells' house and it begins to crumble, the Gypsy coaxes Yvette toward "the back chimney . . . [because] the chimney will stand" (133). At the heart of the house, a sanctuary from destruction, they find Yvette's bedroom, with its narrow fireplace against the wall. Disturbing the opposition of home and freedom, Lawrence stages Yvette's salvation in her own house, in her own room.

In the bedroom, the Gypsy removes his sodden clothes, urges Yvette to do the same, rubs his flesh to warm himself, and then warms her. In a gesture that, in another key, would inevitably be sexual, the Gypsy's ministrations to her are tender, protective, and life-giving: "With his towel he began to rub her, himself shaking all over, but holding her gripped by the shoulder, and slowly, numbedly rubbing her tender body, even trying to rub up into some dryness the pitiful hair of her small head" (135). As they dry themselves and the waters recede, they move to the bed, where, again, the climax that might be sexual appears to be something else. Yvette is shuddering and convulsed, dangerously close to dying of the cold, and the Gypsy wraps his naked limbs around her body to warm her. He, too, shudders, until the warmth they derive from each other relaxes them, and they are revived and "pass[. . .] away into sleep" (138). The emphatic nakedness, the possibility of sexual union, and the language of orgasm—shudder, convulsion—make plausible an ambiguous reading of the scene.[17] I think, however, that Lawrence seduces us into such a reading as a way of heightening his refusal of the cliché (a cliché that he has partly invented and then dilates on in *Lady Chatterley*, not with a raggle-taggle Gypsy, but with a man of the people).

In Lawrence's revision of the conclusion to *The Mill on the Floss*, the heroine not only survives but is able to reconcile with her family as a result of the cataclysm of the flood. But Lawrence's novella reproduces faithfully another aspect of Eliot's novel: the debunking of Gypsy myth. As Carol Siegel puts it, both Maggie and Yvette discover in the end that "beneath the surface strangeness the gypsies are ordinary Englishmen."[18] Maggie learns this after she runs off to Dunlow Common to join a Gypsy band; Yvette, after she receives a letter from the Gypsy once he has left town and moved on. In a gesture that parallels the story's defiance of romantic expectation, the letter explodes a number of myths of Gypsy identity. This man—regarded by Yvette and by the narrative generally as the embodiment of desire and the forces of unsettled, unhoused life that oppose her dreary, trapped existence—turns out to be literate (if not perfectly so), to express himself in an ordinary and homely style, to live according to the rhythms of cattle fairs, and, finally, to have a name.

His signature—"Joe Boswell"—startles the reader as it startles Yvette: "And only then she realised that he had a name" (146). No longer the generic Gypsy, readily and cursorily evoked through his dark looks and colorful scarf, he is now an individual who has been accorded the particularity of his identity. The last line of the story, "And only then . . . ," serves as a rebuke to Yvette, who has yearned for a man she regarded as nameless. Maria DiBattista calls Joe Boswell "the last Laurentian avatar of inviolate humanity," a humanity the writer establishes through naming him.[19] Lawrence's imbuing of Boswell with common literacy and a name sheds light back onto the long lineage of anonymous literary and folkloric Gypsies who stand behind this one. It also offers a curious commentary on the novella's repeated and unrelenting references to Mrs. Fawcett, Major Eastwood's companion, as the "Jewess." It is difficult to say if Lawrence fails to expose or even to recognize as problematic the nasty stereotype of the spoiled Jewish woman he uses or if, rather, he launches a backward-looking critique of this habitual form of identifying her when he gives Joe Boswell a name. In either event, the story's naming of Boswell seems a deliberate redress of the notion of the iconic Gypsy, the Gypsy who is less than human, the Gypsy who lacks individuation or who, as in Conan Doyle's "The Speckled Band," does not even have to be visible in order to signify a generic Gypsy presence.

Boswell's letter, however mundane, also communicates passion and hope and stands as a testament to the power and singularity of human expression. Lawrence would use the same strategy for concluding *Lady Chatterley's Lover*, and, although Mellors's letter to Connie is far more elaborate and suffers from no infelicities of expression, it hints at the primacy of language or, perhaps, the need for language as a conduit for passion when physical contact is impossible. The "ink could stay in the bottle," Mellors writes, if only I could touch you.[20] There is surely a greater likelihood that Connie and Mellors will be reunited than that the Gypsy will return to Yvette, even if, as he says in the letter, he does come her way again. Yvette moans with love for him but is, after all, "acquiescent in the fact of his disappearance" (145). However, the Gypsy's "I live in hopes" is more than a naïve articulation of misplaced dreams; it is an expression of longing that provides a glimpse of Boswell's interior life and vulnerability. Mellors's letter, which ends with the phrase "a hopeful heart," does the same.[21]

The Book of Boswell

D. H. Lawrence did not choose the name of his Gypsy idly or arbitrarily. The Boswells were a well-known clan of British Gypsies, one of the three principal families that Francis Hindes Groome used as sources for *In Gipsy Tents*. British readers would very likely have been able to identify Boswell as a common Gypsy name. Rather like calling a Jewish character Cohen, as George Eliot does the pawnshop owner in *Daniel Deronda*, naming a Gypsy character Boswell casts him as ordinary and, presumably, recognizable. It is mainly, although not wholly, coincidental that the first full-length autobiography produced by a British Gypsy born before the turn of the twentieth century is Silvester Gordon Boswell's *The Book of Boswell: Autobiography of a Gypsy*, a memoir that, as we will see, shares details and motifs other than surname with Lawrence's novella. Partly written and largely dictated, it tells the story of Boswell's life from his birth in 1895, in his own words.[22] Although Gypsy voices and stories can be heard in the writings of the Gypsy lorists and other observers, it is difficult to gain access to sustained Gypsy self-representation for much of the nineteenth and into the twentieth century. Boswell's book follows the shape of autobiography, creating a clear trajectory and interpretation for the events of his life. He offers a narrative of Gypsy existence that might be expected to differ from those considered in this book. The question we must ask, then, concerns the story of identity that one particular Gypsy tells when he tells it himself. Some of the themes that Boswell emphasizes echo those in the works of non-Gypsy writers. He meditates, for example, on the meaning of modernity as it affects a traditional Gypsy existence and laments the passing of a time when a true rambling life was possible. But he also introduces the vexed question of education for the peripatetic Gypsy, and he envisions a way of prospering in the modern world that combines elements of assimilation, accommodation, cultural continuity, and separateness.

When the Boswell family appears in the works of Gypsy lorists, its significance is almost always linked to purity. Groome regards the infrequency of intermarriage between Boswells and *górgios* as the feature that distinguishes them from the Lovell and, especially, Wood clans and remarks that of sixty-eight members on the Boswell family tree, "all of them [were] seemingly full-blooded."[23] Groome tries to correlate this genealogical "purity" with linguistic purity, as well as with the survival of authentic Gypsy culture, and has difficulty in doing so. Nonetheless, the Boswells remained a touchstone of pristine Gypsy identity. In the text where Groome found the Boswell family tree, B. C. Smart and H. T. Crofton's *The Dialect of the English Gypsies*, Gordon Boswell's grandfather Silvester—or Wester—appears in the role of pure Gypsy and pure Romani speaker: "Among these conservators of ancient ways," Smart and Crofton write in their introduction, "we have met with no Gypsy anywhere who can be compared with our friend Sylvester Boswell, for purity of speech and idiomatic style . . . a fine old 'Romani chal'—a regular blue-blooded hidalgo—his father a Boswell, his mother a Herne—his pedigree unstained by a base 'gaujo' admixture."[24] Wester proves invaluable to the authors because he can identify six Romani dialects and is considered an expert in the old ways of speech: "Go to Wester," the young Gypsies tell one another, "he speaks dictionary."[25]

What lies hidden in the back pages of Smart and Crofton's study is that Wester is literate, as well as pure of blood and speech. In the section "Genuine Romany Compositions," the authors include a number of his translations, one into Romani of a passage from Scripture and a few into English of letters that he wrote in Romani.[26] This particular aspect of Wester's knowledge—a form of book learning and not just oral lore—receives no particular attention from the gypsiologists, but takes on enormous significance in his grandson's autobiography. And although Gordon's family tree is extremely important to him and a source of great pride, he never uses the discourse of purity.[27] What distinguishes his pedigree, according to Boswell, is not the absence of intermarriage, but the early appearance of formally educated ancestors. He places at the heart of his narrative not some notion of unsullied race, but the distinction of having a literate grandfather. Because his great-grandfather was forced into military service by a press gang (probably around 1820), his grandfather Wester was schooled by the state along with other soldiers' dependents. This was, Gordon asserts, *"the first instance of any education among Romanies"* (13 [emphasis added]).[28]

The inheritance of literacy is crucial to Boswell's keen awareness of himself not just as a representative Romany who wants to tell his story, but as the author of a book. The title he gives his memoir—*The Book of Boswell*—is itself a signal of his investment in creating a document, a record that will stand for future generations of Romany and *górgios* to consult. The "best of everything" world he inhabited as a boy and young man has disappeared and will now exist "only in a book," according to the poem "On the Road Again," which he uses as an epigraph at the beginning of his narrative. What autobiographer could not say the same? Nonetheless, the capturing of the past in print—the writing of history—sets his efforts apart from the overwhelmingly oral traditions of Romany transmission. An appendix to Gordon's book includes a description of his grandfather Wester's notebook, an annotated record of milestones in his own family and other clans. A source for gypsiologists interested in genealogy, this "Regester Book" and "famaley Memerandum" is the book-within-a-book that confirms Boswell's inheritance not just of literacy but of authorship as well.

Throughout his memoir, Boswell alludes to his own experiences as an educated Gypsy child. The son of a literate man, Gordon's father, Trafalgar, insisted that his children attend school whenever the family settled, however briefly, in a new spot. The family inevitably moved on, but the Boswell children took their couple of weeks or months of learning in periods of settlement. The narrative makes clear the difficulty of reconciling an itinerant life with formal education. Teachers, assuming that Boswell and his siblings were ignorant or at least badly educated, automatically placed them one grade below the level at which they belonged. Boswell, always a big boy among smaller ones, was called a dunce, ridiculed, and snubbed by his peers; his recourse was physical aggression and daily fights. The children eventually learned to lie about their ages, telling teachers that they were one grade ahead in order to be placed in the right one. At school, Boswell believes, they began to tell serious lies, the result of knowing that the non-Gypsy world would never trust their truths (22–23).

Boswell's education, the experience that set him apart from almost all other Gypsy children he knew, also introduced him to the realities of discrimination. However proud he was of his book learning, he understood school as one of the British institutions that taught him the nature of his own inevitable marginality. At the age of twelve, he left home after the school he was attending denied him the recognition his talents warranted simply because he would not be a permanent member of the community. In a contest for the best drawing of an animal, Boswell's work was chosen by a panel of judges as the winner. The schoolmaster ruled that, because he was a Gypsy and would be moving on, Boswell could not receive the first-prize banner, an award that was customarily displayed in the school. If Boswell took the banner with him, there was no point in giving him the prize, and so the runner-up won. This incident convinced Boswell of the irreducibility of his identity as a Gypsy in the view of the settled English community, and he rebelled: "It hurt me. I was a Gypsy again, you see. It was another bit of persecution. And I cried when I got home and I said: 'I will never go to that school again!' And I ran away" (56). Like the hero of many a bildungsroman,

Boswell left school and home to make his way in the world in response to an experience of humiliation and perceived injustice. And like those heroes as well, he would find a means to overcome his debased position and come to consider adversity as the pivot of his life's progress.

"I think the army was the beginning of me," Boswell writes after recounting the story of his service in World War I (92). If school alerted him to his difference, the army convinced him that persecution would haunt him and his people without foreseeable end. At the age of twenty, he signed up and was placed in the veterinary corps. Like Lawrence's Joe Boswell, who serves as a groom during the war, Gordon Boswell drew on his experience with animals—specifically, horses—to make a place for himself in the military. He treated horses for shellshock, wrestled as a representative of the Veterinary Hospital at Boulogne, and went up to serve with the First Cavalry Division. Despite his successes, Boswell suffered the isolation that resulted from having no Gypsy companions in the service, punishment for insubordination, and unnecessarily prolonged confinement in a military hospital. These experiences led him to question the nature of his allegiances and identity and, ultimately, to feel that his interests and Britain's did not coincide. "It used to dawn on me how one British subject can treat another," he writes, and then muses about an alternative national allegiance that would have supplied him with a wholly different military experience: "For we still haven't got a country we can call our own, . . . and I don't suppose there's a spare country anywhere now that can be given us" (78, 84). He searched for anyone dark-skinned to confide in, tried out a few phrases in Romani, and satisfied himself with "swop[ping] words with" Bengalis and Gurkhas (84). Still, he credits this period of war service with the making of him. His resolve was forged in the overcoming of maltreatment and discrimination: "I'd think: if I get free I'll never grumble again—no matter how my life takes me! . . . [F]rom the day of my discharge . . . I've tried to defend myself in persecution. I've lived through it, and I've got through it—and I've conquered something!" (92). His sense of triumph, mixed with regret at the unresolved marginality of his people, sends him back again to the question of education. Although he has achieved some measure of success and equanimity in his life, he still thinks with sadness of the "people on the roads today" who are both persecuted and uneducated. They lack the defenses of literacy and knowledge that his father forced his children to acquire.

Almost every British writer on Gypsy life I have considered thus far associated Gypsies with nostalgia for a pastoral, preindustrial, or lost world and, concomitantly, with the Edenic origins of a vanished England. The Gypsy interlocutors of lorists and other observers also sounded this nostalgic strain, and Boswell proves no exception. At a number of points in his narrative, he expresses regret that "no Gypsy children since the 1914 War finished has had times that we . . . had in my younger days" (21). World War I demarcates a loss of innocence both for himself and for Romany in general. He speaks of "those days of unspoiled England," in which he and his siblings looked forward to spring travels; to lanes full of violets, primroses, and wild roses; and to potatoes roasted over a fire (21). The natural world has been invaded by the machine and, for the Gypsy, nothing exemplifies this more urgently than the disappearance of the horse-drawn caravan and the restrictions placed on free travel. "They've taken our by-ways, our lovely lanes away from us," he laments, "so we've got to revert back [*sic*] to tin cans and iron trailers and that is everything on wheels" (33–34). The juxtaposition of motorcar and Gypsy cart in *The Virgin and the Gipsy* and even in *The Wind in the Willows* marks this particular contrast between mechanical and animal power as a common trope for the shocks of modern life. For Boswell, this change in mode of transportation has its legal and moral corollary in oppressive and constraining rules of movement. "Old England was a wonderful place," he writes, using a term for his nation common to so many non-Gypsy critics and bemoaners of change, "but now it seems to me like a police state. Wherever you go nowadays, you're doing wrong, or you're attempting to do wrong, or you're about to do wrong, and what then? . . . It's all restrictions. Old England isn't like it was when I was a child" (33).

What, then, distinguishes the nostalgia of Gordon Boswell from that of John Clare, Matthew Arnold, George Borrow, or the Gypsy lorists? He appears to accept the trope of a golden age, the reality of a better past, just as the others do. The distinctions are twofold, and they reflect both the difference of Romany subjectivity and the trajectory of Boswell's autobiographical narrative. First, Boswell accepts modernity as his means to prosperity and, second, he manages to find a balance between integration into and aloofness from both modernity and the dominant culture. Boswell's is a story of success and, to some extent, assimilation. His autobiography combines the teleological plot of bildung with an outsider's chronicle of overcoming. "Old England" and the caravan may have been more congenial to Romany life, but iron is what made him.

After earning a living in horse trading, a traditional Romany source of income that he had parlayed into a small international business by buying Russian ponies in Brussels and selling them for pit ponies in England, Boswell realized that tractors were replacing horses in farming. Not wishing to remain a "one-track man," as he believed the average horse dealer to be, he started in the scrap-metal trade (121). He did not resist trailers but actually acquired one as early as 1927. And finally, during World War II, he entered into a contract with the Ministry of Transport that brought him prosperity and launched him on an extensive family business. During the war, when gasoline was at a premium, those who wanted to purchase new trucks or other large vehicles had to turn in their old ones to be made into scrap and melted down. Boswell became the middle man, signing for the old vehicles and cutting them into scrap before sending on the metal to be used in manufacturing. He continued and expanded the business, brought his sons into it, and, as of the time of the writing of his memoir, was dealing with many of the largest farms and tractor firms in the district. The confidence of his clients had become a source of tremendous pride for him: "I've lived for it and we've achieved it and I hope we carry on like this" (153). In an appendix to *The Book of Boswell*, the editor notes that a large number of British Gypsies entered the scrap-metal business in the twentieth century (190–91). Their traditional metalworking skills—tinkering and the like—may have prepared them for this line of work, but there is nonetheless an irony in their resourceful approach to the death of the old ways and the ascendancy of the machine. Nostalgia for the open road did not overwhelm Boswell's sense of enterprise. His narrative makes clear that the cost of romanticizing without qualification the preindustrial past is too high for the Gypsies themselves. While non-Gypsy writers and cultural critics can afford to make a fetish of "Old England," a Gypsy like Boswell cannot.

Still, accommodation to the new ways had limited appeal for Boswell, who was able to withstand assimilation because he fully understood its benefits and costs. Iron to him, he writes, is simply a livelihood—"there's no music attached to it" (155). He awaits longingly the time when he can stop working, leave the scrap business in the hands of his sons, and resume traveling. Only because he has been able to combine his job with his "original life," as he puts it, has he lasted so long as a businessman living a more or less settled existence. His entrepreneurial success is tempered by the refusal of his own father to live in a house. The old man objects to having a toilet upstairs, with waste flushing through the pipes, a detail that recalls Yvette Saywell's disgust at the thought of "indoor sanitation . . . [and the] whole stagnant, sewerage sort of life." Although Boswell does not explain his father's dislike of indoor plumbing, it is most likely connected to prohibitions against contact between food preparation and bodily, as well as other sorts of, waste and, as a result, to the Gypsies' reluctance to have bathrooms in the home, whether stationary or mobile.[29] Whereas for Lawrence, indoor plumbing serves as an avatar of modernity and a symbol of the putrefaction that can be associated with civilized life, for Boswell's father, it signals the compromises attendant on assimilation that he is unwilling to make. Trafalgar Boswell also demonstrates his lack of respect for Gordon's success, permanent dwelling, and wealth by using the teasing and feminizing epithet "millionette" to refer to his son (159).

Gordon Boswell signals his own ambivalence about modern life and entrepreneurial success both by including his father's jaundiced views of wealth and plumbing and by leaving the reader to contemplate the legacy of his sons. Boswell has two, one a settled businessman and the other a "typical Gypsy man" who still travels and is unlikely to stop. This second son, Lewis, an outward confirmation of Boswell's attachment to the old ways, "loves his stick fire, [and] his green grass," although he will send his children to school and, like his father, insist on their getting as much education as their peripatetic life allows (163–64). This Romany vision of life — a combination of practicality, pleasure in achievement, attachment to custom, and qualified aloofness from modernity — emerges only in the Gypsy Boswell's own account. He transforms the rhetoric of nostalgia, characteristic of virtually every text we have considered, into a complex posture toward his own culture and the modern world. With the gift of self-expression that he inherited from family tradition and the means to disseminate his views that late-twentieth-century publication allows, Boswell's narrative supplants the phantom Gypsy, who has no voice and no history and whose silence and even invisibility are often required.

Coda: Myth and History

Gordon Boswell argues for the importance of Romany literacy even as he prizes the culture of rambling and the open road. His ability to narrate and, in part, to write his own story stands as testimony to the virtues of linguistic expression in the cause of self-representation. If nothing else, Boswell's memoir offers a history of nineteenth- and twentieth-century Gypsy life that amplifies and, in some respects, negates the accounts of gypsiologists, literary observers, and even academic historians and social scientists. What Lawrence hints at in *The Virgin and the Gipsy* — that what the Gypsy himself speaks does not conform to the mythology that surrounds him — is borne out by *The Book of Boswell*. Although no absolute line can be drawn between mythology and history, it is fair to say that, without history, mythology is allowed to stand in for the written record. In the case of the Gypsies, the absence of writing — especially by the Gypsies themselves — feeds the dominance of myth in the representation and understanding of Romany existence. The mystery of origin, so crucial to the literary representation of Gypsies, lies at the center of almost all mythologizing of the Romany past. And, as we have seen, it is this deliberately nurtured mystery that has persistently linked the Gypsies to the trope of an ambiguous, hidden, or Edenic genesis. It is tempting to speculate that with the benefit of history — with a written record — the origin of the Gypsies might have been transparent and the Gypsy as potent symbol of the primal past impossible.

I close this book with the reflections of a late-twentieth-century American Gypsy on the paradox of history. In the 1980s, when plans for the United States Holocaust Museum in Washington, D.C., were under way, John Megel from Alexandria, Virginia, became an informal representative from the Romany community to the United States Holocaust Memorial Council. In a paper published by the Gypsy Lore Society, Megel writes movingly of the importance of the museum and of the momentous events in which he participated.[30] For the first time, the United States government was acknowledging the murder of more than 500,000 Gypsies during the Holocaust. But this recognition also marked—and here is where the paradox becomes evident—a coming into self-awareness of the Romany people. Out of the horror of the Nazis' attempted obliteration of the Gypsies had come the beginning of a form of Romany history, a public record of their lives and of the events that had so devastated them. In his introduction to the memoir of Walter Winter, a German Sinto who was interned at Auschwitz and Ravensbrück during World War II, Struan Robertson writes, "[Winter] is convinced that it is only by confronting the past that we can understand the present and secure the future."[31] Like Megel, Winter regards the historical record of cataclysm as crucial to the Gypsies' ongoing need to establish a group identity for themselves and their children.

Megel begins his paper with the admission that many American Romany were themselves ignorant of the devastation of the war, at least in part because they had lost contact with their relatives in Europe. "[M]ost of us could not read or write," he remarks, and so had no way of communicating with their brethren on the Continent (187). It was the trial of Adolf Eichmann, with its overwhelming publicity, that first alerted Megel and others to the events of the Holocaust and prompted them to investigate what had happened. He recalls going to the Smithsonian Institution in the early 1960s in search of more information about the fate of European Gypsies. After museum staff quizzed him aggressively and, regarding him as an anthropological specimen, even tried to measure his skull, he was referred to the German Embassy—of all places. However limited and however much an afterthought might be the Holocaust Museum's inclusion of material on the Sinti and Roma (the two primary Gypsy groups in Germany and eastern Europe targeted for extermination by the Nazis), the museum represents both a public recognition and documentation of Romany suffering and a source of information open to all Gypsies in search of their own history.[32] Megel finds it fitting that his people should now be paired with the Jews. "It seems to me we are always next door," he writes, "whether it comes to immigration, persecution or the Holocaust. . . . We have both been strangers, Rom and Jews. According to the old stereotypes, we would steal the kids and then sell them to the Jews" (189).[33] Both peoples can prepare for the future by understanding their separate and mutual pasts. "Through an awareness of the Holocaust," he concludes, again sounding the note of painful paradox, "we will become aware of our own history" (189). It is this awareness and not simply the history itself that is meaningful. Megel wants others to represent and understand his past, but he wants even more to integrate that past into his own identity and to take possession of the history that knowledge of catastrophe has initiated. For those who read John Megel's words, the phantom Gypsy recedes into the realm of the literary.

Notes

Introduction

1. John Sampson, ed., *The Wind on the Heath: A Gypsy Anthology* (London: Chatto and Windus, 1930), vii.
2. Edward Said, *Orientalism* (New York: Random House, 1979), 3.
3. As the historian George Behlmer writes in an excellent essay, gypsiologists were intent on "advertising an oriental subculture" within Victorian England ("The Gypsy Problem in Victorian England," *Victorian Studies* 28, no. 2 [1985]: 244).
4. B. C. Smart and H. T. Crofton, *The Dialect of the English Gypsies* (London: Asher, 1875), xvi.
5. For a history of English legislation aimed against Gypsies, see David Mayall, *English Gypsies and State Policies* (Hatfield: Gypsy Research Centre and University of Hertfordshire Press, 1995). Mayall's very useful survey suggests that, although harsh measures were on the books throughout the eighteenth and nineteenth centuries, their enforcement was seldom rigorous (46). "Surveillance, discrimination, and harassment" were far more common than prosecution (54).
6. David Mayall, *Gypsy-Travellers in Nineteenth-Century Society* (Cambridge: Cambridge University Press, 1988), 91. One year before she took the throne, Victoria befriended a Gypsy family, the Coopers, who camped near Claremont. She wrote about them extensively in her journal and painted them in watercolor. She insisted in letters that they were not heathens or criminals, but good English Christians. As Lynne Vallone comments, "Victoria reinvents the gypsy outcasts as an English underclass, unrelated, finally, to those others of the race who are not Christians" (*Becoming Victoria* [New Haven, Conn.: Yale University Press, 2001], 188–92).
7. Arthur Morrison, "The Case of the Missing Hand," in *Chronicles of Martin Hewitt* (New York: Appleton, 1896), 165. Hewitt explains later that this man is a Wallachian and, although not the murderer he seeks, is guilty of having cut off

a dead man's hand in order to use it for a ritual that would allow him to thieve without danger of being caught (173–75, 183–85).

8. Jonathan Boyarin, "The Other Within and the Other Without," in *Constructions of Jewish Culture and Identity*, ed. Laurence J. Silberstein and Robert L. Cohen (New York: New York University Press, 1994), 431, 433.

9. John Hoyland, *A Historical Survey of the Customs, Habits, & Present State of the Gypsies: Designed to Develope the Origin of This Singular People, and to Promote the Amelioration of Their Condition* (York: Darton, Harvey, 1816), 191.

10. Francis Hindes Groome, *In Gipsy Tents* (Wakefield, Eng.: EP Publishing, 1973), 279. For a Gypsy's version of this myth, see Silvester Gordon Boswell, *The Book of Boswell: Autobiography of a Gypsy*, ed. John Seymour (London: Gollancz, 1970), 14.

11. Said, *Orientalism*, 27.

12. For a variety of excellent analyses of the figure of the Jew in modern literature, see Michael Ragussis, *Figures of Conversion: "The Jewish Question" and English National Identity* (Durham, N.C.: Duke University Press, 1995); Bryan Cheyette, *Constructions of "the Jew" in English Literature and Society: Racial Representations, 1875–1945* (Cambridge: Cambridge University Press, 1993); and Linda Nochlin and Tamar Garb, eds., *The Jew in the Text: Modernity and the Construction of Identity* (London: Thames and Hudson, 1995).

13. Mayall, *Gypsy-Travellers*, 34–35.

14. Pancks is almost never written about as a Gypsy, largely, I think, because he does not fit the literary stereotype. It is possible that Dickens did not intend him as a Gypsy, but simply as an outsider who refers to himself as such because of his fortune-telling role in the Dorrits' life. The description of Pancks, however, suggests otherwise: "[T]he short dark man held his breath and looked at him. He was dressed in black and rusty iron grey; had jet black beads of eyes; a scrubby little black chin; wiry black hair striking out from his head in prongs, like forks or hair-pins; and a complexion that was very dingy by nature, or very dirty by art, or a compound of nature and art" (Charles Dickens, *Little Dorrit* [Harmondsworth: Penguin, 1967], 189–90).

15. Michael Stewart comments that Gypsies have not thought of themselves as a "diaspora population" waiting to return to a homeland, imagined or real ("The Puzzle of Roma Persistence: Group Identity Without a Nation," in *Romani Culture and Gypsy Identity*, ed. Thomas Acton and Gary Mundy [Hatfield: University of Hertford Press, 1997], 84).

16. Angus M. Fraser, *The Gypsies* (Oxford: Blackwell, 1995), 110–20.

17. Mayall, *English Gypsies*, 25.

18. Holger Pedersen, *Linguistic Science in the Nineteenth Century: Methods and Results*, trans. John Webster Spargo (Cambridge, Mass.: Harvard University Press, 1931), 17.

19. Heinrich Moritz Gottlieb Grellman, *Dissertation on the Gipseys: Representing Their Manner of Life, Family Economy. With an Historical Enquiry Concerning Their Origin & First Appearance in Europe*, trans. Matthew Raper (London: Ballintine, 1807), 199.

20. "A Southern Faunist," *Gentleman's Magazine*, April 1802, 291; Francis Hindes Groome, *Gypsy Folk-Tales* (London: Hurst and Blackett, 1899), xxii.

21. George Henry Borrow, *The Zincali: An Account of the Gypsies of Spain* (London: Dent, 1914), 90.

22. Grellman, *Dissertation on the Gipseys*, 140.

23. Boswell, *Book of Boswell*, 14, 181n.2

24. J. W. Burrow, "The Uses of Philology in Victorian England," in *Ideas and Institutions of Victorian Britain*, ed. Robert Robson (New York: Barnes and Noble, 1967), 185.

25. Burrow, "Uses of Philology," 189.

26. George Henry Borrow, *Lavengro: The Classic Account of Gypsy Life in Nineteenth-Century England* (New York: Dover, 1991), 267, 196.

27. Sheila Salo, "'Stolen by Gypsies': The Kidnap Accusation in the United States," in *Papers from the Eighth and Ninth Annual Meetings of the Gypsy Lore Society, North American Chapter*, ed. Cara DeSilva, Joanne Grumet, and David J. Nemeth (New York: Gypsy Lore Society, 1988), 26–36.

28. Walter Simson and James Simson, *A History of the Gipsies: With Specimens of the Gipsy Language* (London: Sampson, Low, 1866), 45.

29. Michael Holroyd, *Augustus John: A Biography* (Harmondsworth: Penguin, 1976), 15.

30. Simson and Simson, *History of the Gipsies*, 45.

31. Mayall, *Gypsy-Travellers*, 87.

32. Salo, "Stolen by Gypsies," 27.

33. Sigmund Freud, "Family Romances," in *The Standard Edition of the Complete Psychological Works of Sigmund Freud*, trans. James Strachey (London: Hogarth Press, 1955), 9:237–41. "Here the influence of sex is already in evidence," Freud writes, "for a boy is far more inclined to feel hostile impulses toward his father than towards his mother and has a far more intense desire to get free from *him* than from *her*" (238).

34. Holroyd, *Augustus John*, 45.

35. For a discussion of the perception of the Gypsy in France, see Marilyn R. Brown, *Gypsies and Other Bohemians: The Myth of the Artist in Nineteenth-Century France* (Ann Arbor, Mich.: UMI Research Press, 1985). Brown stresses the association between Gypsy and artist-bohemian in French letters and culture. This configuration came relatively late to England. See chapter 6.

36. Hoyland, *Historical Survey of the Customs, Habits, & Present State of the Gypsies*, 125–26. See also, for example, Arthur Symons, "In Praise of Gypsies," *Journal of the Gypsy Lore Society* 1, no. 4 (1908): 297.

37. Behlmer, "Gypsy Problem in Victorian England," 237–44. "Together," Behlmer writes, "the Ryes and their literary friends generated 'a very craze for the Gypsy' that had no European equivalent save perhaps for the celebration of Provençal culture in France" (243).

38. Matthew Arnold, "The Scholar-Gipsy," in *The Poems of Matthew Arnold*, 2d ed., ed. Kenneth Alott and Miriam Alott (London: Longman, 1979), 366 (ll. 203–4), 361 (ll. 77–78).

39. Walter Scott, *Guy Mannering, or, The Astrologer*, ed. Andrew Lang (Boston: Estes and Lauriat, 1892), 1:203, 19.

40. Marianne Hirsch, "Jane's Family Romances," in *Borderwork: Feminist Engagements with Comparative Literature*, ed. Margaret Higonnet (Ithaca, N.Y.: Cornell University Press, 1994), 162–85; Deborah Epstein Nord, "'Marks of Race': Gypsy Figures and Eccentric Femininity in Nineteenth-Century Women's Writing," *Victorian Studies* 41, no. 2 (1998): 189–210.

41. It is uncommon to hear people use the verb "to jew," meaning "to cheat," at least in the United States, but "to gyp," meaning the same thing, is still used, often, I suspect, without any idea of its etymology.

42. Katie Trumpener, "The Time of the Gypsies: A 'People Without History,'" in *Identities*, ed. Anthony Appiah and Henry Louis Gates, Jr. (Chicago: University of Chicago Press, 1995), 344.

43. An almost steady stream of articles about the continuing persecution of Gypsies in eastern Europe appears in newspapers, especially since the "fall" of Communism has made these countries more accessible to the press. See, for example, Steven Erlanger, "Across a New Europe, a People Deemed Unfit for Tolerance," *New York Times*, April 2, 2000, Week in Review, 1, 16, and "The Gypsies of Slovakia: Despised and Despairing," *New York Times*, April 3, 2000, A8.

44. Jane Austen, *Emma* (Harmondsworth: Penguin, 1985), 331. Trumpener refers to this episode in *Emma* as a "violent incident," which it clearly is not.

45. Austen, *Emma*, 333.

46. George Eliot, *The Mill on the Floss* (London: Penguin, 1985), 173.

47. David Mayall makes the valuable point that to distinguish between fiction and fact is not sufficient in the matter of Gypsy representation; one also has to distinguish between nonfictional record and fact and to acknowledge "the significance of shifts [in representation] over time" (*Gypsy Identities, 1500–2000: From Egipcyans and Moon-Men to the Ethnic Romany* [London: Routledge, 2004], 43).

48. John Megel, "The Holocaust and the American Rom," in *Papers from the Sixth and Seventh Annual Meetings of the Gypsy Lore Society, North American Chapter*, ed. Joanne Grumet (New York: Gypsy Lore Society, 1986), 189.

49. Boyarin, "Other Within and Other Without," 431. The Holocaust, he writes, "precludes serious cultural criticism of the situation of Jews before or after World War II" (431).

50. Fraser, *Gypsies*, 2, 8.

51. Judith Okely, *The Traveller-Gypsies* (Cambridge: Cambridge University Press, 1983), 13–14.

52. Okely, *Traveller-Gypsies*, 10.

53. Mayall, *Gypsy-Travellers*, 78–80.

54. Wim Wellems, *In Search of the True Gypsy: From Enlightenment to Final Solution*, trans. Don Bloch (London: Cass, 1997), 4.

55. Fraser, *Gypsies*, 9, 317–18; Thomas Acton, *Gypsy Politics and Social Change: The Development of Ethnic Ideology and Pressure Politics Among British Gypsies from Victorian Reformism to Romany Nationalism* (London: Routledge and Kegan Paul, 1974), esp. chaps. 5 and 7.

56. Grattan Puxon, "The Romani Movement: Rebirth and the First World Romani Congress in Retrospect," in *Scholarship and the Gypsy Struggle: Commitment in Romani Studies*, ed. Donald Kenrick and Thomas Acton (Hatfield: University of Hertfordshire Press, 2000), 94–113.
57. Mayall, *Gypsy Identities*, 7.
58. Frédéric Brenner, *Diaspora: Homelands in Exile*, 2 vols. (New York: HarperCollins, 2003). Brenner, a French anthropologist, set out to answer pictorially the question: What is a Jew? Photographing Jews all over the world, he discovered that diversity of appearance and way of life made the question impossible to answer.
59. George Eliot, *Silas Marner* (London: Penguin, 1996), 5–6.
60. George W. Stocking, Jr., *Victorian Anthropology* (New York: Free Press, 1987), 26–27.
61. George W. Stocking, Jr., *Race, Culture, and Evolution: Essays in the History of Anthropology* (Chicago: University of Chicago Press, 1968), 65.
62. Stocking, *Victorian Anthropology*, 64. See, too, Douglas A. Lorimer, "Race, Science and Culture: Historical Continuities and Discontinuities, 1850–1914," in *The Victorians and Race*, ed. Shearer West (Aldershot, Eng.: Scolar Press, 1997), 12–33. In this excellent and judicious essay, Lorimer writes that when we assess the use of the word "race" in theories and statements of the 1840s, "we need to be wary of a temptation to tease out a more precise meaning, when its ambiguous, and even contradictory, character was the source of its utility" (14). He is at pains to distinguish the use of ideas of "race" from varieties and degrees of racism.

1. A "Mingled Race"

1. Heinrich Moritz Gottlieb Grellmann, *Dissertation on the Gipseys: Representing Their Manner of Life, Family Economy. With an Historical Enquiry Concerning Their Origin & First Appearance in Europe*, trans. Matthew Raper (London: Ballintine, 1807), 109.
2. "A Southern Faunist," *Gentleman's Magazine*, April 1802, 291–92.
3. Walter Simson and James Simson, *A History of the Gipsies: With Specimens of the Gipsy Language* (London: Sampson, Low, 1866), 14.
4. William Marsden, "Observations on the Language of the People Commonly Called Gypsies. In a Letter to Sir Joseph Banks," *Archaeologia, or, Miscellaneous Tracts Relating to Antiquity* 7 (1785): 382–86. Marsden was interested in establishing both that the Gypsies' language was a real one, distinct from cant or fabricated slang, and that it was related to "Hindostanee." He includes a "Table of Comparison" between Romani and "Hindostanic" words (386). The inclusion of this article in the midst of pieces on ancient Britain, Greece, and Rome suggests the seriousness with which philologists and antiquarians regarded the study of Romani in the late eighteenth century.
5. Grellman, *Dissertation on the Gipseys*, i.
6. Grellman, *Dissertation on the Gipseys*, iii.

7. Grellman, *Dissertation on the Gipseys*, 2.

8. Grellman, *Dissertation on the Gipseys*, 84–85.

9. Grellman, *Dissertation on the Gipseys*, 14.

10. John Hoyland, *A Historical Survey of the Customs, Habits, & Present State of the Gypsies: Designed to Develope the Origin of This Singular People, and to Promote the Amelioration of Their Condition* (York: Darton, Harvey, 1816), 47, 95.

11. Hoyland, *Historical Survey of the Customs, Habits, & Present State of the Gypsies*, 103.

12. For a discussion of the frequency of Gypsy–*górgio* (non-Gypsy) marriage, see David Mayall, *Gypsy-Travellers in Nineteenth-Century Society* (Cambridge: Cambridge University Press, 1988), 84–86.

13. Mayall, *Gypsy-Travellers*, 82, 87.

14. Simson and Simson, *History of the Gipsies*, 45.

15. Sigmund Freud, "Family Romances," in *The Standard Edition of the Complete Psychological Works of Sigmund Freud*, trans. James Strachey (London: Hogarth Press, 1955), 9:237–41.

16. Simson and Simson, *History of the Gipsies*, 117. Common Gypsy names, although often recognizable as such, tended to be indistinguishable from non-Gypsy names: for example, Boswell, Buckley, Clayton, Heron, Holland, Stanley, and Wood. See Mayall, *Gypsy-Travellers*, 85.

17. Simson and Simson, *History of the Gipsies*, 184.

18. Simson and Simson, *History of the Gipsies*, 287, 303.

19. George Behlmer, "The Gypsy Problem in Victorian England," *Victorian Studies* 28, no. 2 (1985): 240–44.

20. Simson and Simson, *History of the Gipsies*, 218.

21. For Scott's antiquarianism, see Iain Gordon Brown, *The Hobby-Horsical Antiquary: A Scottish Character, 1640–1830* (Edinburgh: National Library of Scotland, 1980), and George W. Stocking, Jr., *Victorian Anthropology* (New York: Free Press, 1987), 53–55. On Scott as a pioneer of the mass-culture industry that embodied a new "sensibility for the past," see Peter Mandler, *The Fall and Rise of the Stately Home* (New Haven, Conn.: Yale University Press, 1997), 21–22.

22. Walter Scott, *Guy Mannering, or, The Astrologer*, ed. Andrew Lang (Boston: Estes and Lauriat, 1892), 1:22. Subsequent references are cited in the text.

23. John Keats, "Meg Merrilies," in *Selected Poems and Letters*, ed. Douglas Bush (Boston: Houghton Mifflin, 1959), 158; Charles Lamb, "The Gipsy's Malison," *Blackwood's Edinburgh Review* 25 (1829): 64. For Meg Merrilies's life after *Guy Mannering*, see Joan Coldwell, "'Meg Merrilies': Scott's Gipsy Tamed," *Keats–Shelley Memorial Bulletin* 32 (1981): 30–37; Peter Garside, "Meg Merrilies and India," in *Scott in Carnival*, ed. J. H. Alexander and David Hewitt (Aberdeen: Association for Scottish Literary Studies, 1993), 154–71; Catherine Gordon, "The Illustrations of Sir Walter Scott: Nineteenth-Century Enthusiasm and Adaptation," *Journal of the Warburg and Courtauld Institute* 34 (1971): 297–317; and Claire Lamont, "Meg the Gipsy in Scott and Keats," *English: The Journal of the English Association* 36 (1987): 137–45.

24. Garside, "Meg Merrilies and India," 156.

25. Katie Trumpener discusses the European tendency, whether in literary texts or in visual displays, to imagine Gypsies in static set pieces or tableaux ("The Time of the Gypsies: A 'People Without History,'" in *Identities*, ed. Anthony Appiah and Henry Louis Gates, Jr. [Chicago: University of Chicago Press, 1995], 341–43).

26. George Eliot quotes Meg Merrilies at least twice in letters to close friends, on April 27, 1852, and December, 30, 1859, and does so without referring to her source (*The George Eliot Letters*, ed. Gordon S. Haight [New Haven, Conn.: Yale University Press, 1954], 2:21, 3:238). This suggests a general familiarity with the novel and the character.

27. John Sutherland, *The Life of Walter Scott: A Critical Biography* (Oxford: Blackwell, 1995), 4.

28. Sutherland, *Life of Walter Scott*, 1, 3.

29. Simson and Simson, *History of the Gipsies*, 241; Walter Simson, "Notices Concerning the Scottish Gypsies," *Blackwood's Edinburgh Magazine* 1 (1817): 54–56. Simson identifies Walter Scott as the author of a description of Jean Gordon in one of his articles.

30. Simson, "Notices," 54. Jean Gordon was referring to Bonnie Prince Charlie, the Pretender and next best hope for the Jacobites, who were centered in the Scottish Highlands.

31. Andrew Lang, "Editor's Introduction," in Scott, *Guy Mannering*, 1:xxi.

32. Sutherland, *Life of Walter Scott*, 182; Graham McMaster, *Scott and Society* (Cambridge: Cambridge University Press, 1981), 159.

33. J. G. Lockhart, *Memoirs of the Life of Sir Walter Scott, Bart.* (Edinburgh: Cadell, 1844), 277.

34. Sutherland, *Life of Walter Scott*, 181.

35. In his notes to *Guy Mannering*, Lang identifies Grimm's fairy tales and other German fables as possible sources for Meg's spinning (1:282).

36. In a suggestive essay, Jana Davis discusses characters' habits of glancing through apertures in *Guy Mannering* in connection with the theme of limited perception and mental confusion ("Landscape Images and Epistemology in *Guy Mannering*," in *Scott and His Influence*, ed. J. H. Alexander and David Hewitt [Aberdeen: Association for Scottish Literary Studies, 1983], 125–26). My emphasis is slightly different, associating this kind of vision in the novel with seeing or spying; with something forbidden, mysterious, ritualistic, and only partly decipherable; and, ultimately, with memory.

37. Sigmund Freud, "The Paths to the Formation of Symptoms," in *The Complete Introductory Lectures on Psychoanalysis*, trans. James Strachey (New York: Norton, 1966), 371.

38. In the preamble to his study of the poor of London, Henry Mayhew discusses the "wandering tribes" that exist on the periphery of "civilized" nations as the prototype for his London street folk (*London Labour and the London Poor* [New York: Dover, 1968], 1:1–2). He cites the work of ethnologists Andrew Smith and James Prichard and uses language very similar to Scott's to define a pariah culture.

39. Lamb's poem about Meg Merrilies is called "The Gipsy's Malison," the word "malison" meaning "curse." Keats's poem includes a reference to Margaret of

Anjou—"Old Meg she was brave as Margaret Queen / And as tall as Amazon"—
with whom the narrator of *Guy Mannering* compares Meg directly after she utters
her curse (1:72–73). Coldwell suggests that it was Sarah Siddons's performance of
Margaret of Anjou in a minor play, rather than in Shakespeare's *Henry VI*, that
probably influenced Scott's comparison ("Meg Merrilies," 34–35). Later in the
novel, the tragic Meg is likened to Sarah Siddons (2:284), which would tend to
confirm Coldwell's hypothesis.

40. David Mayall, *English Gypsies and State Policies* (Hatfield: Gypsy Research Centre and University of Hertfordshire Press, 1988), 29–31.
41. Katie Trumpener, *Bardic Nationalism: The Romantic Novel and the British Empire* (Princeton, N.J.: Princeton University Press, 1997), 184.
42. Garside, "Meg Merrilies and India," 162–64.
43. Trumpener, *Bardic Nationalism*, 183–92.
44. Edward Said, *Culture and Imperialism* (New York: Knopf, 1993), 62.
45. Trumpener, *Bardic Nationalism*, 192.
46. Georg Lukács dismisses both the critical belief that Scott's art "propagated feudal tendencies" and the equally "false theory," disseminated by "vulgar sociology," that he was a poet "of the English merchants and colonizers of contemporary English imperialism" (*The Historical Novel* [Harmondsworth: Penguin, 1969], 51).
47. Ian Duncan, *Modern Romance and Transformations of the Novel: The Gothic, Scott, Dickens* (Cambridge: Cambridge University Press, 1992), 116. My reading and Duncan's converge at many points, although his emphasis is on the form of romance.
48. Duncan refers to Guy Mannering and Meg Merrilies as Harry's "symbolic parents—authors of his destiny—far more powerful than his dim biological parents" (*Modern Romance and Transformations of the Novel*, 126).
49. Garside, "Meg Merrilies and India," 160.
50. Duncan, *Modern Romance and Transformations of the Novel*, 131.
51. The Bertram motto is "Our Right Makes Our Might," while the motto that Glossin has invented to replace it is "He who takes it, makes it" (2:138–39).
52. Trumpener mistakenly attributes the kidnapping to the Ellangowan Gypsies ("Time of the Gypsies," 362).
53. Lukács, *Historical Novel*, 31.
54. Lukács, *Historical Novel*, 32, 61.
55. Patrick Brantlinger, *Dark Vanishings: Discourses on the Extinction of Primitive Races, 1800–1930* (Ithaca, N.Y.: Cornell University Press, 2003), 61–63. Brantlinger describes James Fenimore Cooper's novels as just such stories of extinction and compares them with Scott's historical fictions about the origins of modern Britain.
56. Garside argues, on the contrary, that Meg is effectively and brutally written out of the end of the novel: "The final un-figuring of Meg could represent a betrayal more devastating in its effects that the elder Bertram's original sin in evicting the Gypsies" ("Meg Merrilies and India," 168).
57. Michael Ragussis, *Figures of Conversion: "The Jewish Question" and English National Identity* (Durham, N.C.: Duke University Press, 1995), 100.

58. Freud, "Paths to the Formation of Symptoms," 371; C. G. Jung, "On the Psychology of the Unconscious," in *The Essential Jung*, ed. Anthony Storr (Princeton, N.J.: Princeton University Press, 1983), 69.

59. Discussing the patterns of father–son relations in Scott's Waverley novels, Alexander Welsh speculates on the influence of nineteenth-century fiction on Freud's theorizing and marshals an especially apt formulation from Terence Cave's *Recognition: A Study in Poetics*: "psychoanalysis is the elaboration of a plot structure according to rules which are already demonstrated by literary texts" (quoted in *The Hero of the Waverley Novels, with New Essays on Scott* [Princeton, N.J.: Princeton University Press, 1992], 223).

60. Charles Dickens, *David Copperfield* (London: Penguin, 2004), 72. Note that both Scott's memory of the outsize Jean Gordon and Lang's recollection of her similarly larger-than-life granddaughter, Madge, are rooted in childhood.

61. Dickens, *David Copperfield*, 28.

62. Grellman, *Dissertation on the Gipseys*, 92; Hoyland, *Historical Survey of the Customs, Habits, & Present State of the Gypsies*, 125–26.

63. Deborah Epstein Nord, "'Marks of Race': Gypsy Figures and Eccentric Femininity in Nineteenth-Century Women's Writing," *Victorian Studies* 41, no. 2 (1998): 189–210. Harry's tutor, Dominie Sampson, another beloved character from the novel, is Meg's mirror image: a feminized and sentimental male. He is also, in many ways, Harry's other parent. For Dominie, see Peter Garside, "Scott, the Eighteenth Century, and the New Man of Sentiment," *Anglia* 103 (1985): 71–98.

64. Charlotte Brontë, *Jane Eyre* (London: Penguin, 1996), 221–28. See also Nord, "Marks of Race," 194–97. Bronte was plainly thinking of Meg Merrilies here: Rochester's gypsy is referred to as a "Sybil" (221) and shares "elf-locks" with Meg (1:20).

65. Brontë, *Jane Eyre*, 227.

66. That the masculinized Gypsy figure had already become a mythic figure or literary convention is underscored by comparing Dorothy Wordsworth's description of the real-life model for the Gypsy in William's poem "Beggars"—"a very tall woman, much beyond the measure of tall women"—with her brother's opening line (entry for June 10, 1800, in *Journals of Dorothy Wordsworth: The Alfoxden Journal, 1798; the Grasmere Journals, 1800–1803*, ed. Mary Moorman [London: Oxford University Press, 1971], 26). William compares her not with a tall woman, but with a tall man.

67. Trumpener, "Time of the Gypsies," 344.

2. Vagrant and Poet

1. George Eliot, *The Mill on the Floss* (London: Penguin Books, 1985), 171.

2. David Mayall, *English Gypsies and State Policies* (Hatfield: Gypsy Research Centre and University of Hertfordshire Press, 1995), 31. For a succinct history of legislation relating to Gypsies, see 17–26. Beginning in the early nineteenth century,

Gypsies were persecuted not simply for being "Egipcians," but for living in tents, telling fortunes, and camping in the wrong place.

3. Mayall, *English Gypsies*, 25, chap. 3.

4. For literary responses to enclosure, see, especially, Raymond Williams, *The Country and the City* (London: Chatto and Windus, 1973), chap. 10, and Elizabeth K. Helsinger, *Rural Scenes and National Representation: Britain, 1815–1850* (Princeton, N.J.: Princeton University Press, 1997).

5. John Clare, "[Gipseys]," in *John Clare by Himself*, ed. Eric Robinson and David Powell (Ashington, Eng.: Carcanet Press, 1996), 87.

6. See chap. 1, note 38.

7. Williams, *Country and City*, 96.

8. Williams, *Country and City*, 96, 128, 130.

9. Helsinger, *Rural Scenes and National Representation*, 7.

10. David G. Riede, *Matthew Arnold and the Betrayal of Language* (Charlottesville: University Press of Virginia, 1988), 59.

11. Anne Williams remarks that Gypsies had become a "cliché of the picturesque" by the end of the eighteenth century ("Clare's 'Gypsies,'" *Explicator* 39, no. 3 [1981]: 10). On the picturesque and its associations with, among other things, Gypsies, see Peter Mandler, *The Fall and Rise of the Stately Home* (New Haven, Conn.: Yale University Press, 1997), 12.

12. Mary Russell Mitford, *Our Village: Sketches of Rural Characters and Scenery* (London: Bell, 1876), 451. Subsequent references are cited in the text.

13. For a discussion of another, much later case of displacing ostensible characteristics of Gypsies onto animals, especially dogs, in Virginia Woolf's story "Gipsy, the Mongrel," see Katie Trumpener, "The Time of the Gypsies: A 'People Without History,'" in *Identities*, ed. Anthony Appiah and Henry Louis Gates, Jr. (Chicago: University of Chicago Press, 1995), 370–74.

14. "Pastoral at its simplest," writes Roger Sales, "represents an escape to another country where things are done differently as blissful innocence and homespun simplicity rule" ("The Politics of Pastoral," in *Peasants and Countrymen in Literature*, ed. Kathleen Parkinson and Martin Priestman [London: Roehampton Institute, 1982], 92). William Empson complicates this idea by reminding us that all pastoral is "based on a double attitude of the artist to the worker [or peasant or shepherd], of the complex man to the simple one ('I am in one way better, in another not so good')" (*Some Versions of Pastoral* [New York: New Directions, 1974], 14).

15. Helsinger, *Rural Scenes and National Representation*, 159.

16. Clare, "[Gipseys]," 83. Eric Robinson describes Clare's vast and eclectic knowledge of ballads and ballad music; dances and dance tunes ("some of which he collected from gypsies"), including Morris dances; local festivals, such as May Day, Valentine's Eves, and Plough Mondays; bull-runnings; local flora and fauna; and Gypsy and London slang (introduction to *John Clare's Autobiographical Writings*, ed. Eric Robinson and John Lawrence [Oxford: Oxford University Press, 1983], xiv). For the Boswells, see Jonathan Bate, *John Clare: A Biography* (New York: Farrar, Straus, 2003), 94.

17. Bate, *John Clare*, 94. For Clare and the Gypsies, see 93–99.
18. Clare, "[Gipseys]," 83–86
19. Clare, "Cousins," in *Autobiographical Writings*, 65.
20. John Clare, "The Gipsies Evening Blaze," in *The Early Poems of John Clare, 1804–1822*, ed. Eric Robinson and David Powell (Oxford: Clarendon Press, 1989), 1:33.
21. John Clare, "October," in *The Shepherd's Calendar* (Oxford: Oxford University Press, 1964), 112–13.
22. On Clare's love of secret, hidden spots, see Helsinger, *Rural Scenes and National Representation*, 152.
23. John Clare, "The Gipsy Camp," in *The Later Poems of John Clare, 1837–1864*, ed. Eric Robinson and David Powell (Oxford: Clarendon Press, 1984), 1:29. This poem is also referred to as "Gypsies," according to Williams, "Clare's 'Gypsies.'"
24. Williams, "Clare's 'Gypsies,'" 11.
25. Clare, "Journey out of Essex," in *Autobiographical Writings*, vii, 153.
26. Clare, "Journey out of Essex," 153.
27. Trumpener observes that Wordsworth and Clare mark opposite responses to Gypsies among Romantics. The former, she writes, belongs with those who "still seem to harbor eighteenth-century fears for the forces of civilization," and the latter with those who "celebrate in the Gypsies a community united by a love of liberty and a tradition of political resistance" ("Time of the Gypsies," 360–61). See, too, her discussion of Clare's "The Gipsy's Song."
28. David Simpson, "Criticism, Politics, and Style in Wordsworth's Poetry," *Critical Inquiry* 11, no. 1 (1984): 62. Both this essay and David Simpson, "Figuring Class, Sex, and Gender: What Is the Subject of Wordsworth's 'Gipsies'?" *South Atlantic Quarterly* 88, no. 3 (1989): 541–69, are among the most interesting critical statements about the poem. In the latter article, Simpson reads "Gypsies" as an incest fantasy.
29. John O. Hayden, notes to "Beggars," in William Wordsworth, *Poems*, ed. John O. Hayden (Harmondsworth: Penguin Books, 1977), 1:975–76.
30. Entry for June 10, 1800, in *Journals of Dorothy Wordsworth: The Alfoxden Journal, 1798; the Grasmere Journals, 1800–1803*, ed. Mary Moorman (London: Oxford University Press, 1971), 26–27.
31. Wordsworth, "Beggars," in *Poems*, 1:516–17 (emphasis added).
32. The contradictoriness of Wordsworth's stance is also reflected in what he purportedly told Henry Crabb Robinson about "Beggars." He wrote it, he said, to "exhibit the power of physical beauty and health and vigour in childhood even in a state of moral depravity" (quoted in Hayden, notes to "Beggars," 1:976).
33. Wordsworth, "Sequel to 'Beggars' Composed Many Years After," in *Poems*, 1:17–18 (l. 14).
34. I am using the original 1807 version of "Gypsies." In response to complaints about its callousness, Wordsworth added the following lines in 1820: "In scorn I speak not;— they are what their birth / And breeding suffer them to be; / Wild outcasts of society" (Wordsworth, "Gypsies," in *Poems*, 1:735 [ll. 26–28], 1025). The first version, without this awkward apology, is a better poem.

35. According to physicist Edward Groh, the poet is making his journey one day past a full moon, evident from his remark that the moon comes up one hour after sunset. The almost new moon brightens the scene and makes the Gypsies visible, and the renewal of the monthly cycle emphasizes the activity and constancy of nature, as opposed to the sloth and stagnation of the Gypsy group.

36. According to Simpson, "The speaker *cannot* thus project with any complete confidence the persona of honest laborer. . . . He can hardly accuse them [the Gypsies] of wasting time in leisure when his own occupation is so darkly ambiguous in precisely the same way" ("Criticism, Politics, and Style," 65–66).

37. Samuel Taylor Coleridge, *Biographia Literaria* (New York: Macmillan, 1926), 289.

38. William Hazlitt, "On Manner," in *The Complete Works of William Hazlitt*, ed. P. P. Howe (London: Dent, 1930), 4:45–46n.2.

39. Simpson, "Criticism, Politics, and Style," 66.

40. Wordsworth, "Resolution and Independence," in *Poems*, 1:553 (ll. 33–35).

41. According to Mayall, "Anyone found begging, being a lewd or disorderly prostitute, sleeping in the open, or having no visible means of subsistence, could be prosecuted as a vagrant" (*English Gypsies*, 29).

42. Isobel Armstrong, *Victorian Poetry: Poetry, Poetics, and Politics* (London: Routledge, 1993), 219

43. Armstrong, *Victorian Poetry*, 221. "Clare's pastoral," Armstrong writes, "and the educated pastoral of Arnold's 'The Scholar-Gipsy' and 'Thyrsis,' poems which Arnold hoped could become a therapeutic antidote to the 'confusion' of the nineteenth century, strangely reduplicate one another" (171).

44. Matthew Arnold, "Resignation (To Fausta)," in *The Poems of Matthew Arnold*, 2d ed., ed. Kenneth Alott and Miriam Alott (London: Longman, 1979), 88–100 (ll. 132–35).

45. Riede, *Matthew Arnold and the Betrayal of Language*, 57–59.

46. The "unbroken knot" of bodies in Wordsworth's "Gypsies" provides Simpson with the starting point for his interpretation of the poem as an incest fantasy involving the poet's sister ("Figuring Class, Sex, and Gender," 558). Simpson suggests that Wordsworth associated Dorothy with dark Gypsy looks. This reading raises another possibility for understanding the Arnold–Wordsworth connection in "Resignation."

47. The lines read "they rubbed through / Yesterday in their hereditary way" (ll. 138–39). Arnold's use of the word "hereditary" suggests both a cultural and a biological inheritance.

48. Traditional Arnold critics tend to think and write of the scholar-gypsy as "the scholar," while critics interested in Gypsies tend not to register the fact that the scholar-gypsy is not a Gypsy or, rather, not simply a Gypsy. For the latter interpretation, see Antony Harrison, "Matthew Arnold's Gipsies: Intertextuality and the New Historicism," *Victorian Poetry* 29, no. 4 (1991): 365–83.

49. Quoted in Nicholas Murray, *A Life of Matthew Arnold* (London: Hodder and Stoughton, 1996), 140–41.

50. Dwight Culler, *Imaginative Reason: The Poetry of Matthew Arnold* (New Haven, Conn.: Yale University Press, 1966), 183.

51. Joseph Glanvill, *The Vanity of Dogmatizing: Reproduced from the Edition of 1661* (New York: Columbia University Press, 1931), 196. Arnold spells the author's name with only one *l*.

52. Glanvill, *Vanity of Dogmatizing*, 197.

53. Arnold, "The Scholar-Gipsy," in *Poems of Matthew Arnold*, 355–96 (l. 62).

54. Riede comments that "The Scholar-Gipsy" contains "the most lush descriptive verse Arnold ever wrote" and almost certainly includes allusions to Tennyson's "Lotus-Eaters" and Keats's "To Autumn" (*Matthew Arnold and the Betrayal of Language*, 139).

55. Trumpener, "Time of the Gypsies," 355–56.

56. Critics have pondered the significance of this apparent rejection of Greek civilization. James Harrison asks, "How can Arnold the Hellenist intend us to see Greeks as in any way the equivalent of those afflicted with 'this strange disease of modern life'?" and concludes that in doing so the poet signals the "immoderation of his indictment of contemporary society" ("Arnold's 'The Scholar-Gipsy,'" *Explicator* 45, no. 3 [1987]: 35). G. Wilson Knight's reading of the coda seems more consistent with what I have been trying to say about Arnold's unconventional representation of the Gypsies: "Arnold's poem confronts our western tradition with suggestions of a wisdom, lore, or magic of oriental affinities or origin. The intellectual legacy of ancient Greece has clamped down with too exclusive a domination, too burning a weight of consciousness, or intellect. . . . Our consciousness has become . . . too purely 'Apollonian,' too heated, and needs fertilization again from the cool depths of the 'Dionysian,' the more darkly feminine, and eastern, powers" ("The Scholar-Gipsy," in *Matthew Arnold: Modern Critical Views*, ed. Harold Bloom [New York: Chelsea House, 1987], 72).

57. Arnold, "Thyrsis," in *Poems of Matthew Arnold*, 537–50.

3. In the Beginning Was the Word

1. George Henry Borrow, *The Romany Rye* (London: Dent, 1906), 343. Subsequent references are cited in the text, with the abbreviation *RR*.

2. The title of one of the most recent biographies of Borrow, by Michael Collie, is *George Borrow: Eccentric* (Cambridge: Cambridge University Press, 1982).

3. Ian Duncan, "Wild England: George Borrow's Nomadology," *Victorian Studies* 41, no. 3 (1998): 394. Duncan's superb essay is the best piece of writing on Borrow to have appeared in recent years.

4. On Borrow's work for the British and Foreign Bible Society, see Collie, *George Borrow*, chap. 3, and *Letters of George Borrow to the British and Foreign Bible Society*, ed. T. H. Darlow (London: Hodder and Stoughton, 1911). The books that made Borrow's reputation were *The Zincali, or, An Account of the Gypsies of Spain* (1841) and *The Bible in Spain* (1843). It is difficult to know exactly where Borrow traveled because,

as is true about many things in his life, the relationship between his actual experience and its representation in writing is unclear (Collie, *George Borrow*, 51–52).

5. Borrow to the Bible Society, September 1835, in *Letters*, 94.

6. Michael Collie, "George Borrow and Claude Lorrain," *English Studies in Canada* 9, no. 3 (1983): 326–27. Collie notes that *The Bible in Spain* "made Borrow's
reputation overnight" and appeared in four English editions in the year it was
published (326).

7. Collie, "George Borrow and Claude Lorrain," 335–36.

8. William Ireland Knapp, *Life, Writings and Correspondence of George Borrow
(1803–1881); Based on Official and Other Authentic Sources*, 2 vols. (London:
Murray, 1899); Collie, "George Borrow and Claude Lorrain," 326n.4. Between
1909 and 1914, articles on Borrow included "The Wanderer: George Borrow,"
Edinburgh Review, October 1909, 303–28; C. M. Bowen, "George Borrow," *West-
minster Review*, March 1910, 286–304; "Musings Without Method," *Blackwood's*,
March 1912, 417–21; and Urbanus Sylvan [pseud.], "The Borrow Commemora-
tion at Norwich," *Cornhill*, September 13, 1913, 330–35, as well as many in less
prominent journals. Even earlier appeared "The Borrow Revival," *Outlook*, January 5, 1901, 55–58.

9. Jan Marsh, *Back to the Land: The Pastoral Impulse in Victorian England from
1880 to 1914* (London: Quartet Books, 1982); Alun Howkins, "The Discovery of
Rural England," in *Englishness: Politics and Culture, 1880–1920*, ed. Robert Colls
and Philip Dodd (London: Croom Helm, 1986), 62–88.

10. Marsh, *Back to the Land*, 87.

11. Marsh, *Back to the Land*, 78, 88–89.

12. John Sampson, ed., *The Wind on the Heath: A Gypsy Anthology* (London: Chatto and Windus, 1930); George Henry Borrow, *Lavengro: The Classic Account of
Gypsy Life in Nineteenth-Century England* (New York: Dover, 1991), 164. Subsequent references are cited in the text, with the abbreviation *L*. The passage
from *Lavengro* amounts to a Gypsy credo and is uttered by Jasper Petulengro,
Lavengro's Romany brother.

13. *Borrow Selections, with Essays by Richard Ford, Leslie Stephen, and George
Saintsbury*, ed. Humphrey S. Milford (Oxford: Clarendon Press, 1924).

14. George Saintsbury, "George Saintsbury on George Borrow," in *Borrow Selections*,
33.

15. Leslie Stephen, "Leslie Stephen on George Borrow," in *Borrow Selections*, 25–26.

16. Stephen, "Leslie Stephen on George Borrow," 20.

17. Augustine Birrell, "George Borrow," in *Res Judicatae: Papers and Essays* (New
York: Scribner, 1897), 120.

18. George Henry Borrow, *Wild Wales: The People, Language and Scenery* (London:
Dent, 1906), viii. Theodore Watts-Dunton also wrote the introduction to an edition of *The Romany Rye* (London: Ward, Lock, n.d.). In it he describes a comical
episode involving Borrow's decision, prompted by a friend, to read Arnold's "The
Scholar-Gipsy" aloud to a Romany beauty (xiv–xx). Watts-Dunton lived for some
twenty years with Algernon Swinburne and married very late in life, nine years
before his death at the age of eighty-two.

19. Duncan, "Wild England," 391.
20. Peter Brooks, *Reading for the Plot: Design and Intention in Narrative* (New York: Vintage, 1985), 39.
21. The female plot, Brooks comments, "takes a more complex stance toward ambition": for the heroine, selfhood is asserted "in resistance to the overt and violating male plots of ambition" (*Reading for the Plot*, 39).
22. Critics who have explored the Victorian construction of masculinity point to a number of routes to the realization of masculine ambition, prophecy and celibacy among them. See, especially, James Eli Adams, *Dandies and Desert Saints: Styles of Victorian Masculinity* (Ithaca, N.Y.: Cornell University Press, 1995), 27, 35, and Herbert Sussman, *Victorian Masculinities: Manhood and Masculine Poetics in Early Victorian Literature and Art* (Cambridge: Cambridge University Press, 1995), 47.
23. Duncan, "Wild England," 397.
24. The last eighteen chapters of *Lavengro* and first sixteen chapters of *The Romany Rye* were published together in a single volume: George Borrow, *Isopel Berners*, ed. Thomas Secombe (London: Hodder and Stoughton, 1901).
25. Lavengro urges the same thing again a few pages later, echoing the scene in Genesis 18:1–15 when Abraham asks Sarah to prepare food and drink for the strangers who have appeared at their tent in the desert. Sarah herself does not come out at first, and, when she hears the visitors' prediction that she will give birth to a son, she laughs from inside the tent. Another biblical woman who is urged to appear before visitors but refuses is Vashti, whose unwillingness to bend to men's wishes inspired Charlotte Brontë's character in *Villette* (1853) and is shared, to a degree, by Belle.
26. Duncan refers to Lavengro's "gifted, mildly autistic weirdness" ("Wild England," 397).
27. W. E. Henley, "Borrow," in *Views and Reviews: Essays in Appreciation* (New York: Scribner, 1890), 137.
28. A. S. Byatt, "The Scholar Gypsy," review of *A World of His Own: The Double Life of George Borrow*, by David Williams, and *Lavengro*, by George Borrow, *The Times*, December 2, 1982, 10.
29. As Duncan has phrased it, comparing Lavengro with Harry Bertram, Scott's reinstated laird, "*Lavengro* refuses the romance of a homecoming in modernity" ("Wild England," 394). No fortune, estate, bride, or title awaits him.
30. Duncan, "Wild England," 397.
31. Duncan sees this moment as a possible indication that Lavengro "would appear to be electing himself as the forerunner of those secret servants of empire . . . imagined by Kipling and Buchan and enacted by Burton and Lawrence" ("Wild England," 400). He asserts, however, that we cannot know what Lavengro will do next. I would add that Lavengro's difficulties with the recruiting agent suggest that he would be unlikely to work within any institutional frame, imperial or otherwise.
32. J. W. Burrow, "The Uses of Philology in Victorian Britain," in *Ideas and Institutions of Victorian Britain*, ed. Robert Robson (New York: Barnes and Noble,

1967), 187. See also, on Max Müller, J. W. Burrow, *Evolution and Society: A Study in Victorian Social Theory* (Cambridge: Cambridge University Press, 1970), 149–53, and Holger Pedersen, *Linguistic Science in the Nineteenth Century: Methods and Results*, trans. John Webster Spargo (Cambridge, Mass.: Harvard University Press, 1931), esp. 12–17.

33. Burrow, "Uses of Philology," 189.

34. In a well-known letter, written in October 1900, Freud told Wilhelm Fliess that Dora's case "has opened smoothly to my collection of picklocks" (quoted in Philip Rieff, introduction to Sigmund Freud, *Dora: An Analysis of a Case of Hysteria*, ed. Philip Rieff [New York: Collier Books, 1963], 7).

35. We might also consider that Moll falls in with and lives for a brief time with Gypsies at the very beginning of *Moll Flanders*. For a discussion of this episode, see Ellen Pollak, *Incest and the English Novel, 1684–1814* (Baltimore: Johns Hopkins University Press, 2003), 127–28.

36. George Borrow, *The Bible in Spain; or, the Journeys, Adventures, and Imprisonments of an Englishman, in an Attempt to Circulate the Scriptures in the Peninsula* (London: Ward, Lock, n.d.), 20.

37. Sussman, *Victorian Masculinities*, 47. Sussman discusses two models of Victorian brotherhood, the Carlylean and the Pre-Raphaelite, which illuminate but do not fully correspond to Borrow's fraternal narratives. In Carlyle's *Sartor Resartus*, for example, male desire is channeled into production, which cannot be said of *Lavengro*, and for the Pre-Raphaelites, nonbourgeois, bohemian heterosexuality dominates relations between the sexes. In this respect, the Pre-Raphaelite Brotherhood is closer to the late-nineteenth-century ryes, like Augustus John and John Sampson, than to Borrow.

38. Andrew Motion, review of "George Borrow: A Centenary Lecture," Cheltenham Festival of Literature, *Times Literary Supplement*, October 30, 1981, 1266.

39. Michael Mason, "A Philologist in the Wild," review of *A World of His Own: The Double Life of George Borrow*, by David Williams, and *George Borrow: Eccentric*, by Michael Collie, *Times Literary Supplement*, December 10, 1982, 1353.

40. E. P. Thompson, *The Making of the English Working Class* (New York: Vintage, 1963), 700–709. Thompson actually cites Borrow's *The Romany Rye* as a source on Thistlewood (701).

4. "Marks of Race"

1. In her recent book, Alicia Carroll devotes a chapter to tracing Eliot's use of the Gypsy figure (*Dark Smiles: Race and Desire in George Eliot* [Athens: Ohio University Press, 2003], chap. 2).

2. Raymond Williams, *The Country and the City* (London: Chatto and Windus, 1973), 165–81. For a related analysis of Eliot that employs Ferdinand Tönnies's terms *Gemeinschaft* and *Gesellschaft* with great effectiveness, see Susan Graver, *George Eliot and Community: A Study in Social Theory and Social Form* (Berkeley: University of California Press, 1984), esp. 14–25.

3. Williams, *Country and City*, 165–81.

4. Steven Marcus, "Literature and Social Theory: Starting in with George Eliot," in *Representations: Essays on Literature and Society* (New York: Random House, 1975), 190.

5. Williams, *Country and City*, 174.

6. Gillian Beer, "Beyond Determinism: George Eliot and Virginia Woolf," in *Women Writing and Writing About Women*, ed. Mary Jacobus (London: Croom Helm, 1979), 88.

7. Michael Ragussis, *Figures of Conversion: "The Jewish Question" and English National Identity* (Durham, N.C.: Duke University Press, 1995), esp. chaps. 4 and 6; Bernard Semmel, *George Eliot and the Politics of National Inheritance* (New York: Oxford University Press, 1994), esp. chap. 5. I am indebted to Semmel's excellent book, which suggests that Eliot's emphasis on nationality and "national inheritance" in *The Spanish Gypsy* and *Daniel Deronda* is the final phase in her long-standing concern with the problem of disinheritance.

8. Walter Scott, *Ivanhoe* (London: Penguin, 1986), 117.

9. George Eliot, *Silas Marner* (London: Penguin, 1996), 5–6. Subsequent references are cited in the text, with the abbreviation *SM*.

10. Jonathan Boyarin, "The Other Within and the Other Without," in *Constructions of Jewish Culture and Identity*, ed. Laurence J. Silberstein and Robert L. Cohen (New York: New York University Press, 1994), 424–49. In theorizing the Jew as "the Other inside Europe," Boyarin mentions in passing that the transnational or non-national Romany are analogous to the Jews in this sense (433). This pairing is an old one, but Scott and Eliot seem to be the two nineteenth-century writers most compelled by this comparison.

11. George Eliot, *The Mill on the Floss* (London: Penguin, 1985), 59–60. Subsequent references are cited in the text, with the abbreviation *MF*.

12. For the chronology of Eliot's writing, see Gordon S. Haight, *George Eliot: A Biography* (Oxford: Oxford University Press, 1968), 385, 402, 420. Eliot began work on *The Spanish Gypsy* in 1864 and finished *Felix Holt* in 1866. *Middlemarch* had been in her mind since completing *Holt*.

13. George Eliot, *Middlemarch* (New York: Penguin, 1994), 366. Subsequent references are cited in the text, with the abbreviation *M*.

14. Lydgate's full comment is that Will is "sort of a gypsy; he thinks nothing of leather and prunella." The editor's note explains that this phrase, from Alexander Pope's *An Essay on Man* (1733–1734), refers to social distinction, leather being a material for the cobbler's apron, and prunella a cloth for a parson's robe.

15. Thomas Pinney, "Another Note on the Forgotten Past of Will Ladislaw," *Nineteenth-Century Fiction* 17 (1962): 69–73. Pinney takes issue with the position of Jerome Beatty, who regarded Will as at least partly Jewish, and believes that "genetic speculation" is unnecessary in light of what is really important in *Middlemarch*: that Eliot created a series of characters all "cut off from their rightful inheritances" (72–73). While I think that Pinney is right to stress that Will's ostensible Jewishness is attributed to him by unreliable and small-minded gossips, I hope to show that Daniel Deronda's and Fedalma's actual

genetic—or "racial"—difference is crucial to Eliot's representation of their respective inheritances.

16. Semmel, *George Eliot and the Politics of National Inheritance*, esp. 103–4.

17. George Eliot, "The Modern Hep! Hep! Hep!" in *Impressions of Theophrastus Such* (Edinburgh: Blackwood, 1879), 347 (emphasis added). Subsequent references are cited in the text, with the abbreviation "MH." The "State" to which the text refers is Italy. Eliot was an admirer of Giuseppe Mazzini, leader of the movement to reunite Italy as a republican state and a refugee in London for a number of years. See Haight, *George Eliot*, 99.

18. There has been a good deal of critical debate about the "imperialist" implications of Eliot's notion of a Jewish homeland. Views of the current Israeli–Palestinian conflict have colored and distorted this issue, but recently some more lucid and historically informed voices have been heard. See, for example, Amanda Anderson, *The Powers of Distance: Cosmopolitanism and the Cultivation of Detachment* (Princeton, N.J.: Princeton University Press, 2001), chap. 4, and Nancy Henry, *George Eliot and the British Empire* (Cambridge: Cambridge University Press, 2002), chap. 4.

19. George Eliot, *Daniel Deronda* (Harmondsworth: Penguin, 1970), 592, 594. Subsequent references are cited in the text, with the abbreviation *DD*. Daniel himself talks about Mazzini and his vision for a reunited Italy just after Mordecai's declaration. Shortly thereafter, Mordecai's sister Mirah, Deronda's future wife, sings Giacomo Leopardi's "O patria mia," an ode to Italy (619).

20. As Anderson puts it, "the best result of a lamentable diaspora is that it issues in a deliberate and chosen affirmation of those previously tacit communal and cultural bonds that have been subjected to such fragmenting and destructive forces" (*Powers of Distance*, 131)

21. Benedict R. Anderson, *Imagined Communities: Reflections on the Origin and Spread of Nationalism* (London: Verso, 1991), 5–6.

22. Anderson, *Imagined Communities*, 11.

23. Anderson, *Imagined Communities*, 12.

24. Irene Tucker argues that in *Daniel Deronda*, Eliot redefines what it means to read a novel by inviting us to imagine a place that does not yet exist—a utopia— and a "world that she has not yet written" at the novel's end (*A Probable State: The Novel, the Contract, and the Jews* [Chicago: University of Chicago Press, 2000], 119). This is a large claim, but it offers an interesting new gloss on the idea of "imagined" communities.

25. Beer, "Beyond Determinism," 88.

26. It is interesting to note that Eppie rejects her biological inheritance—and the prosperity and status that it would bring her—in favor of remaining the daughter of Silas, her adoptive father. Fedalma and Deronda do the opposite, severing filial ties to those who raised them and answering the call of blood. For them, of course, biological inheritance is associated with a national cause and a people to help redeem. See Semmel's discussion of *Silas Marner*, in *George Eliot and the Politics of National Inheritance*, 24–26.

27. Semmel, *George Eliot and the Politics of National Inheritance*, 75.

28. George Eliot, *The Spanish Gypsy* (Edinburgh: Blackwood, 1868), 147 (emphasis added). Subsequent references are cited in the text, with the abbreviation SG.

29. *George Eliot's Life as Related in Her Letters and Journals*, ed. J. W. Cross (Boston: Estes and Lauriat, 1895), 3:32.

30. *George Eliot's Life*, 3:35.

31. *George Eliot's Life*, 3:33, 35.

32. *George Eliot's Life*, 3:33.

33. Ragussis, *Figures of Conversion*, 136–59.

34. Ragussis, *Figures of Conversion*, 155.

35. Carroll, *Dark Smiles*, 51.

36. One can easily imagine that Eliot meant to stress this parallel: Zarca is denied entry into the Promised Land, as is Moses, and both are punished, partly for their excesses, and replaced by more temperate leaders.

37. As Anderson puts it: "Deronda cannot imagine that perhaps his mother's experience of tradition was in fact profoundly alienating and could not accommodate her individuality, her art, or her gender; his more capacious dialogical model narrows and hardens in the face of a direct challenge to its underlying investments in family and nation" (*Powers of Distance*, 142). When she goes on to say that a "recuperation" of Deronda's character "should not be made at the expense of Leonora, who represents a viable and deeply felt response to her own cultural context," I think she is offering an extra-textual, ethical analysis that departs from Eliot's own ethical convictions as expressed in the novel, however vexing and contradictory those convictions may seem to us.

38. The best known argument *against* the idea that Deronda freely chooses his Jewishness is in Cynthia Chase, "The Decomposition of the Elephants: Double-Reading *Daniel Deronda*," PMLA 93 (1978): 215–25. For a critique of Chase's analysis, see Anderson, *Powers of Distance*, 132–33.

39. For Philip's affinity with Philoctetes, see *The Mill on the Floss*, bk. 2, chap. 6. Eliot extends the connection between male effeminacy and bodily stigma in the episode of Tom Tulliver's accident with a sword while pretending to be the duke of Wellington. Tom drops the sword on his foot, making himself into a kind of Philoctetes and bringing him closer to Philip, and faints (255–56). All this happens at Mr. Stelling's school, where Tom "became more like a girl than he had ever been in his life before," largely because he feels inadequate and quite vulnerable as a student (210).

40. The first to make this observation was Marcus, who attributes it to Lennard Davis, then his graduate student: "In order for the plot to work, Deronda's circumcised penis must be invisible, or nonexistent—which is one more demonstration in detail of why the plot does not in fact work" ("Literature and Social Theory," 212).

41. George Eliot, unsigned autograph manuscript notes on the persecution of the Jews in Spain, 53, Parrish Collection, box 9, folder 15, Firestone Library, Princeton University, Princeton, N.J.

42. Katie Trumpener, "The Time of the Gypsies: A 'People Without History,'" in *Identities*, ed. Anthony Appiah and Henry Louis Gates, Jr. (Chicago: University of Chicago Press, 1995), 344

43. *George Eliot's Life,* 3:32.

44. Semmel, *George Eliot and the Politics of National Inheritance,* 107. Haight was perhaps the first to wonder if Eliot had been influenced by Bulwer-Lytton's novel, but he notes as well that she does not mention it as a source (*George Eliot,* 376).

45. The Gypsies of Spain did not, in fact, suffer grave persecution at the hands of the Inquisition. George Borrow, whose *Zincali* Victorian readers might well have known, asserts that the "Inquisition, which burnt so many Jews and Moors, and conscientious Christians . . . seems to have exhibited the greatest clemency and forbearance to the Gitanos" (*The Zincali: An Account of the Gypsies of Spain* [London: Dent, 1914], 95). Angus M. Fraser, in a history of the Gypsies, concurs, pointing out that the Gypsies were not perceived as heretics because they apparently lacked any religious faith and that those who were hounded by the Inquisitors had been baptized (*The Gypsies* [Oxford: Blackwell, 1992], 184–85). As Borrow further remarks, it was the secular authorities rather than the ecclesiastical courts that took responsibility for reigning in Gypsies (*Zincali,* 95).

46. For Eliot's sources, see *George Eliot's Life,* 3:58. August Friedrich Pott was a German philologist who practiced the Indo-Germanic science of language and was especially interested in the Gypsies. Ann Ridler identifies the allusion to Borrow reading the New Testament to Gypsies in *Middlemarch* (305) as a reference to his book *Zincali* ("George Eliot and George Borrow," *George Eliot–George Henry Lewes Newsletter,* September 1984, 3–4).

47. Semmel, *George Eliot and the Politics of National Inheritance,* 108; Eliot, unsigned autograph manuscript notes.

48. For Eliot's knowledge of a variety of aspects of Judaism and Jewish life, including proto-Zionist aspirations to return to a homeland in Palestine, see William Baker, *George Eliot and Judaism* (Salzburg: Institut für Englische Sprache und Literatur, Universität Salzburg, 1975), 134–42.

49. In the well-known passage that begins chapter 3 of *Daniel Deronda,* the narrator implies that Gwendolen's rootlessness is the basis for future failures and deficits of character: "Pity that Offendene was not the home of Miss Harleth's childhood, or endeared to her by family memories! A human life, I think, should be well rooted in some spot of a native land. . . . [B]ut this blessed persistence in which affection can take root had been wanting in Gwendolen's life" (50). Eliot's use of the phrase "native land" immediately establishes the connection between Gwendolen's lack of a home and Daniel's discovery of a homeland.

5. "The Last Romance"

1. For an account of Sampson's funeral, see Anthony Sampson, *The Scholar Gypsy: The Quest for a Family Secret* (London: Murray, 1997), 166–74, and Dora Yates, *My Gypsy Days: Recollections of a Romany Rawnie* (London: Phoenix House, 1953), 117–22. Subsequent references are cited in the text, with the abbreviation GD.

2. Sampson, *Scholar Gypsy,* 166.

3. The Gypsy Lore Society was established in 1888 by founding members Henry Crofton, Francis Hindes Groome, Charles Leland, David MacRitchie, and Archduke Joseph of Austria-Hungary. The first run of the *Journal of the Gypsy Lore Society* went from 1888 to 1892; it was revived in 1907 and lasted until 1914; its third and longest run went from 1922 to 1973. After all its early members were dead, the fourth series was published from 1974 to 1978 and the fifth, from 1991 to 1999. Currently, a successor to the journal is published in the United States as *Romani Studies*. For a brief history of the society, see Angus Fraser, "A Rum Lot," in *One Hundred Years of Gypsy Studies: Papers from the Tenth Annual Meeting of the Gypsy Lore Society, North American Chapter*, ed. Matt T. Salo (Cheverly, Md.: Gypsy Lore Society, 1990), 1–15.

4. For the best introduction to the British folklore movement, see Richard M. Dorson, *The British Folklorists: A History* (Chicago: University of Chicago Press, 1968).

5. George Lawrence Gomme, "The Science of Folk-Lore," *Folk-Lore Journal* 3 (1885): 1.

6. David Mayall, *Gypsy-Travellers in Nineteenth-Century Society* (Cambridge: Cambridge University Press, 1988), 83.

7. David Nemeth, "'To Preserve What Might Otherwise Perish': The *JGLS*, Gypsy Studies, and a New Challenge," in *Papers from the Sixth and Seventh Annual Meetings of the Gypsy Lore Society, North American Chapter*, ed. Joanne Grumet (New York: Gypsy Lore Society, 1986), 7.

8. Charles Leland refers to Arnold's "The Scholar-Gipsy" in *The Gypsies* (Boston: Houghton, Mifflin, 1882), 223, and even seems to take seriously the "faculty . . . as strange as divination" that scholar-gypsies acquire. Subsequent references are cited in the text, with the abbreviation G. On Leland, see Regenia Gagnier, "Cultural Philanthropy, Gypsies, and Interdisciplinary Scholars: Dream of a Common Language," *19: Interdisciplinary Studies in the Long Nineteenth Century* 1 (2005), http://www.nineteen.bbk.ac.uk.

9. John Sampson, *The Dialect of the Gypsies of Wales: Being the Older Form of British Romani Preserved in the Speech of the Clan of Abram Wood* (Oxford: Clarendon Press, 1968), vii. Subsequent references are cited in the text, with the abbreviation *DGW*.

10. George Henry Borrow, *Lavengro: The Classic Account of Gypsy Life in Nineteenth-Century England* (New York: Dover, 1991), 164.

11. Charles Godfrey Leland, *Memoirs* (New York: Appleton, 1893), 417.

12. Thomas Acton, introduction to *Scholarship and the Gypsy Struggle: Commitment in Romani Studies*, ed. Thomas Acton (Hatfield: University of Hertfordshire Press, 2000), xx.

13. Fraser, "Rum Lot," 2; George Borrow, *The Romany Rye*, ed. John Sampson (London: Methuen, 1903), xxviii; Francis Hindes Groome, *In Gipsy Tents* (Wakefield, Eng.: EP Publishing, 1973), 7. Subsequent references are cited in the text, with the abbreviation *GT*.

14. Quoted in Elizabeth Bradburn, *Dr. Dora Yates: An Appreciation* (Liverpool: University of Liverpool Press, 1975), 29.

15. Nemeth, "To Preserve What Might Otherwise Perish," 11.

16. Walter Starkie, in *Journal of the Gypsy Lore Society* [Festschrift for Dora Yates's eightieth birthday], 3rd ser., 39 (1960): 18. For Kenrick's debt to Yates and Sampson, whose informants' descendants he used for his own language study, see Acton, introduction to *Scholarship and the Gypsy Struggle*, xx, xxii.

17. Fraser, "Rum Lot," 7.

18. For the connection between French writers and Gypsies, see Marilyn R. Brown, *Gypsies and Other Bohemians: The Myth of the Artist in Nineteenth-Century France* (Ann Arbor, Mich.: UMI Research Press, 1985).

19. Brown cites this essay by Charles Dickens, "The True Bohemians of Paris," *Household Words*, November 15, 1851, 190–92 (*Gypsies and Other Bohemians*, 2).

20. Lisa Tickner, *Modern Life and Modern Subjects: British Art in the Early Twentieth Century* (New Haven, Conn.: Yale University Press, 2000), 53–54. Elizabeth von Arnim documents the early-twentieth-century craze for caravanning in *The Caravaners* (1909; reprint, London: Penguin-Virago, 1990). The Edelgards, a German couple on vacation in the south of England, travel about in a caravan "bearing a strong resemblance to the gipsy carts that are continually (and very rightly) being sent somewhere else by our local police." Unlike the harassed Gypsies, the Edelgards plan to "lead a completely free and Bohemian existence . . . wandering through the English lanes . . . and drawing up for the night in a secluded spot near some little streamlet" (14).

21. Michael Holroyd, *Augustus John: A Biography* (Harmondsworth: Penguin, 1976), 358.

22. Holroyd, *Augustus John*, 360; Augustus John, *Chiaroscuro: Fragments of Autobiography* (New York: Pellegrini & Cudahy, 1952), 63–64.

23. For the marriage of Groome and Lock, see Yates, *My Gypsy Days*, 102, and John, *Chiaroscuro*, 60. Henry Crofton kept a scrapbook of clippings from both British and foreign newspapers that touched on Gypsy matters. The book includes at least two on the scandal of Groome's marriage, as well as a number on Esmeralda Lock's first marriage, to Hubert Smith, also a gypsiologist (clippings, *Daily Telegraph*, March 2, 1876; *Manchester Critic*, March 10, 1876, K-35, Gypsy Lore Society Archive, University of Liverpool).

24. Herbert Samuel, in *Journal of the Gypsy Lore Society* [Festschrift for Dora Yates's eightieth birthday], 3rd ser., 39 (1960): 5.

25. Patrick Brantlinger, *Dark Vanishings: Discourse on the Extinction of Primitive Races, 1800–1930* (Ithaca, N.Y.: Cornell University Press, 2003), 4–5.

26. John Sampson, preface to *The Wind on the Heath: A Gypsy Anthology*, ed. John Sampson (London: Chatto & Windus, 1930), vii.

27. George Henry Borrow, *The Romany Rye* (London: Dent, 1906), 82.

28. Mayall, *Gypsy-Travellers*, 87–88.

29. Borrow, *Romany Rye*, 343–44.

30. Arthur Symons, "In Praise of Gypsies," *Journal of the Gypsy Lore Society* 1, no. 4 (1908): 298. It is important to note that Symons has none of Lamb's irony.

31. Symons, "In Praise of Gypsies," 295–96. In a letter to Edward Hutton, Symons described this essay as "a violent attack on civilisation" (Karl E. Beckson, *Arthur*

Symons: A Life [Oxford: Clarendon Press, 1987], 251). In a letter to Augustus John, written in 1910, Symons included a "Gypsy proverb" that he had translated and punctuated with the comment "Splendid!": "We are not used to live as a Christian log: / We are used to live as a savage dog" (*Arthur Symons: Selected Letters, 1880–1935*, ed. Karl Beckson and John Munro [London: Macmillan, 1989], 214).

32. Symons, "In Praise of Gypsies," 296 (emphasis added).
33. Symons, "In Praise of Gypsies," 298.
34. R. A. R. Wade, obituary for Dora Yates, *Journal of the Gypsy Lore Society*, 3rd ser., 52 (1974): 100.
35. Quoted in Bradburn, *Dr. Dora Yates*, 39.
36. Dorson, *British Folklorists*, 440.
37. Mary Beard, "Frazer, Leach, and Virgil: The Popularity (and Unpopularity) of *The Golden Bough*," *Comparative Studies in Society and History* 34, no. 2 (1992): 219.
38. Beard, "Frazer, Leach, and Virgil," 219. On the anthropologist Edward Tylor's use of the analogy between peasant and savage, see Dorson, *British Folklorists*, 212.
39. Christopher Herbert, "Frazer, Einstein, and Free Play," in *Prehistories of the Future: The Primitivist Project and the Culture of Modernism*, ed. Elazar Barkan and Ronald Bush (Stanford, Calif.: Stanford University Press, 1995), 144–45.
40. Herbert, "Frazer, Einstein, and Free Play," 155.
41. Quoted in Herbert, "Frazer, Einstein, and Free Play," 164.
42. Dorson, *British Folklorists*, 160–66.
43. William R. Bascom, "Folklore and Anthropology," in *The Study of Folklore*, ed. Alan Dundes (Englewood Cliffs, N.J.: Prentice Hall, 1965), 54.
44. Dorson, *British Folklorists*, 205–8.
45. A. J. Cinch, foreword to Groome, *In Gipsy Tents*, xi.
46. Dorson, *British Folklorists*, 270. See also Francis Hindes Groome, *Gypsy Folk-Tales* (London: Hurst and Blackett, 1899), lxxxiii.
47. Dorson identifies three "illustrious newcomers" to the Folk-Lore Society in the late 1880s who were all strong diffusionists: Groome; Joseph Jacobs, a Judaic scholar from Australia; and Moses Gaster, a rabbi from Romania (*British Folklorists*, 266–77). It makes sense that a Gypsy lorist and two Jewish refugees, scholars who studied and, in two cases, belonged to dispersed groups of people, would automatically be sympathetic to the theory of diffusion.
48. Groome, *Gypsy Folk-Tales*, lxiii, lxix.
49. Groome, *Gypsy Folk-Tales*, lxxxii–iii. Throughout his collection, Groome offers commentary on the resemblance of certain tales to stories from other cultural traditions. He refers, for example, to "Two Thieves," a Romanian Gypsy tale, as a "curious combination of the 'Rhampsinitus' story in Herodotus and of Grimm's 'Master Thief'" (52).
50. Dorson, *British Folklorists*, 273.
51. Michael Owen Jones, "Francis Hindes Groome: 'Scholar Gypsy' and Gypsy Scholar," *Journal of American Folklore* 80 (1967): 76–77.
52. Dorson, *British Folklorists*, 333.
53. Bradburn, *Dr. Dora Yates*, 19–21; Wade, obituary for Dora Yates, 102.

54. Mayall, *Gypsy*-Travellers, 83–87.

55. Quoted in James Douglas, *Theodore Watts-Dunton: Poet, Novelist, Critic* (New York: Lane, 1905), 390.

56. In notes on Groome's life, Yates indicated that Rossetti had painted Esmeralda as Victor Hugo's heroine on the parapet of Notre Dame, dancing with a tambourine (GLS C.8.38, Gypsy Lore Society Archive). I have found no evidence that the Rossetti story is true, although he did do at least one drawing called *La Gitana*, whose present whereabouts are unknown. See Virginia Surtees, *The Painting and Drawings of Dante Gabriel Rossetti (1828–1882): A Catalogue Raisonné* (London: Oxford University Press, 1971), 130. Rossetti's father was a passionate reader of Hugo. Rossetti himself was both a reader and a translator of Hugo and the author of a poem, "The Staircase of Notre Dame, Paris," that may allude to Hugo's *Notre Dame de Paris*. Theodore Watts-Dunton became Rossetti's close friend in the early 1870s and was at his bedside when he died. For the poem, see *Dante Gabriel Rossetti: Collected Poetry and Prose*, ed. Jerome McGann (New Haven, Conn.: Yale University Press, 2003), 349; for Rossetti's life, see Oswald Doughty, *A Victorian Romantic: Dante Gabriel Rossetti* (London: Oxford University Press, 1960), 46, 122, 559, 667.

57. Symons, "In Praise of Gypsies," 297.

58. Lee MacCormick Edwards, *Herkomer: A Victorian Artist* (Aldershot, Eng.: Ashgate, 1999), 32–33.

59. A collection of illustrations, largely from newspapers like the *Illustrated London News*, in the Gypsy Archive at the University of Liverpool, includes many such images of women with babies and children. These representations of maternal love and labor offer an interesting contrast to common images of kidnapping, such as "The Stolen Child—From a Picture by Schlesinger," *Illustrated Times*, January 18, 1862. In this picture, a group of swarthy people gather around their chief, who holds a pale-complexioned baby.

60. Tickner, *Modern Life and Modern Subjects*, 73.

61. Theodore Watts-Dunton, "The Coming of Love," in *The Coming of Love and Other Poems* (London: The Bodley Head, n.d.), 20.

62. Arthur Symons, "Ballad of the Tent of Yester-Year," typescript, C13.15, Gypsy Lore Society Archive. Sampson's biography of his grandfather makes the identity and parentage of this child the central mystery of the family's history; Sampson and Imlach named the child Mary Arnold, in homage, the grandson believes, to the author of "The Scholar-Gipsy" (*Scholar Gypsy*, 197). Yates appears to have been the keeper of this secret, and her letters suggest that it remained a secret until as late as the 1950s (see, for example, Augustus John to Dora Yates, March 10, 1952, GLS D9-39, Gypsy Lore Society Archive).

63. Renée Christine Furst takes a debunking and, to my mind, ungenerous look at Yates in "Dora Yates: Prominent Female Gypsiologist and Liverpool Academic or 'the Wretched Dora'? A Critical View of Her Life and Work" (M.A. thesis, University of Liverpool, 1999), H.3.440, Scott Macfie Collection, University of Liverpool. Although an unsung heroine of the Gypsy Lore Society, Furst writes, Yates's scholarship was unimpressive, she was not a feminist or a "new woman," she was

a romantic folklorist with no political instincts, and the driving force behind her work was really a man: John Sampson (18–19, 46–50, 57–60).

64. Bradburn, *Dr. Dora Yates*, 8.

65. Yates was recording secretary of the Refugee Students Committee at the University of Liverpool from 1938 to 1940. Liverpool welcomed and granted scholarships to many refugees from Nazism in the 1930s, a history that Yates recounted in a speech about the university that she delivered after World War II (GLS DY2.1.20, Gypsy Lore Society Archive). Yates's father had been involved in similar work with Russian-Jewish refugees in the 1880s (GLS DY1.1.3, Gypsy Lore Society Archive).

66. Wade, obituary for Dora Yates, 103.

67. The degree to which Yates has been neglected in accounts of the Gypsy Lore Society is striking. Fraser's "Rum Lot" does not mention her at all.

68. Thomas Acton, *Gypsy Politics and Social Change: The Development of Ethnic Ideology and Pressure Politics Among British Gypsies from Victorian Reformism to Romany Nationalism* (London: Routledge and Kegan Paul, 1974), 68–69, 83–84.

69. Acton refers to Groome's attempt to "reconcile his own observations of outmarriage with the racist genetic determinism which was, as with most Victorians, his normal frame of reference" (*Gypsy Politics and Social Change*, 68).

70. See, especially, Mayall, *Gypsy-Travellers*, 97–150, and Acton, *Gypsy Politics and Social Change*, 106–23.

71. Mayall, *Gypsy-Travellers*, 135.

72. Mayall, *Gypsy-Travellers*, 138, 142, 145.

73. Mayall, *Gypsy-Travellers*, 131–32.

74. Acton, *Gypsy Politics and Social Change*, 110–11, 126.

75. Acton, *Gypsy Politics and Social Change*, 128. Given that the work of the Gypsy lorists is filled with contradictions, it is no surprise that their critics' commentary should be so as well.

76. Mayall, *Gypsy-Travellers*, 132.

77. Acton, *Gypsy Politics and Social Change*, 125.

78. Mayall, *Gypsy-Travellers*, 91.

79. For a concise chronology of German racist actions in relation to Sinti and Roma, beginning with the end of the nineteenth century, see Walter Winter, *Winter Time: Memoirs of a German Sinto Who Survived Aushwitz*, trans. Struan Robertson (Hatfield: University of Hertfordshire Press, 2004), 142–49. Winter emphasizes the degree to which Gypsies and Jews were paired in racial laws and decrees.

80. Fraser, "Rum Lot," 8.

81. Clipping, "Anthropometrical Measurements," *The Times*, 1879, Crofton scrapbook, K-35, Gypsy Lore Society Archive.

82. Fraser, "Rum Lot," 10. Fraser has seen a copy of Dillman's *Zigeuner-Buch* for 1905 (identifying some 3350 individual German Gypsies), which Augustus John gave to Scott Macfie and inscribed with a reference to this "revolting book."

83. Michael Burleigh and Wolfgang Wipperman, *The Racial State: Germany, 1933–1945* (Cambridge: Cambridge University Press, 1991), esp. 119, 127.

84. John, *Chiaroscuro*, 39–40.

85. Dora E. Yates, "Hitler and the Gypsies," *Commentary*, November 1949, 455–59. The typescript, which differs from the published article, is called "The Nazi Persecution of the Gypsies" (GLS D11-6, Gypsy Lore Society Archive).

86. Yates, "Hitler and the Gypsies," 459.

87. Quoted in Yates, "Nazi Persecution of the Gypsies," 15.

6. The Phantom Gypsy

1. Katie Trumpener offers a very similar vision of the increasingly literary representation of Gypsies. She calls this a "process of 'literarization'" and refers to "a progressive dissociation and conflation of literary traditions with living people" ("The Time of the Gypsies: A 'People Without History,'" in *Identities*, ed. Anthony Appiah and Henry Louis Gates, Jr. [Chicago: University of Chicago Press, 1995], 344).

2. In two recent British novels, Gypsies figure in a self-consciously literary and allusive way. Margaret Drabble describes two young friends as "angel fair" and "dark as a gypsy": "light and dark were they, the princesses of a Walter Scott romance" (*The Peppered Moth* [San Diego, Calif.: Harcourt, 2001], 31). The parents of Ian McEwan's ill-fated protagonist spend their honeymoon picking hops and living in a Gypsy caravan. In a photograph from that time, his father wears a neck scarf and a rope belt, "playful Romany touches" (*Atonement* [London: Vintage, 2001], 83).

3. For the popularity of the story, see John A. Hodgson, "The Recoil of 'The Speckled Band': Detective Story and Detective Discourse," in Arthur Conan Doyle, *Sherlock Holmes: The Major Stories, with Contemporary Critical Essays*, ed. John A. Hodgson (New York: St. Martin's Press, 1994), 335–36.

4. Arthur Conan Doyle, "The Adventure of the Speckled Band," in *Sherlock Holmes: The Complete Novels and Stories* (New York: Bantam, 1986), 1:352. Subsequent references are cited in the text.

5. Kenneth Grahame, *The Wind in the Willows* (New York: Scribner, 1908), 29.

6. Rosemary Hennessy and Rajeswari Mohan, "'The Speckled Band': The Construction of Woman in a Popular Text," in *Sherlock Holmes: The Major Stories*, 391 (emphasis added).

7. Cyndy Hendershot points out that, in fact, none of the animals on Roylott's estate is indigenous to India and that there is no such creature as an Indian puff adder ("The Animal Without: Masculinity and Imperialism in *The Island of Doctor Moreau* and 'The Adventure of the Speckled Band,'" *Nineteenth-Century Studies* 10 [1996]: 22). Conan Doyle requires that they be Indian for a number of reasons, one of which is their link to the Gypsies.

8. Walter Scott, *Guy Mannering, or, The Astrologer*, ed. Andrew Lang (Boston: Estes and Lauriat, 1892), 1:204.

9. Bram Stoker, *Dracula* (Mattituck, N.Y.: Amereon House, 1985), 43.

10. D. H. Lawrence, *The Virgin and the Gipsy* (New York: Vintage, 1992), 33. Subsequent references are cited in the text.

11. Although written before *Lady Chatterley's Lover*, *The Virgin and the Gipsy* was not published until 1930, after Lawrence's death. Many have compared the two.

See, for example, Keith Cushman, "The Virgin and the Gypsy and the Lady and the Gamekeeper," in *D. H. Lawrence's "Lady": A New Look at "Lady Chatterley's Lover,"* ed. Dennis Jackman and Michael Squires (Athens: University of Georgia Press, 1985), 154–69.

12. For a related and similar reading of Lawrence's story, see Janet Lyon, "Gadže Modernism," *Modernism/modernity* 11 (2004): 517–38. Lyon is interested in the modernist trope of the Gypsy as marker of sociability and in the modernist investigation of the "incommensurability" between Gypsy and non-Gypsy cultures (532).

13. On Yvette, the Lady of Shalott, and the Sleeping Beauty plot, see Cushman, "The Virgin and the Gypsy and the Lady and the Gamekeeper," 155.

14. For Lawrence's debt to George Eliot's *The Mill on the Floss*, see Carol Siegel, "Floods of Female Desire in Lawrence and Eudora Welty," in *D. H. Lawrence's Literary Inheritors*, ed. Keith Cushman and Dennis Jackson (Basingstoke, Eng.: Macmillan, 1991), 114.

15. For this version of "The Raggle Taggle Gypsy," see http://www.lecairde/Lieder/Raggle_Taggle_ Gypsy.html.

16. The fact of Mellors's service in the military remakes his image as well: it recalibrates his class position, adds world travel and foreign languages to his experience and knowledge, and makes him a more cosmopolitan and worldly figure.

17. Critics have differed about what transpires between Yvette and the Gypsy during the flood. Cushman agrees that their encounter is "not romantic or even sexual" ("The Virgin and the Gypsy and the Lady and the Gamekeeper," 165), but Jeffrey Meyers, who represents the other camp, writes that Lawrence's "description of their regenerative embrace and consummation . . . is a superb example of a rippling, rhythmic, energetic prose that approximates their sexual union" ("The Voice of Water: Lawrence's *The Virgin and the Gipsy*," *English Miscellany* 21 [1970]: 205).

18. Siegel, "Floods of Female Desire," 114. Siegel also discusses the influence of Charlotte Brontë's *Jane Eyre*.

19. Maria DiBattista, *First Love: The Affections of Modern Fiction* (Chicago: University of Chicago Press, 1991), 58.

20. D. H. Lawrence, *Lady Chatterley's Lover* (London: Penguin, 1994), 301.

21. Lawrence, *Lady Chatterley*, 302.

22. Silvester Gordon Boswell, *The Book of Boswell: Autobiography of a Gypsy*, ed. John Seymour (London: Gollancz, 1970). Subsequent references are cited in the text.

23. Francis Hindes Groome, *In Gipsy Tents* (Wakefield, Eng.: EP Publishing, 1973), 250–51.

24. B. C. Smart and H. T. Crofton, *The Dialect of the English Gypsies* (London: Asher, 1875), ix.

25. Smart and Crofton, *Dialect of the English Gypsies*, x–xi.

26. Smart and Crofton, *Dialect of the English Gypsies*, 229, 248.

27. Boswell's family tree is displayed on both the front and back end papers of his memoir, and an appendix contains a detailed account of his genealogy (169–74). In this narrative, he mentions, among other things, that the son-in-law of his grandfather Tyso Boswell was the fiddler who taught John Clare to play (169). See

Jonathan Bate, *John Clare: A Biography* (New York: Farrar, Straus, 2003), 94, and chapter 3.

28. Groome comments on the prevalence of illiteracy among Gypsies, although he acknowledges variations from place to place. He attributes this illiteracy to the reluctance of schoolmasters to educate Gypsy children (Boswell's account bears this out), as well as to Gypsies' reluctance to send their children to school. Groome wants to promote the idea that families that settle for even a period of months might send their offspring to be educated or, alternatively, that teachers might circulate among Gypsy tents to teach reading (*In Gipsy Tents*, 254, 258–59).

29. For the spatial organization of contemporary Gypsy domestic life and its connections to rituals of purity, see Judith Okely, *The Traveller-Gypsies* (Cambridge: Cambridge University Press, 1983), 85–89. "Whereas Gorgio hygiene consists to some extent in containing, covering or hiding dirt," Okely writes, "for the Gypsies, polluting dirt can be visible, but it must be a clear distance from the clean" (86). Lawrence clearly knew about such taboos ("If Gypsies had no bathrooms, at least they had no sewerage") and transferred them to Yvette's more general disgust at the hypocrisies of modern, sanitized life.

30. John Megel, "The Holocaust and the American Rom," in *Papers from the Sixth and Seventh Annual Meetings of the Gypsy Lore Society, North American Chapter*, ed. Joanne Grumet (New York: Gypsy Lore Society, 1986), 187–90. Subsequent references are cited in the text.

31. Walter Winter, *Winter Time: Memoirs of a German Sinto Who Survived Auschwitz*, trans. Struan Robertson (Hatfield: University of Hertfordshire, 2004), x.

32. There have been ongoing disputes about the degree to which the United States Holocaust Memorial Museum has excluded groups other than Jews who were systematically murdered by the Nazis. According to Ian Hancock, an official representative from the Gypsy community was first appointed to the United States Holocaust Memorial Council in 1987, presumably after the period of Megel's unofficial or informal service; in 2002, however, President George Bush canceled Romany representation to the council (*We Are the Romany People [Ame sam e Rromane džene]* [Hatfield: University of Hertfordshire Press, 2002], 50). For Hancock's views on the museum, his anger at the exclusion of the Gypsies from discussions of the Holocaust—or Porrajmos, as he prefers to call it, emphasizing the Gypsy experience as unique—and his belief in the modest progress that has been made in rectifying these omissions, see "Jewish Responses to the Porrajmos (The Romani Holocaust)," http://www.chgs.umn.edu/Histories Narratives Documen/Roma Sinti Gypsies / Jewish Responses to the Porraj/jewish responses to the porraj.html.

33. With considerable justification, Hancock bitterly criticizes Jewish accounts of the Holocaust that ignore or minimize Gypsy suffering, but he also remarks that only Jews and Gypsies can come close to understanding each other's experiences. Nonetheless, he concludes, neither group can fully grasp the other's history or interpret it with full authority ("Jewish Responses to the Porrajmos," 2). Megel may be expressing a naïve sentiment, but the two people's sufferings are better twinned than placed in a hierarchy of victimization.

Bibliography

Primary Texts

Arnold, Matthew. *The Poems of Matthew Arnold.* 2d ed. Edited by Kenneth Alott and Miriam Alott. London: Longman, 1979.

Austen, Jane. *Emma.* Harmondsworth: Penguin, 1985.

Birrell, Augustine. *Res Judicatae: Papers and Essays.* New York: Scribner, 1897.

Borrow, George. *Borrow Selections, with Essays by Richard Ford, Leslie Stephen, and George Saintsbury.* Edited by Humphrey S. Milford. Oxford: Clarendon Press, 1924.

Borrow, George Henry. *The Bible in Spain; or, the Journeys, Adventures, and Imprisonments of an Englishman, in an Attempt to Circulate the Scriptures in the Peninsula.* London: Ward, Lock, n.d.

——. *Lavengro: The Classic Account of Gypsy Life in Nineteenth-Century England.* New York: Dover, 1991.

——. *Letters of George Borrow to the British and Foreign Bible Society.* Edited by T. H. Barlow. London: Hodder and Stoughton, 1911.

——. *The Romany Rye.* London: Dent, 1906.

——. *Wild Wales: The People, Language and Scenery.* London: Dent, 1906.

——. *The Zincali: An Account of the Gypsies of Spain.* London: Dent, 1914.

Boswell, Silvester Gordon. *The Book of Boswell: Autobiography of a Gypsy.* Edited by John Seymour. London: Gollancz, 1970.

Brenner, Frédéric. *Diaspora: Homelands in Exile.* 2 vols. New York: HarperCollins, 2003.

Brontë, Charlotte. *Jane Eyre.* London: Penguin, 1996.

Clare, John. *The Early Poems of John Clare, 1804–1822.* 2 vols. Edited by Eric Robinson and David Powell. Oxford: Clarendon Press, 1989.

——. *John Clare by Himself.* Edited by Eric Robinson and David Powell. Ashington, Eng.: Carcanet Press, 1996.

——. *John Clare's Autobiographical Writings*. Edited by Eric Robinson and John Lawrence. Oxford: Oxford University Press, 1983.

——. *The Later Poems of John Clare, 1837–1864*. 2 vols. Edited by Eric Robinson and David Powell. Oxford: Clarendon Press, 1984.

——. *The Shepherd's Calendar*. Oxford: Oxford University Press, 1964.

Coleridge, Samuel Taylor. *Biographia Literaria*. New York: Macmillan, 1926.

Dickens, Charles. *David Copperfield*. London: Penguin, 2004.

——. *Little Dorrit*. Harmondsworth: Penguin, 1967.

Doyle, Arthur Conan. *Sherlock Holmes: The Complete Novels and Stories*. Vol. 1. New York: Bantam, 1986.

Drabble, Margaret. *The Peppered Moth*. New York: Harcourt, 2001.

Eliot, George. *Daniel Deronda*. Harmondsworth: Penguin, 1970.

——. *The George Eliot Letters*. 9 vols. Edited by Gordon S. Haight. New Haven, Conn.: Yale University Press, 1954–1978.

——. *George Eliot's Life as Related in Her Letters and Journals*. 3 vols. Edited by J. W. Cross. Boston: Estes and Lauriat, 1895

——. *Impressions of Theophrastus Such*. Edinburgh: Blackwood, 1879.

——. *Middlemarch*. London: Penguin, 1994.

——. *The Mill on the Floss*. London: Penguin, 1985.

——. *Silas Marner*. London: Penguin, 1996.

——. *The Spanish Gypsy*. Standard ed. Edinburgh: Blackwood, 1868.

——. Unsigned autograph manuscript notes on the persecution of the Jews in Spain. Parrish Collection, box 9, folder 15. Firestone Library, Princeton University, Princeton, N.J.

Freud, Sigmund. *The Complete Introductory Lectures on Psychoanalysis*. Translated by James Strachey. New York: Norton, 1966.

——. *Dora: An Analysis of a Case of Hysteria*. Edited by Philip Rieff. New York: Collier Books, 1963.

——. "Family Romances." In *The Standard Edition of the Complete Psychological Works of Sigmund Freud*, translated by James Strachey, 9:237–41. London: Hogarth Press, 1955.

Glanvill, Joseph. *The Vanity of Dogmatizing: Reproduced from the Edition of 1661*. New York: Columbia University Press, 1931.

Grahame, Kenneth. *The Wind in the Willows*. New York: Scribner, 1908.

Grellmann, Heinrich Moritz Gottlieb. *Dissertation on the Gipseys: Representing Their Manner of Life, Family Economy. With an Historical Enquiry Concerning Their Origin & First Appearance in Europe*. Translated by Matthew Raper. London: Ballintine, 1807.

Groome, Francis Hindes. *Gypsy Folk-Tales*. London: Hurst and Blackett, 1899.

——. *In Gipsy Tents*. Wakefield, Eng.: EP Publishing, 1973.

Hazlitt, William. *The Complete Works of William Hazlitt*. Centenary ed. 21 vols. Edited by P. P. Howe. London: Dent, 1930.

Henley, William Ernest. *Views and Reviews: Essays in Appreciation*. New York: Scribner, 1890.

Hoyland, John. *A Historical Survey of the Customs, Habits, & Present State of the Gypsies: Designed to Develope the Origin of This Singular People, and to Promote the Amelioration of Their Condition*. York: Darton, Harvey, 1816.

John, Augustus. *Chiaroscuro: Fragments of Autobiography*. New York: Pellegrini & Cudahy, 1952.

——. Letter to Dora Yates, March 10, 1952. GLS D9-39, Gypsy Lore Society Archive, University of Liverpool.

Jung, C. G. *The Essential Jung*. Edited by Anthony Storr. Princeton, N.J.: Princeton University Press, 1983.

Keats, John. *Selected Poems and Letters*. Edited by Douglas Bush. Boston: Houghton Mifflin, 1959.

Lamb, Charles. "The Gipsy's Malison." *Blackwood's Edinburgh Review* 25 (1829): 64.

Lawrence, D. H. *Lady Chatterley's Lover*. London: Penguin, 1994.

——. *The Virgin and the Gipsy*. New York: Vintage, 1992.

Leland, Charles Godfrey. *The Gypsies*. Boston: Houghton Mifflin, 1882.

——. *Memoirs*. New York: Appleton, 1893.

Lockhart, J. G. *Memoirs of the Life of Sir Walter Scott, Bart*. New ed. Edinburgh: Cadell, 1844.

Marsden, William. "Observations on the Language of the People Commonly Called Gypsies. In a Letter to Sir Joseph Banks." *Archaeologia, or, Miscellaneous Tracts Relating to Antiquity* 7 (1785): 382–86.

Mayhew, Henry. *London Labour and the London Poor*. Vol. 1. New York: Dover, 1968.

McEwan, Ian. *Atonement*. London: Vintage, 2001.

Megel, John. "The Holocaust and the American Rom." In *Papers from the Sixth and Seventh Annual Meetings of the Gypsy Lore Society, North American Chapter*, edited by Joanne Grummet, 187–90. New York: Gypsy Lore Society, 1986.

Mitford, Mary Russell. *Our Village: Sketches of Rural Life and Scenery*. London: Bell, 1876.

Morrison, Arthur. *Chronicles of Martin Hewitt*. New York: Appleton, 1896.

Rossetti, Dante Gabriel. *Collected Poetry and Prose*. Edited by Jerome J. McGann. New Haven, Conn.: Yale University Press, 2003.

Sampson, John. *The Dialect of the Gypsies of Wales: Being the Older Form of British Romani Preserved in the Speech of the Clan of Abram Wood*. Oxford: Clarendon Press, 1968.

——, ed. *The Wind on the Heath: A Gypsy Anthology*. London: Chatto and Windus, 1930.

Scott, Sir Walter. *Guy Mannering, or, The Astrologer*. 2 vols. Edited by Andrew Lang. Boston: Estes and Lauriat, 1892.

——. *Ivanhoe*. London: Penguin, 1986.

Simson, Walter. "Notices Concerning the Scottish Gypsies." *Blackwood's Edinburgh Magazine* 1 (1817): 54–56.

Simson, Walter, and James Simson. *A History of the Gipsies: With Specimens of the Gipsy Language*. London: Sampson, Low, 1866.

Smart, B. C., and H. T. Crofton. *The Dialect of the English Gypsies*. London: Asher, 1875.

"A Southern Faunist." *Gentleman's Magazine*, April 1802, 292–93.

Stoker, Bram. *Dracula*. Mattituck, N.Y.: Amereon House, 1985.

Symons, Arthur. *Arthur Symons: Selected Letters, 1880–1935*. Edited by Karl Beckson and John Munro. London: Macmillan, 1989.

——. "Ballad of the Tent of Yester-Year." Typescript. C13.15, Gypsy Lore Society Archive, University of Liverpool.

——. "In Praise of Gypsies." *Journal of the Gypsy Lore Society* 1, no. 4 (1908): 295–98.

von Arnim, Elizabeth. *The Caravaners*. 1909. Reprint, London: Penguin-Virago, 1990.

Watts-Dunton, Theodore. *The Coming of Love and Other Poems*. London: The Bodley Head, n.d.

Winter, Walter Stanoski. *Winter Time: Memoirs of a German Sinto Who Survived Auschwitz*. Translated by Struan Robertson. Hatfield: University of Hertfordshire Press, 2004.

Wordsworth, Dorothy. *Journals of Dorothy Wordsworth: The Alfoxden Journal, 1798; the Grasmere Journals, 1800–1803*. Edited by Mary Moorman. London: Oxford University Press, 1971.

Wordsworth, William. *Poems*. 2 vols. Edited by John O. Hayden. Harmondsworth: Penguin, 1977.

Yates, Dora. *My Gypsy Days: Recollections of a Romany Rawnie*. London: Phoenix House, 1953.

——. "The Nazi Persecution of the Gypsies." GLS, D11-6, Gypsy Lore Society Archive, University of Liverpool.

——. Undated speech delivered at the University of Liverpool after the Second World War. GLS DY2.1.20, Gypsy Lore Society Archive, University of Liverpool.

Yates, Dora E. "Hitler and the Gypsies." *Commentary*, November 1949, 455–59.

Selected Secondary Texts

Acton, Thomas. *Gypsy Politics and Social Change: The Development of Ethnic Ideology and Pressure Politics Among British Gypsies from Victorian Reformism to Romany Nationalism*. London: Routledge and Kegan Paul, 1974.

Acton, Thomas, and Gary Mundy, eds. *Romani Culture and Gypsy Identity*. Hatfield: University of Hertfordshire Press, 1997.

Adams, James Eli. *Dandies and Desert Saints: Styles of Victorian Masculinity*. Ithaca, N.Y.: Cornell University Press, 1995.

Anderson, Amanda. *The Powers of Distance: Cosmopolitanism and the Cultivation of Detachment*. Princeton, N.J.: Princeton University Press, 2001.

Anderson, Benedict R. *Imagined Communities: Reflections on the Origin and Spread of Nationalism*. London: Verso, 1991.

Armstrong, Isobel. *Victorian Poetry: Poetry, Poetics, and Politics*. London: Routledge, 1993.

Baker, William. *George Eliot and Judaism*. Salzburg: Institut für Englische Sprache und Literatur Universität Salzburg, 1975.

Bate, Jonathan. *John Clare: A Biography*. New York: Farrar, Straus, 2003.

Beckson, Karl E. *Arthur Symons: A Life*. Oxford: Clarendon Press, 1987.

Beer, Gillian. "Beyond Determinism: George Eliot and Virginia Woolf." In *Women Writing and Writing About Women*, edited by Mary Jacobus, 80–99. London: Croom Helm, 1979.

Behlmer, George. "The Gypsy Problem in Victorian England." *Victorian Studies* 28, no. 2 (1985): 231–53.

Boyarin, Jonathan. "The Other Within and the Other Without." In *Constructions of Jewish Culture and Identity*, edited by Laurence J. Silberstein and Robert L. Cohen, 424–50. New York: New York University Press, 1994.

Bradburn, Elizabeth. *Dr. Dora Yates: An Appreciation*. Liverpool: University of Liverpool Press, 1975.

Brantlinger, Patrick. *Dark Vanishings: Discourse on the Extinction of Primitive Races, 1800–1930*. Ithaca, N.Y.: Cornell University Press, 2003.

Brown, Marilyn R. *Gypsies and Other Bohemians: The Myth of the Artist in Nineteenth-Century France*. Ann Arbor, Mich.: UMI Research Press, 1985.

Burleigh, Michael, and Wolfgang Wippermann. *The Racial State: Germany, 1933–1945*. Cambridge: Cambridge University Press, 1991.

Burrow, J. W. *Evolution and Society: A Study in Victorian Social Theory*. Cambridge: Cambridge University Press, 1970.

——. "The Uses of Philology in Victorian Britain." In *Ideas and Institutions of Victorian Britain*, edited by Robert Robson, 180–204. New York: Barnes and Noble, 1967.

Carroll, Alicia. *Dark Smiles: Race and Desire in George Eliot*. Athens: Ohio University Press, 2003.

Cheyette, Bryan. *Constructions of "the Jew" in English Literature and Society: Racial Representations, 1875–1945*. Cambridge: Cambridge University Press, 1993.

Collie, Michael. *George Borrow: Eccentric*. Cambridge: Cambridge University Press, 1982.

Cushman, Keith. "The Virgin and the Gypsy and the Lady and the Gamekeeper." In *D. H. Lawrence's "Lady": A New Look at "Lady Chatterley's Lover,"* edited by Dennis Jackman and Michael Squires, 154–69. Athens: University of Georgia Press, 1985.

DiBattista, Maria. *First Love: The Affections of Modern Fiction*. Chicago: University of Chicago Press, 1991.

Dorson, Richard Mercer. *The British Folklorists: A History*. Chicago: University of Chicago Press, 1968.

Douglas, James. *Theodore Watts-Dunton, Poet, Novelist, Critic*. New York: Lane, 1905.

Duncan, Ian. *Modern Romance and Transformations of the Novel: The Gothic, Scott, Dickens*. Cambridge: Cambridge University Press, 1992.

——. "Wild England: George Borrow's Nomadology." *Victorian Studies* 41, no. 3 (1998): 381–403.

Dundes, Alan. *The Study of Folklore*. Englewood Cliffs, N.J.: Prentice Hall, 1965.

Edwards, Lee M. *Herkomer: A Victorian Artist*. Aldershot, Eng.: Ashgate, 1999.

Fraser, Angus. "A Rum Lot." In *One Hundred Years of Gypsy Studies: Papers from the Tenth Annual Meeting of the Gypsy Lore Society, North American Chapter*, edited by Matt T. Salo, 1–15. Cheverly, Md.: Gypsy Lore Society, 1990.

Fraser, Angus M. *The Gypsies*. Oxford: Blackwell, 1995.

Furst, Renée Christine. "Dora Yates: Prominent Female Gypsiologist and Liverpool Academic or 'the Wretched Dora'? A Critical View of Her Life and Work." M.A. thesis, University of Liverpool, 1999. H.3.440, Scott Macfie Collection, University of Liverpool.

Gagnier, Regenia. "Cultural Philanthropy, Gypsies, and Interdisciplinary Scholars: Dream of a Common Language." *19: Interdisciplinary Studies in the Long Nineteenth Century* 1 (2005). http://www.nineteen.bbk.ac.uk.

Graver, Suzanne. *George Eliot and Community: A Study in Social Theory and Fictional Form*. Berkeley: University of California Press, 1984.

Haight, Gordon S. *George Eliot: A Biography*. Oxford: Oxford University Press, 1968.

Hancock, Ian F. *We Are the Romany People (Ame sam e Rromane džene)*. Hatfield: University of Hertfordshire Press, 2002.

Helsinger, Elizabeth K. *Rural Scenes and National Representation: Britain, 1815–1850*. Princeton, N.J.: Princeton University Press, 1997.

Henry, Nancy. *George Eliot and the British Empire*. Cambridge: Cambridge University Press, 2002.

Hodgson, John A. "The Recoil of 'The Speckled Band': Detective Story and Detective Discourse." In *Sherlock Holmes: The Major Stories, with Contemporary Critical Essays*, edited by John A. Hodgson, 335–52. New York: St. Martin's Press, 1994.

Holroyd, Michael. *Augustus John: A Biography*. Harmondsworth: Penguin, 1976.

Howkins, Alun. "The Discovery of Rural England." In *Englishness: Politics and Culture, 1880–1920*, edited by Robert Colls and Philip Dodd, 62–88. London: Croom Helm, 1986.

Jones, Michael Owen. "Francis Hindes Groome: 'Scholar Gypsy' and Gypsy Scholar." *Journal of American Folklore* 80 (1967): 71–81.

Kenrick, Donald, and Thomas A. Acton, eds. *Scholarship and the Gypsy Struggle: Commitment in Romani Studies*. Hatfield: University of Hertfordshire Press, 2000.

Lorimer, Douglas A. "Race, Science and Culture: Historical Continuities and Discontinuities, 1850–1914." In *The Victorians and Race*, edited by Shearer West, 12–33. Aldershot, Eng.: Scolar Press, 1997.

Lukács, Georg. *The Historical Novel*. Harmondsworth: Penguin, 1969.

Mandler, Peter. *The Fall and Rise of the Stately Home*. New Haven, Conn.: Yale University Press, 1997.

Marcus, Steven. "Literature and Social Theory: Starting in with George Eliot." In *Representations: Essays on Literature and Society*, 183–214. New York: Random House, 1975.

Marsh, Jan. *Back to the Land: The Pastoral Impulse in England, from 1880 to 1914*. London: Quartet Books, 1982.

Mayall, David. *English Gypsies and State Policies*. Hatfield: Gypsy Research Centre and University of Hertfordshire Press, 1995.

——. *Gypsy Identities, 1500–2000: From Egipcyans and Moon-Men to the Ethnic Romany*. London: Routledge, 2004.

——. *Gypsy-Travellers in Nineteenth-Century Society*. Cambridge: Cambridge University Press, 1988.

Nemeth, David. "'To Preserve What Might Otherwise Perish': The *JGSL*, Gypsy Studies, and a New Challenge." In *Papers from the Sixth and Seventh Annual Meetings
of the Gypsy Lore Society, North American Chapter*, edited by Joanne Grumet, 5–17.
New York: Gypsy Lore Society, 1986.

Nord, Deborah Epstein. "'Marks of Race': Gypsy Figures and Eccentric Femininity in
Nineteenth-Century Women's Writing." *Victorian Studies* 41, no. 2 (1998): 189–210.

Okely, Judith. *The Traveller-Gypsies*. Cambridge: Cambridge University Press, 1983.

Pedersen, Holger. *Linguistic Science in the Nineteenth Century: Methods and Results*.
Translated by John Webster Spargo. Cambridge, Mass.: Harvard University Press,
1931.

Pollak, Ellen. *Incest and the English Novel, 1684–1814*. Baltimore: Johns Hopkins University Press, 2003.

Ragussis, Michael. *Figures of Conversion: "The Jewish Question" and English National
Identity*. Durham, N.C.: Duke University Press, 1995.

Riede, David G. *Matthew Arnold and the Betrayal of Language*. Charlottesville: University Press of Virginia, 1988.

Sampson, Anthony. *The Scholar Gypsy: The Quest for a Family Secret*. London: Murray, 1997.

Semmel, Bernard. *George Eliot and the Politics of National Inheritance*. New York:
Oxford University Press, 1994.

Siegel, Carol. "Floods of Female Desire in Lawrence and Eudora Welty." In *D. H.
Lawrence's Literary Inheritors*, edited by Keith Cushman and Dennis Jackson, 109–
31. Basingstoke, Eng.: Macmillan, 1991.

Simpson, David. "Criticism, Politics, and Style in Wordsworth's Poetry." *Critical Inquiry* 11, no. 1 (1984): 60–81.

——. "Figuring Class, Sex, and Gender: What Is the Subject of Wordsworth's 'Gipsies'?" *South Atlantic Quarterly* 88, no. 3 (1989): 541–67.

Stocking, George W., Jr. *Victorian Anthropology*. New York: Free Press, 1987.

Sussman, Herbert L. *Victorian Masculinities: Manhood and Masculine Poetics in Early
Victorian Literature and Art*. Cambridge: Cambridge University Press, 1995.

Sutherland, John. *The Life of Walter Scott: A Critical Biography*. Oxford: Blackwell,
1995.

Tickner, Lisa. *Modern Life and Modern Subjects: British Art in the Early Twentieth
Century*. New Haven, Conn.: Yale University Press, 2000.

Trumpener, Katie. *Bardic Nationalism: The Romantic Novel and the British Empire*.
Princeton, N.J.: Princeton University Press, 1997.

——. "The Time of the Gypsies: A 'People Without History.'" In *Identities*, edited by
Anthony Appiah and Henry Louis Gates, Jr., 338–79. Chicago: University of Chicago Press, 1995.

Tucker, Irene. *A Probable State: The Novel, the Contract, and the Jews*. Chicago: University of Chicago Press, 2000.

Willems, Wim. *In Search of the True Gypsy: From Enlightenment to Final Solution*.
Translated by Don Bloch. London: Cass, 1997.

Williams, Raymond. *The Country and the City*. London: Chatto and Windus, 1973.

Index

representation. *See* literary representation of Gypsies

Res Judicate (Birrell), 75

"Resignation (To Fausta)" (Arnold), 44, 56–60, 63, 67, 93, 132, 155

Riede, David G., 45, 57

Robertson, Struan, 174

Robinson Crusoe (Defoe), 89

Rochester, Edward (*Jane Eyre*), 1, 14, 41

Romani (language), 7, 8, 19, 21, 128, 134, 150; dictionaries of, 141

Romani Archives and Documentation Center, 19

Romany. *See* Gypsies

Romany Rye, The (Borrow), 16, 71–72; Abraham story in, 81–82, 189n.25; anti-Catholicism in, 90, 94; as anti-pastoral, 80–84; influence of, on Gypsy lorists, 134; language in, 85–91; man in black in, 72–73, 90; as mock memoir, 73–74; origins in, 86–91; romantic desire in, 80–84; Sampson's introduction to, 130

Romany ryes, 13, 16, 24, 92, 127, 177n.37; Borrow's invention of, 71, 73–75. *See also* Gypsy lorists; scholar-gypsy

Rossetti, Dante Gabriel, 144, 150, 198n.56

Said, Edward, 2, 6, 34

Saintsbury, George, 74, 94

Sampson, Anthony, 125

Sampson, John, 1–2, 9, 74, 128, 147, 198n.62; as auto-didact, 129; caravaning by, 134; *The Dialect of the Gypsies of Wales*, 125, 129, 134, 142; funeral of, 125; introduction to *The Romany Rye* by, 130; *The Wind on the Heath*, 1–2, 9, 74, 128, 143; Yates's research for, 141–42

Sampson, Margaret, 125

Sanskrit, 8

Sartor Resartus (Carlyle), 94, 190n.37

"Scholar-Gipsy, The" (Arnold), 9, 16, 44–45, 93, 155, 186n.48, 187n.54; gender in, 13, 63–64; Gypsies as

mythic beings in, 45, 68, 157; kidnapping plot in, 10, 61–62; memory in, 60–61; observation in, 62–63

scholar-gypsy, 24, 128; as feminized, 64, 71; susceptibility of, to change, 65–66. *See also* Romany ryes

scholar-gypsy ("The Scholar-Gipsy"), 131; as exile, 60–62; as feminized, 63–64; as prototype for Gypsy lorist, 68–69

Scott, Walter, 6, 25, 72, 93, 182n.46; ancestry of, 26–27; conservatism of, 38–39; *Ivanhoe*, 6, 39, 102; *Waverly*, 26. See also *Guy Mannering, or, The Astrologer*

Scott Macfie Collection of Books on Gypsy Lore, 147

Scottish Gypsies: as hybrid and ancestral people, 25–27, 30–31, 36, 39, 40; inclusion of, in history, 38–39, 41–42

Semmel, Bernard, 102, 110, 121, 122

sewage metaphor, 163–64, 172, 202n.29

sexuality: exotic, 143–44; expressed through language, 81, 83–84; passive, 144, 145–47; promiscuous, attributed to Gypsies, 40–41, 58

Sharp, Cecil, 74

Shepherd's Calendar, The ("October" section) (Clare), 48–49, 56–57

Siddons, Sarah, 26, 182n.39

Siegel, Carol, 166

Silas Marner (Eliot), 20, 101, 102–3, 109–10, 159, 192n.26

Simpson, David, 50, 54, 186nn.36, 46

Simson, Walter, 24, 25, 26–27

skin color, 11, 20, 23, 47, 51, 77, 99. *See also* physical difference

Smart, B. C.: *The Dialect of the English Gypsies*, 168

Smith, Adam, 10–11, 23–24; referred to in *Guy Mannering*, 30, 33, 38

Smith, George, 150–51

Smith, Harriet (*Emma*), 3, 4–5

Spanish Gypsy, The (Eliot), 6, 7, 10, 16; ambivalence of, 112–14; family romance in, 100, 107, 113; homeland for

DATE DUE

GAYLORD | No. 2333 | | PRINTED IN U.S.A.